NO TIME
— FOR —
SERGEANTS
AND OTHER MILITARY PLAYS BY
IRA LEVIN

WORKS BY IRA LEVIN

NOVELS

Son of Rosemary

Sliver

The Boys from Brazil

The Stepford Wives

This Perfect Day

Rosemary's Baby

A Kiss Before Dying

PLAYS

Footsteps

Cantorial

Break A Leg

Deathtrap

Veronica's Room

Dr. Cook's Garden

General Seeger

Critic's Choice

Interlock

No Time For Sergeants

(from the novel by Mac Hyman)

MUSICALS

Drat! The Cat!

(music by Milton Schafer)

NO TIME FOR SERGEANTS

AND OTHER MILITARY PLAYS BY

IRA LEVIN

AN ARMED FORCES–THEMED TRIAD OF COMEDY, TRAGEDY, AND DRAMA: *NO TIME FOR SERGEANTS*, *GENERAL SEEGER*, AND *NOTEBOOK WARRIOR*

BLACK STONE
PUBLISHING

Printed in the United States of America

ISBN 979-8-212-64282-8
Drama / American / General

Version 1

Blackstone Publishing
31 Mistletoe Rd.
Ashland, OR 97520

www.BlackstonePublishing.com

CONTENTS

NO TIME FOR SERGEANTS

INTRODUCTION

(NO TIME FOR SERGEANTS)

Even if you're unfamiliar with *No Time For Sergeants*, you're familiar with it. Everything from *The Beverly Hillbillies* to *Forrest Gump* has been influenced to some degree by the benignly guileless, modern-day *Huckleberry Finn* that is *Will Stockdale*—the lead character from Mac Hyman's 1954 novel, and Ira Levin's two subsequent television and stage adaptations of it.

Hyman, a former Air Force navigator, had great success with his novel immediately upon its publication. A year later, a writer was sought to adapt it for television. Who better than Levin—himself an active-duty draftee (just like Stockdale), and at that, one who'd created this volume's armed forces–themed *Notebook Warrior* just a year earlier for the *United States Steel Hour*—the Emmy-winning series on which *Sergeants* would also air. As Levin noted, *"It's interesting, the way one thing leads to another."*

But while *Notebook Warrior* was a joint effort between the military and all concerned, *Sergeants* was not—so Levin wrote his one-hour TV script on his own time—during three weeks of accumulated leave time.

A then mostly unknown Andy Griffith was cast to play the confounding, but good-hearted Will. The rehearsals were proving so riotously funny, the show's producers added seating for an audience (a first for the *Steel Hour*) to capture their genuine laughter during the live broadcast.

The New York Times praised the final television offering's "hilarious escapades," with the *Philadelphia Inquirer* dubbing it a "Smash Comedy Hit," and Sturgis Hedrick of the *Buffalo Times* proclaiming "A new comedy star was born" in Griffith.

The rights to adapt Mac Hyman's novel for the live stage (as opposed to the small screen) had already been purchased by theatrical producer Maurice Evans—who was also a noted Shakespearean actor, as well as a general in the U.S. Army (though born in Britain, he became a naturalized citizen in 1941). Evans would, over the course of his career, like Levin, amass his own small arsenal of military-themed works.

To scribe his theatrical adaptation, Evans had originally contracted the creators of the hard-edged war comedy *Stalag 17*, Donald Bevan and Edmund Trzcinski. Dissatisfied with their first draft, private Levin received a call while on duty at Fort Monmouth, New Jersey; he recounted the experience in the 1956 *New York Times*:

"I was called to the telephone and a clipped British voice said, 'Mr. Levin? This is Maurice Evans.' I have a friend who does impersonations, so in a clipped British voice I told him to drop dead, old chap. Maurice Evans pondered that for a moment, then asked me whether—personal feelings aside—I would care to write a stage version of Mac Hyman's novel, *No Time For Sergeants*. 'Yes,' I said."

The result is the play you now hold in your hands.

While it might appear that adapting a book dramatically is a straightforward matter, its successful bringing-off requires mastery of many elements: structure, characterization, comedy (in this instance), and so forth. *The Saturday Review* at the time called out Levin as "a brilliant technician"; indeed, successfully adapting Mac Hyman's novel in both condensed (one-hour) and full-length (two-act) form speaks—beyond the laughs and all—to the level of behind-the-scenes expertise Levin brought to the matter.

There was one complication however in Evans' hiring of Levin—the young draftee still had three months of his two-year service remaining—and no amount of accumulated leave could satisfy the demands of the job at hand. So, Evans successfully petitioned the army for Levin's early release, on the basis that commercial theater constituted a form of *seasonal employment* (as it indeed did), such as in the agricultural trades. The release was granted, and Levin became a civilian again—three months ahead of schedule—with an honorable discharge, and the National Defense Service Medal (for having been drafted during wartime). He immediately set to work, and Broadway made time for *Sergeants* in the same year the television adaptation aired, 1955. But—owing to the show's subject matter—not before the Pentagon had fully OK'd its script.

Andy Griffith reprised his TV role of Will Stockdale, with the superb Roddy McDowall cast anew as his bespectacled chum *Ben Whitledge*. And making his Broadway debut in two featured parts (one per act) was Don Knotts—who'd go on with Griffith to form one of the great enduring comedy duos.

The *New York Post* called Levin's adaptation "one of the funniest plays ever seen on Broadway." And Levin's softening of some of Stockdale's originally more barbed contours (in both of his adaptations) resulted in further praise from the *Post* for the play's "warm and affectionate quality that is rare in comedies."

On the strength of *Sergeants'* source material, Levin's writerly skill, and Griffith's performance, the Broadway production proved as big a success as they come, running for two years, then being adapted into the classic Hollywood film, a short-lived TV series—even a comic book, and board game.

Sergeants—in all its various incarnations—also helped take "down-home" entertainment mainstream, playing an outsized role in engendering all manner of later "countrified" fare, as well as a phalanx of military-themed comedies.

A footnote: just as the earlier *Notebook Warrior*'s co-star Sidney Blackmer would go on to portray *Roman Castevet* in the iconic 1968 film adaptation of Levin's novel *Rosemary's Baby*, Maurice Evans (*Sergeants*' Broadway producer) would also appear in that film—as *Rosemary's* father figure, *Edward (Hutch) Hutchins*. As Levin said, *"It's interesting, the way one thing leads to another."*

Nicholas Levin
New York
March 2025

Left to right:
Myron McCormick,
Andy Griffith, and
Roddy McDowall
in *No Time For
Sergeants*, 1955
(Credit: Fred Fehl)

Ira Levin (2nd from left) with Andy Griffith and Maurice Evans (both seated) in rehearsal for *No Time For Sergeants* (1955)

NO TIME FOR SERGEANTS

Adapted from the novel by Mac Hyman

No Time For Sergeants was presented by Maurice Evans, in association with Emmett Rogers, at the Alvin Theatre, New York City, October 20, 1955, with the following cast:

(IN ORDER OF APPEARANCE)

PREACHER . . . . Don Knotts
WILL STOCKDALE. . . . . Andy Griffith
PA STOCKDALE . . . . Floyd Buckley
DRAFT MAN . . . . O. Tolbert-Hewitt
BUS DRIVER . . . . Michael Thoma
IRVIN BLANCHARD . . . . Robert Webber
ROSABELLE. . . . . Maree Dow
INDUCTEES . . . . Cecil Rutherford
                                        Robert McQuade
                                        Carl Albertson
                                        Arthur P. Keegan
                                        Van Williams
                                        Jules Racine
                                        Wynn Pearce
BEN WHITLEDGE . . . . Roddy McDowall
SERGEANT KING. . . . . Myron McCormick
A CAPTAIN . . . . Ed Peck
A NURSE . . . . Maree Dow
FIRST CLASSIFICATION CORPORAL . . Robert McQuade
SECOND CLASSIFICATION CORPORAL . . . Don Knotts
THIRD CLASSIFICATION CORPORAL . . . . Ray Johnson
A LIEUTENANT . . . . Earle Hyman
A PSYCHIATRIST . . . . James Millhollin
CIGARETTE GIRL . . . . Maree Dow
AN INFANTRYMAN. . . . . Arthur P. Keegan

AIR FORCE POLICEMAN . . . . Jules Racine
A COLONEL . . . . .Rex Everhart
LT. BRIDGES (PILOT). . . . . Hazen Gifford
LT. GARDELLA (CO-PILOT) . . . . Carl Albertson
LT. KENDALL (ENGINEER). . . . . Cecil Rutherford
LT. COVER (NAVIGATOR). . . . . .Bill Hinnant
GENERAL BUSH. . . . . Howard Freeman
GENERAL POLLARD . . . . Royal Beal
A SENATOR. . . . . O. Tolbert-Hewitt
AIDE TO GENERAL POLLARD. . . . . .Ray Johnson
LT. ABEL. . . . . .Rex Everhart
LT. BAKER . . . . Edmund Johnston
CAPT. CHARLES . . . . Wynn Pearce

The action of the play takes place in and above the
United States of America. Some of it is happening now and
some of it happened a while back. There are two acts.

ACT ONE

The house curtain rises on a second curtain, that of the "Callville Township Meeting Hall," on which is depicted a horde of Confederate soldiers surging on toward victory. The house lights dim, amateur musicians are heard, and the PREACHER *enters from the wings, applauding solicitously.*

PREACHER

Thank you, members of the Civic Orchestra, for fillin' in so beautifully, but now our speaker has finally arrived. And here he is, Callville's favorite son in uniform—Will Stockdale.

    (*He motions toward the wings, coaxes applause from audience—but no one appears.*)

Will Stockdale!

    (WILL STOCKDALE *enters, wearing a private's uniform. He watches the* PREACHER *exit, then finds the mark at the center of the stage and faces the audience. He would rather be anywhere else in the world.*)

WILL

Howdy. How I Won My Medal.

    (*Pause.*)

There's this medal that I got in the draft and I'm supposed to tell you how I won it. Well I didn't *win* it exactly; more like this fellow just *slipped* it to me. I tell you the truth, I'd just as soon somebody come up here and sung a song or somethin'.

(*He heads for the wings, stops, nods obediently several times and returns to center stage.*)

Well, How I Won My Medal. The whole thing begun, of course, when I went into the draft. Well, I didn't exactly *go in* to the draft, neither. What it was, was the draft *come out* to me. Last spring that was, one evenin' around the time the chickens was quietin' down. You know.

(*Through the backlit "Meeting Hall" curtain, a ramshackle cabin is seen, surrounded by scrubby trees.* PA STOCKDALE *is sitting on the porch steps, his chin in his hands, angry-looking. An ancient radio on a shelf is straining out hill-billy music. A rifle is propped against the front of the cabin; near it, a sleeping hound-dog whose head droops over the edge of the porch.*)

Pa and I had gone fishin' that day and he was settin' on the front steps of our place with his neck all red and his foot tappin'— angry, kind of. I'd caught a bigger fish than him. Anyhow, things was right peaceful, with my dog Blue asleep there, and the radio playin' some good music and all.

(PA *has heard something. He stands and looks* OFFSTAGE RIGHT.)

And then, all of a sudden, Pa stood up. Now that surprised me a good bit right there, because usually when we go fishin' it takes Pa two-three hours to get over it.

PA

(*Calling, still looking* OFFSTAGE.)

Will!

(*"Meeting Hall" curtain rises as* WILL *turns* UPSTAGE.)

WILL

What is it, Pa?
(*Starts to undo his tie.*)

PA

Come over here!

(WILL *heads for porch, taking off tie.*)

WILL

(*To audience.*)
I warn't in uniform then.
(*Goes up to* PA, *unbuttoning shirt.*)

PA

Listen. Your ears are better than mine. Somebody's comin'.

WILL

I don't hear nothin'.

PA

Turn off that whatchamacallit.

WILL

Radio.

PA

I know what you call it. Turn it off.
(WILL *turns it off, drops shirt and tie on porch. He is now
in T-shirt and khaki trousers.*)
First I heared one of them cars, and then it stopped, and now
somebody's comin'.

(*Sound of twigs breaking and mumbled cursing* OFFSTAGE
RIGHT.)

Hear?

DRAFT MAN
(OFFSTAGE.)
You stay right here and if I call come a'running.

(PA *snatches up rifle, holds it ready.*)

WILL
(*Trying to restrain him.*)
Pa . . . That ain't no way to welcome folks. Maybe it's kin.

PA
Kin don't come in cars. See if you can wake that hound-dog.

WILL
(*Crouching beside dog.*)
Hey, Blue. C'mon Blue. Got a big old hambone for you. C'mon
Blue . . .

(*Approaching sounds have been growing louder. Now* DRAFT MAN
*comes bursting in; a short, fat man in a white linen suit. He is
sweating, fuming, and picking branches from his ankles.*)

DRAFT MAN
Never seen such a prickly path in all my whole life! . . . Damn!
(*Coming up for air before* WILL, *who is still crouching.*)
You Will Stockdale?

WILL

(*Rising.*)

Howdy . . .

DRAFT MAN

(*Pointing vigorously.*)

Three damn times I been out here this month!

PA

(*Raising rifle.*)

Don't you pint your finger in my boy's face!

DRAFT MAN

(*Retreating a step.*)

Are you threatening me with a firearm? I'm a government rep-
resentative on government business!

PA

Bustin' up here without sayin' Howdy or nothin' . . . What
government?

DRAFT MAN

U.S. Government! The draft board! This boy's been called for
the April draft and never reported. He's a draft-dodger!

(*He points again.*)

PA

Fold in that finger, sir! I'm warnin' you, fold in that finger!

DRAFT MAN

(*Lowering his hand.*)

He can be put in jail for that. He's in tomorrow's group.

(*Turning to* WILL.)

This is your last chance, and by God, if you don't leave with that group at seven a.m. you're gonna be in more trouble than you ever seen! You already got one offense against you for not answering my letters!

WILL

I never got no letters.

DRAFT MAN

And don't tell me you can't read because you could've got somebody to read 'em to you, so that ain't no excuse!

(WILL, *shocked, turns to* PA.)

PA

Do you mean to stand here and say to my face that my son can't read?

DRAFT MAN

Now look . . .

PA

Do you think my son, who has *gone to school* and who has read *more times* than you could shake a stick at, couldn't read a puny little ole letter if he wanted to? By God, sir!

WILL

I never *got* no letters.

PA

I don't think I can stand to *listen* to any more of this, by God! Get that book!

(WILL *exits into cabin. To* DRAFT MAN:)

No sir! What you think don't mean nothin' to me . . .

(*Levels rifle again.*)

But we're gonna settle this here question here and now, and not have no more foolishness about it!

(WILL *enters from cabin with book.*)

Read at 'im!

WILL

(*Clears throat. Reads slowly:*)

Once there was a boy named Tony who wanted a pony. He went to his Mama and said, "May I have a pony?" and his Mama said,

(*Turns page.*)

"No, Tony, you may not have a pony."

(*Looks at* PA, *who signals him to continue.*)

So he went to his Papa and said, "May I have a pony?" and his Papa said, "No, Tony, you may not have—

(*Turns page.*)

—a pony."

(PA *lifts hand grandly.* WILL *closes book. To* DRAFT MAN:)

End of the book, he gets the pony anyhow.

PA

(*Advancing on* DRAFT MAN.)

Now that we've settled whether or not my boy can read . . .

WILL

Pa . . .

PA

. . . you best be gettin' off'n my property and into that car of yourn and out of range of—

WILL

Pa . . . Be Christian to him.

PA

Christian? You know what Christ woulda done if a man come
stompin' onto *His* property . . . not sayin' Howdy or nothin' . . .
sayin' folks couldn't read? *I* know what He woulda done. He
woulda sent that man straight to *hell*, by God!

WILL

Pa!
          (*Taking* PA's *shoulder, gently:*)
Now, I want to talk to you for a minute. Come here.
          (PA *turns to* WILL, *who backs toward cabin.* PA *looks back*
          at DRAFT MAN, *lowers rifle reluctantly and joins* WILL.
          They sit on porch steps.)
Now, Pa, listen. I don't think this here draft is such a bad idea.
I mean, I'd kind of like to go. There's a whole bunch of fellows
there and they all march along right snappy-like—

PA

You listen to me, boy. Goin' into the draft don't mean just goin'
into town. It means Macon and Atlanta, and farther still. I been
to Atlanta—you know that—when I was no older than you. I
told you how them folks . . . laughed at me and called me smart
names. You don't want that, boy.

WILL

Pa, now ain't the same as it was then.

PA

The hell it ain't.

WILL

But they *want* me. They even sent a man to come and fetch me, didn't they? And that ain't all. Last spring I seen this sign out on the sidewalk down there in town. This big picture of Uncle Sam. And "*Uncle Sam* wants you," he's sayin'—just like this fellow here, Pa, pintin' straight in my face. And don't you think this soldier fellow come up to me right then and there, invitin' me to come along with all the other fellows? I told him how you was ailin' then and would he kindly wait a while.

    (*Pause.*)

You been tearin' up them letters, haven't you, Pa? And you ain't ailin' no more.

    (*He rises.*)

Say good-bye to Blue for me when he wakes up, will you?

    (*Holds out his hand.*)

PA

You'll see, thing's ain't no different. They'll make fun of you . . . and talk sassy 'cause you ain't a town boy . . .

    (*Rises, grabs* WILL'*s hand.*)

Write to me regular, you hear?

WILL

Sure, Pa.

    (WILL *backs toward* DRAFT MAN.)

PA

Print big!

DRAFT MAN

All right now . . .

PA

Draft man! You tell them folks out there to be nice to that boy, hear?

(DRAFT MAN *mutters an impatient affirmative.*)
He's a *good* boy. And it's my fault he didn't come when he should'a.

(WILL *and* DRAFT MAN *start* OFFSTAGE.)

DRAFT MAN

Yeah, yeah . . .

WILL

'Bye, Pa.

PA

'Bye, Will . . .
(*He picks up "Tony and The Pony", holds it out.*)
You want your book?

WILL

No, Pa . . . 'Bye.

(PA *watches them off, looks at book, wipes it slowly with his sleeve. The lights dim out.*)

(*Lights come up on the town square. A bus stands* UPSTAGE. *There is a statue at* STAGE RIGHT *and a gas station with two pumps at* STAGE LEFT. INDUCTEES *are lounging around; one strumming a guitar and singing softly, one embracing a girl. As more* INDUCTEES *drift in, a civilian* BUS DRIVER *takes forms which they carry and gives them blue cards in exchange.*)

DRIVER

Fill it out. Last name first, first name, middle name last.
(*Gives a card to another* INDUCTEE.)
Fill it out. Last name first, first name, middle name last.

(IRVIN BLANCHARD *enters, wearing a leather jacket and dark glasses. He looks about disdainfully.*)

IRVIN

This the group going to the Air Force?

DRIVER

That's where I'm driving the bus to. You want me to reserve you a seat?

IRVIN

All right, save the jokes for the plowboys.

DRIVER

(*Glaring at* IRVIN, *giving him card.*)
Fill it out. Last name first, first name, middle name last.

IRVIN

I know.

(IRVIN *moves aside and begins writing as* DRAFT MAN *enters, his right wrist handcuffed to* WILL'*s left.*)

DRAFT MAN

Stand back, everybody. Stand back. Don't come too close. Keep away from him.

(INDUCTEES *who have been lying down, sit up. Guitar stops.* WILL *looks shamefaced as* DRAFT MAN *transfers cuff from his own wrist to gas pump.*)
Reckon this'll hold you.

                    WILL

Yes, sir.

                    DRIVER

Have any trouble bringing him over, Mr. McKinney?

                    DRAFT MAN
          (*Finished with handcuffs, stepping back and surveying* WILL.)
Uh-uh. Night in jail simmered all the wildness out of him.
          (*Takes forms and cards from* DRIVER, DRAFT MAN *gives card and pencil to* WILL.)
Fill it out. Last name first, first name, middle name last. Lean on the pump there.

                    WILL

Last name first . . .

                    DRAFT MAN

First name, middle name last.
          (WILL, *looking confused, holds card against pump and begins to write.*)
Any of you boys had any R.O.T.C.?

                    IRVIN

I did. Close to a year.

DRAFT MAN

What's your name?

IRVIN

Blanchard, Irvin S.

DRAFT MAN

Okay, Irvin, I'm setting you in charge of the group. When the bus gets to the Classification Center, report to the Sergeant there. Give him these here forms.

IRVIN

(*Nodding toward* WILL.)
What about *him*?

DRAFT MAN

Better keep the cuffs on him. Here's the key. It took me two months to flush him out of the hills, so see that he don't get away.

DRIVER

Mr. McKinney . . .

(DRAFT MAN *goes over to* DRIVER. IRVIN *goes to* WILL.)

IRVIN

You hear what he said, plowboy? I don't want any trouble, you understand?

WILL

Oh, me neither, Irvin.

IRVIN

My name to you is Blanchard.

WILL

(*Extending his hand.*)

It's a real pleasure.

IRVIN

Are you getting smart with me, plowboy?

(WILL *shakes his head.*)

I don't want to hear one peep out of you. Not a peep!

(IRVIN *moves aside.* WILL *resumes writing.*)

DRAFT MAN

All right, boys. Irvin here is in charge. Do like he tells you and don't give him any trouble. Callville is proud of her sons in uniform. Show them what kind of men we raise down here. Be good, and if you can't be good, be careful.

(*He laughs uproariously at his joke, then catches sight of the* INDUCTEE *and* GIRL *embracing by bus.*)

Rosabelle!

ROSABELLE

(*Breaking away from the* INDUCTEE.)

Pa!

DRAFT MAN

Get on home!

ROSABELLE

Yes, Pa!

(*She runs* OFFSTAGE.)

DRAFT MAN

I told you to stay home this time. Now git! Ma'll kill you!
(*To* INDUCTEES:)
Well, 'bye, boys. Don't take any wooden nickels!

(*This line really kills him. He exits in a roar of laughter, which is echoed mockingly by the* INDUCTEES. IRVIN *moves to center and silences them.*)

IRVIN

Okay. Okay! Into the bus when I call your name. DeRoy, Richard S.

FIRST INDUCTEE

Here!

(*Gives card to* IRVIN *and exits around bus. Other* INDUCTEES *do the same when their names are called.*)

IRVIN

Farnum, Robert E.

SECOND INDUCTEE

Here!

IRVIN

Hooper, Junior C.

THIRD INDUCTEE

Here!

IRVIN

Lemon, Henry P.

FOURTH INDUCTEE

Here!

IRVIN

Stockdale, Will.

WILL

(*Pause.*)

Here . . .

IRVIN

Swinburne, Armand A.

FIFTH INDUCTEE

Here!

IRVIN

Whitledge, Benjamin B.
(*Pause.*)
Whitledge, Benjamin B.!

(WHITLEDGE, BENJAMIN B., *comes running in, an overnight bag in one hand, a pink envelope in the other. He is small, spindly and frenetic.*)

BEN

Here! Here! Whitledge! Here! Benjamin B.! Is Mr. McKinney here? Mr. McKinney—the man on the draft board! Where is he?

IRVIN

Who?

BEN

Mr. McKinney, the man on the draft board! Where'd he go?
I got a letter for him!

IRVIN

Take it easy, sonny. You just missed him.

BEN

I got to find him! I got a letter for him!

IRVIN

He left *me* in charge.
(*Plucks the letter out of* BEN's *hand.*)

BEN

Hey, give me that! That's a private letter! You can't take that! It's
official business, for Mr. McKinney! Give it back!

(IRVIN *pushes* BEN *away from him roughly.* WILL *extends his free
arm and keeps* BEN *from falling over backwards.*)

IRVIN

Don't you understand English? *I'm* in charge.
(*Shoves card at* BEN.)
Fill out this card.

BEN

That's a private letter . . .
(IRVIN *glares at him, moving* UPSTAGE.)
You big . . .

WILL

Don't get sore at Irvin, fellow. He's had R.O.T.C.

BEN

That don't give him no right to push me around.
(*Starts to fill out card.*)

WILL

You put your last name, and then your first name, and then . . .
(*Shows his card to* BEN.)
Like this.

BEN

(*Reading:*)
Stockdale, Will, Will, Stockdale, Stockdale, Stockdale . . .
(*Shaking head.*)
All you need is one of each.

WILL

That's all?
(*Scratches head, begins crossing out extra names.*)

BEN

(*Glaring toward* IRVIN.)
Wise guy . . .

(WILL *drops pencil, has difficulty retrieving it because of handcuffs,*
BEN *picks it up for him, notices handcuffs.*)

BEN

What's the matter with you?

WILL

They think I'm a draft-dodger, but I ain't.

BEN

(*Taking* WILL's *card.*)

Here, give me . . . You can't write good with handcuffs.

WILL

Thanks. Can't write much good *without* 'em, neither.

BEN

(*Glares at* IRVIN.)

Big shot!

(*To* WILL:)

Ever have measles?

WILL

No.

BEN

(*Making checks on card.*)

The mumps?

WILL

No.

BEN

Chicken pox . . .

WILL

No.

BEN

Any other communicable diseases?

WILL

Reckon not.
>   (*Watches* BEN *write.*)
You figger they're gonna make me go back home?

IRVIN

>   (*Reading letter.*)
Hey Wiggins, come here!

(INDUCTEE *comes to* IRVIN, *reads over his shoulder.*)

BEN

Ever break any bones?

WILL

Leg bone once.

BEN

Which leg?

WILL

The right. No, it was the left. Yeh, the left.

BEN

>   (*Writing.*)
Any member of your family belong to groups planning to overthrow the government by unconstitutional means?

WILL

(*Thinks.*)

No, we're pretty satisfied.

(BEN *writes.* WILL *thinks.*)

He still limps a mite.

BEN

Who does?

WILL

That fellow whose leg bone I broke.

(BEN *looks annoyedly at* WILL, *begins erasing.*)

He hit me first . . .

WIGGINS

Hey, Young!

(*Another* INDUCTEE *joins* IRVIN *and* WIGGINS. *They chuckle over the letter.*)

BEN

Did you ever have R.O.T.C.?

WILL

No.

(*Pause.*)

Irvin had it—close to a year. I figure he still got a touch of it in him.

BEN

Look, Stockdale—

                              WILL

Will's my name.

                              BEN

Listen . . .

                              WILL

What's yours again?

                              BEN

Ben Whitledge.

                              WILL

Howdy.
            (*He extends his hand.* BEN *shakes it.*)

                              BEN

Hi. Look, Will, R.O.T.C. ain't a disease. It's training. Reserve,
Officer, Training—uh—Corporation.

                              WILL

Is that the truth . . .

                              BEN

Sure. There's different kinds. There's Cavalry R.O.T.C., Artillery
R.O.T.C., Infantry R.O.T.C . . . Infantry's the best.

                              WILL

Yeh. . . that's what I always thought . . .
            (BEN *writes on his own card.*)
Ben, Irvin ain't sick?

BEN

No. And he don't rank no higher than we do, neither, 'cause
R.O.T.C. don't mean nothing unless you finish the course.

IRVIN

(*Removing glasses and holding up sheet of pink paper.*)
"So I beg of you, Mr. McKinney, please get my enclosed letter
to the Commanding Officer in the Air Force."

BEN

Hey, you . . .

(BEN *flies at* IRVIN *but* WIGGINS *and* YOUNG *grab him.*)

IRVIN

". . . so that my son Ben will be put into the Infantry the same
as his six brothers . . ."

BEN

Give me that! You big—let go! Let go of me!

IRVIN

"All his life little Ben has been dreaming of being a real Infan-
try soldier like all the men in our family."
(INDUCTEES *roar.*)
Little Ben wanna be a big soldier!

WILL

(*Loud. Silencing them:*)
Irvin! That there letter belongs to Ben. You give it to him.

IRVIN

I told you to keep your mouth shut, plowboy!
(*Resumes reading:*)
"It will break his poor heart if he's put in the Air Force in-
stead of—"

(WILL *wrenches his arm free, along with a piece of the gas pump.*)

WILL

Give Ben his letter, Irvin.

IRVIN

(*A bit pale.*)
I'm in charge here . . . I'm warning you . . .

WILL

Ben, are you absolutely sure about that R.O.T.C.?
(BEN, *still held captive, nods,* WILL *hits* IRVIN; *a blockbuster.*
As IRVIN *collapses,* WILL *plucks the letter out of his hand*
and gives it to BEN. *Light irises down to a pin-spot on* WILL.
He turns, comes DOWNSTAGE *and addresses audience, at-*
tempting to conceal the handcuffs, which embarrass him.)
After laying there in that jail till seven o'clock in the morning it
was right good to finally git some exercise. Well anyhow, we had
a real nice ride up to the Classification Center. Ben and I got us
a seat in the back of the bus and what we done was every fifteen
minutes we switched around—you know, so there wouldn't be
neither one of us settin' next to the window no longer than the
other. We rode up through Pinehurst, and then another town
just as big, and then another town as big as Pinehurst and Callville put together! You never seen nothin' like it. And then we
come to Macon. Whew! Half an hour to get through it! And it

was real fun, with all the fellows hangin' out the bus windows, whistlin' at the gals and hollerin' "Oh, you kid" and "I want you in my stockin' for Christmas" and a whole lot of funny sayings like that. I did enjoy it that day. But somewhere between Macon and Atlanta, Ben and I both dozed off and didn't wake up until we was at the Classification Center.

(*Lights fade on him. Whistle blows in darkness. Light comes up on* SERGEANT KING, *standing before a section of wall on which is a bulletin board marked "Barracks #10—Sgt. King."* KING *looks very tired and somewhat pained by it all. He gives another blast on the whistle.*)

KING

Please . . . let's keep it quiet . . .
> (*He waits for silence, glances at his wrist watch, and starts unreeling his orientation speech in a somnambulistic monotone, avoiding any inflection that might give meaning to the words. He takes a breath whenever he feels the need—usually in mid-sentence.*)

On behalf of the President of the United States, the Secretary of the Air Force and the Commanders of the base and this squadron, I want to welcome you gentlemen to the United States Air Force. This is a classification center where you will undergo a series of tests both physical and mental designed to determine your abilities and potentialities so that you may be trained for the position from which you and the Air Force will derive the greatest benefit, tests are for your own good so do your best in every test. My name is King, K-I-N-G, *Sergeant* King, and I'm in charge of this barracks in which you will be billeted for approximately two weeks. During this period the barracks *will* be kept spotlessly clean, maybe it's just a stopping place to you, but to me—*it's home.* Before turning in tonight every one of you will write a letter to your nearest of kin informing them that you have arrived safely and *are in the best of health.* If at any time a problem should arise, feel free to consult me about its solution.

 (Opens door of his room.)

I am here to help you during these first difficult days of military service. *Knock before entering.*

(He exits, closing door. Blackout. Lights come up in KING'*s room, a cosy place with many homelike touches.* KING *stands just within door, garrison cap in hand, wiping his forehead. He hangs cap on hook, goes to radio on shelf and turns it on. Pausing to straighten framed sampler on which "Mother" is embroidered in prominent letters, he goes down to small table with hotplate and percolator.* KING *jiggles percolator, nods, sets it on hotplate, flicks switch, and looks at his watch. Knock on door.)*

KING

Come in.

*(*IRVIN *enters, still in civilian clothes, holding the forms that* DRAFT MAN *gave him. He comes to attention.)*

IRVIN

Private Blanchard delivering forms on eight inductees as ordered.

KING

 (A contemplative pause.)

You keep standing like that, you're gonna pull a muscle.

 (Starts taking off tie.)

Just put them down.

 *(*IRVIN *starts to put forms on bunk.)*

Not on the bed please.

(IRVIN *looks around for someplace else.* KING *nods toward the table.* IRVIN *puts forms there, hesitates.*)
Anything else?

IRVIN

Sergeant, I feel it's my duty to tell you about one of the men. Fellow named Stockdale. A draft-dodger. He gave me a lot of trouble.
(*Takes handcuffs out of pocket.*)
They brought him to the bus in these.

KING

(*A bit taken aback by handcuffs.*)
I'll make a note of it.

IRVIN

I think he ought to be given disciplinary action. He took a swing at—one of the men. Even knocked him out. He jumped this man from behind and knocked him out.

KING

In the barracks here?

IRVIN

Back at the bus.

KING

(*Pause.*)
I'll make a note of it.

IRVIN

I thought he ought to be reported to the Squadron Commander, that's what.

(KING *freezes for a moment.*)
I mean, I think it's my duty to see that he—

KING

Any reporting is done around here, I do it.

IRVIN

Sure you do, and this fellow Stockdale is a real troublemaker
and he—

KING

(*Sitting on bed.*)
Sonny, look; how long have you been in the service?

IRVIN

About six hours, I guess. I had R.O.T.C., though.

KING

Uh-huh . . . And they told you it was all efficiency and getting things done and standing at attention and running
around?
(*Taking off shoes.*)
I been in for eighteen years, and it ain't like you think at all.
It's a quiet, peaceful life . . . if everybody minds their own business. It's like there's a big lake, nice and calm; I'm in one canoe,
you're in another, the Captain's in a canoe, the Colonel . . . You
know what you do when you complain to somebody, or report
somebody, or request something?
(IRVIN *shakes his head.*)
You make waves.

(*Puts his feet into big woolly slippers, rises, goes to table, takes cup and saucer from shelf, pours coffee. IRVIN, meanwhile, puts handcuffs on forms and goes to door.*)

IRVIN

Well, I thought the Captain would want to know, if he's got a troublemaker in the outfit.

KING

Look, Sonny, I hate to pull rank, but for your information, you got the smallest canoe in the whole damn lake! Good afternoon, Private.

(IRVIN *exits, closing door.* KING *stretches out on his bunk.*)

RADIO ANNOUNCER

Our next request comes from Master Sergeant Orville C. King at the Air Force Classification Center. Here you are, Sergeant.

(KING *beams. The radio plays* "Flow Gently, Sweet Afton," KING *sips his coffee thoughtfully, and the lights slowly fade.*)

(*Lights come up on a double-decker bunk.* BEN, *in underwear, manages to climb on to upper bunk, with* WILL'*s assistance.*)

BEN

Don't boost—I can make it.

WILL

Ben, I wish you would take the bottom one.

BEN

No, sir. Just hand me my bag.

WILL

(*Doing so.*)
Honest, I like sleeping high.

BEN

No, sir. You sat on the bottom bunk first.

WILL

I didn't mean nothin' by it. Honest I didn't.

BEN

First come, first served. That's the military way.

VOICE

(OFFSTAGE.)
Lights out in five minutes.

WILL

(*Pulling on* BEN's *bag.*)
C'mon, Ben.

BEN

I won't, I tell you!

(IRVIN *and two* INDUCTEES *enter from* RIGHT.)

IRVIN

Let that man alone, Stockdale! Get your hands off that man's
things!

(WILL, *wide-eyed, withdraws his hand.* BEN *falls back on bunk.*)
They brought you to the bus in handcuffs and I'm beginning to think I never should've taken 'em off you!

WILL

Irvin, I wasn't doin' anythin'. I was just—

IRVIN

I've stood about as much as I'm *gonna* stand out of you! One lucky punch don't make no champion. If you want to start some more fighting go after somebody your own size, not some skinny little—

BEN

(*Swinging his feet off top bunk.*)
You watch your mouth! Why don't you mind your own business anyhow?

IRVIN

Look, this fellow was going to—

BEN

That's between him and me! Nobody asked you to butt in!

WILL

Now, Ben, don't . . .

IRVIN

I was only trying to do you a favor, Junior!

BEN

Who you calling Junior? Who asked you anything anyhow?

IRVIN

All right. If that's the way you feel about it, all right. You want to be buddies with the draft-dodger, *be* buddies with the draft-dodger. Go ahead . . .

BEN

That's the way I feel about it.

IRVIN

(*Backing away.*)
You better just get into bed and *don't start no trouble in this barracks!* Get into bed!

WILL

I was just goin' to, Irvin.

FIRST INDUCTEE

Give him time, Irvin. Beds is strange to Plowboy; he's used to sleepin' with the hogs!

(INDUCTEES *laugh,* WILL *joins in,* BEN *glares.* IRVIN *and* INDUCTEES, *laughing, move* OFFSTAGE.)

BEN

(*Livid.*)
What's the matter with you anyhow?

WILL

Me?

BEN

Taking their insults all day and hee-hawing like a danged donkey!

WILL

Ah, they don't mean nothin', Ben. And besides, that one about sleepin' with the hogs was kind of funny.
(*Starts taking off pants.*)

BEN

(*Getting under blankets.*)
Aw . . .

WILL

I figger if we just laugh with 'em, Ben, pretty soon they'll get tired of carryin' on, and that way there won't be no ruckus or nothin'.

BEN

You think laughing is gonna stop these guys? A good licking is all they understand!

WILL

(*Hangs pants on end of bunk.*)
You think so?

BEN

I know so! . . . And you hee-hawing like a danged donkey!

(*He turns over, putting his back to* WILL. WILL *scratches his head, sits on bottom bunk. Lights dim down and a bugle starts playing "Taps."* WILL *listens for a moment.*)

WILL

(*To audience:*)
Somebody brung their trumpet.

(THIRD INDUCTEE *crosses.*)

FIRST INDUCTEE

Lonesome for the hogs, Plowboy?

(WILL *laughs half-heartedly.*)

WILL

(*To audience:*)
I reckon Ben knew what he was talkin' about when he said laughin' warn't gonna do no good. But I figgered I couldn't start bangin' away at 'em with no reason so I set around waitin' for someone to give me a reason.

FOURTH INDUCTEE

(*Passing* WILL.)
Ain't used to sleeping indoors, are you, Plowboy?

WILL

(*To audience:*)
I didn't feel as how that was quite enough.

(IRVIN *and his two sidekicks return.*)

IRVIN

Get in bed, Plowboy.

WILL

(*To audience:*)

That warn't enough.

IRVIN

(*To* WILL:)

That is, if you can lift those big clumsy feet of yours.

WILL

(*To audience:*)

That warn't enough either.

IRVIN

(*To* BEN:)

Don't wet the bed, Junior, or Mama will spank.

WILL

(*To audience:*)

That were.

(*He slugs* IRVIN *and* IRVIN *goes down.*)

No stayin' power at all.

(*Other* INDUCTEES *attack.* BEN *hops onto one's shoulders and pummels his head.* WILL *dispatches the others with great ease, punctuating the action with the following lines:*)

No more muscle than a rabbit . . . Livin' in town, that's what does it . . . They stay up till close on to ten o'clock every night! Eat all them fancy foods . . . Orange juice . . . Won't touch green peas unless the shells is off 'em! Surprises me they got what little strength they have . . .

(*All the assailants are floored by now. They stagger away.* WILL *comes* DOWNSTAGE, *brushing off his hands.*)

But there was a whole lot of 'em, so it was a pretty good fight anyhow!

>   (*Turning up to* BEN.)

Warn't it, Ben?

                    BEN

Aww . . .

                    WILL

Could've been better, but it wasn't bad.

                    BEN

Dog it, Will. This will mess up everything!

                    WILL

What will, Ben?

                    BEN

Fighting—in the barracks.

                    WILL

But you said a lickin' was all they'd understand.

                    BEN

Not in the barracks! One of them's bound to talk about it. Dog it, I'll never get into the Infantry now . . . starting a big ruckus . . . I figgered if we kept our mouths shut and didn't do nothin to nobody we might get transferred—but now—

                    WILL

Both of us?

BEN

But now they're sure to talk about the fight—they're bound to!

WILL

No they won't, Ben. If one of them says anythin', I'll take him out back and whomp him good.

BEN

Now there you go again, Will! You think they want folks in the Infantry that acts like that? No sir, they want folks who can take it and keep their mouths shut, the way a man ought to do. Transfer? We'll be lucky if they don't transfer us into the Navy— walking around in them li'l ole white uniforms!

WILL

You want both of us to transfer, Ben?

BEN

Don't you understand, Will? It's the Infantry does the real fight-ing . . . the rest is just helpers. Look at The War Between The States. How about that?

WILL

Yeh! How about that!

BEN

See what I mean? Listen, every man in my whole family's been in the Infantry, clear back to Great-Grandpa! You know what he done? Fought with Stonewall Jackson at Chancellorsville, that's what!

WILL

Licked him good too, I bet!

BEN

By dog, first thing tomorrow morning I'm going to get the Sergeant's permission to see the Captain. I'll give him Ma's letter . . .

(*Takes letter from under pillow, looks at it.*)

Aww . . .

(*Throws letter disgustedly on floor.*)

What's the use!

(*Climbs into bunk and under blankets.*)

WILL

But, Ben, maybe you'll get to like the Air Force. Zoomin' all over the sky, shoutin' Roger and Wilco and everythin'. Maybe it won't be so bad.

BEN

Bad! You know what they call men in the Air Force? Airmen! Like something out of a danged funny book! How you gonna like it when somebody calls you Airman?

WILL

By God, I just don't think I'd stand for it.

BEN

AIRMAN!

(*He buries his head in the pillow.*)

WILL

Ben!

(*No response.*)

Hey, Ben!

(*Still no reply.* WILL *picks up the letter which* BEN *has discarded. He looks at the envelope.*)

By dog!

(*Lights fade, leaving only a pin-spot on* WILL *as he takes trousers from bunk, pulls them on, tiptoes down to door of* KING'S *room and knocks lightly. He buttons trousers and knocks again, harder. He fastens belt and knocks once more, a real rafter-shaker. There is an excited bumping and fumbling from* KING'S *room.*)

KING

All right! I'm up! I'm up! All right!
    (*More bumping and fumbling. Lights come up;* KING'S
    table lamp. He almost knocks it over. One leg is in his
    trousers, one arm in his shirt. WILL *enters room.*)
All right! I'm up!

WILL

Howdy! I'm Will Stockdale.

KING

    (*Struggling into uniform.*)
I didn't hear no whistle. Tell the men to line up in back. If the Captain comes around tell him I'm checking on who overslept. I'll be out as soon as I . . .
    (*Looks at* WILL, *looks around, looks at wrist watch.*)
It's ten o'clock . . . at night.

WILL

It is?
    (KING *shoves his wrist watch under* WILL's *nose.*)
Ooh! That's the prettiest watch . . .

KING
(*Dazed by the enormity of the sin.*)
You woke me.

WILL
You said to knock before enterin'.

KING
(*Sinking on bunk, removing uniform.*)
Why did you wake me?

WILL
Well, this ain't nothin' personal against you, Sergeant, or that we don't like your barracks or nothin' like that. What it is is Ben's got these six brothers that are all Infantry—that's my new buddy Ben that's sleepin' out there—so naturally he don't want to be in the Air Force, I mean with the Infantry doin' the real fightin' and the Air Force just bein' the helpers. You know, like in The War Between The States. So he wants to transfer to the Infantry and he asked me to go along with him. I figgered you could do it for us. I heared what you said out there, about how you was here to help us durin' these first difficult days of military service.

KING
(*Stares, turns away.*)
Why do they send all the bums and idiots to my barracks?

WILL
They do?

KING
(*Turning to him again.*)
Yes. Yes, they do.

WILL

Sho' must be a mess.

KING

(*Rising.*)
Now look, whatever-your-name-is, I want you to get—

WILL

Stockdale.

KING

Stockdale. I want you to get out of this room and—Stock-
dale . . .
(*Turns to table, lifts handcuffs.*)
Stockdale . . .
(*Turning to* WILL *again.*)
Now don't start anything with me, you hear. Just get out of here
and go to sleep, that's all.

WILL

Yes, sir.
(*As he exits:*)
Ben *did* say the Captain was the one to see.

KING

STOCKDALE!
(*Rushes after him.*)
Where are you going?

WILL

To the Captain.

KING

No . . . no . . . You can't . . .
(*Pushes* WILL *back into room.*)

WILL

Ben knows all about doin' things military-like, and he said the
Captain was—

KING

Stockdale, you're . . . you're . . .
(*Makes wave-making gesture.*)
You can't *do* this. This Captain'll rip off your stripes as soon as
look at you.

WILL

I ain't got no stripes.

KING

You'll never get transfers waking him up. He won't understand;
believe me, he won't!

WILL

I'll go over it real slow.

KING

Oh Lord . . . Look, this Captain . . . he . . . he won't do a favor
for anybody unless they do a favor for him first! That's it. Now
how would you like to do a big favor for the Captain?

WILL

Me?

KING

Come on.

(*Virtually drags* WILL *across stage.*)

You do one for him, he'll do one for me, and I do one for you.
That's the way it works in the service.

(*Lights come up in latrine and fade out in* KING*'s room.*)

KING

Do you know what this is, Stockdale?

WILL

Well, it's kind of a big outhouse, ain't it?

KING

We call it the latrine.

WILL

(*Looking around.*)

La-trine . . . How about that . . .

KING

You might say it's the Captain's hobby. He inspects it every
chance he gets, and when everything is sparkling, the Captain
sparkles too.

(*Takes long-handled brush from wall and gives it to* WILL.)

You stay in here and get things all cleaned up. You are the Officer in Charge.

WILL

(*Overwhelmed.*)

In charge?

KING

Every last one! All yours!

WILL

Golly!

KING

(*Going to door.*)

Now stay in here, you understand? Don't go no place.

WILL

You bet! Good night!

KING

(*Incredulously.*)

Good night . . .

(*Exits, shaking head wonderingly.*)

WILL

(*Calling after him.*)

Say, thanks!

(*He tucks handle of brush under his belt and begins collecting trash from floor. Door of* KING*'s room is heard slamming. To audience:*)

Well! It just goes to show you how good things happen to you when you least expect 'em.

(*Hums at his work.*)

I stayed Officer in Charge of this here la-trine all night, a'rubbin' and a'scrubbin' and doin' my best to make things sparkle like Sergeant King said.

(*Puts trash in can.*)

And by the time mornin' come—if you'll excuse my braggin'—I

think I done a right good job of it. Sergeant King was real pleased with how things come out.

(KING *enters latrine.*)

KING

Beautiful! Beautiful . . . beautiful . . .
  (*At commodes.*)
. . . beau—ti—ful!

WILL

Shucks, it ain't hard . . .

KING

(*Looks around incredulously.*)
Wait till the *Captain* sees this! He inspects this place like it was an operating room where they was getting ready to *cut out his heart!* Never in your life have you seen such a man for sticking his head *right down into* things!

WILL

You figger he'll like what I done?

KING

He'll be a new man . . .
  (KING *stares some more, then goes to* WILL *and puts his hand solemnly on his shoulder.*)
Will . . . How would you like to be . . . Permanent Latrine Orderly?

WILL

Permanent Latrine Orderly . . .

KING

P.L.O.!

WILL

Golly . . .

KING

You'll keep this place all the time like it is now, the Captain'll get off my back . . .

WILL

Gee, I sure would like to do it, Sergeant. Only I was set on helpin' Ben get those transfers. He's my buddy.

KING

Ain't I your buddy?

WILL

You are?

KING

You help me, I'll help Ben. But don't say a word about this outside of this room, you understand? I'm going straight over to the Record Section and fix it with some friends of mine.

WILL

Don't I have to go get them tests you talked about yesterday, to get myself classified?

KING

(At door.)
No, Will . . .

(*A final enraptured look at latrine.*)
. . . you've *been* classified.

(*He exits.* WILL *turns happily to audience.*)

WILL

Well, didn't *that* make me feel pretty good?
    (*Hangs brush on wall, takes tie and khaki shirt from hook,
    puts them on during following.*)
I worked just as hard as I could all week long. Of course, every time I seen Ben, he took on right fierce about how it was against the rules for me to be permanent in the latrine. He didn't mean nothin' by it, though. Anyhow I worked real hard; I scrubbed what was for scrubbin' and polished what was for polishin', and what was left over, I painted. And by Saturday, when the Captain come to inspect, I had everythin' so white and shiny you couldn't hardly look at it without squenchin' up your eyes. Them faucets for instance; I polished them so hard they don't say hot and cold no more!

(*Smooths down his hair and comes to attention facing the door. Door flies open.*)

KING

Ten-hut!
    (KING *holds door for* CAPTAIN, *then follows him in.*)

WILL

    (*Saluting.*)
Latrine ready for inspection, sir!

(CAPTAIN *returns salute, sees glittering latrine, lowers arm slowly.* WILL *drops salute.* CAPTAIN, *wide-eyed, turns to* KING. KING *smiles complacently.* CAPTAIN *moves incredulously about latrine.*)

CAPTAIN

This is incredible . . . This is absolutely . . . incredible! I'm
pleased! No, no . . . no, I'm *happy*!

KING

Thank you, sir, thank you.

CAPTAIN

 (Inspects commodes, thoroughly, then beams at WILL.)
You the one on latrine duty today, Private?

WILL

Yes, sir. All week, sir.

(KING *clears his throat forebodingly.*)

CAPTAIN

Well, you are to be congratulated.
 (Examines sink.)
Just look at the—
 (Turns to WILL.)
What did you say?

WILL

Me? Nothin', sir.

CAPTAIN

Something about all week.

WILL

Well, I done my best in one day, but to be fair with you it took
a week of rubbin' and scrubbin' to get it like this.

CAPTAIN

(*To* KING.)

Is this man being punished for—

WILL

Heck no, sir! I'm P.L.O.!

CAPTAIN

What?

WILL

Permanent Latrine Orderly.

KING

Stockdale . . .

WILL

Don't credit me none, sir. It's *all* Sergeant King's doin'. He's even got it fixed up so's I don't have to get classified!

KING

Sir—

CAPTAIN

That's . . . that's impossible!

WILL

Oh no, sir. He fixed it with some friends of his.

KING

Stockdale . . .

WILL

It was him got me to work so hard, tellin' me how latrines is
your hobby and stickin' your head into things and all.

KING

Sir, I can . . .

WILL

Now don't be bashful, Sergeant! Sir, I been wantin' to tell you
what a good sergeant he is. He solves our problems for us, and
he helps us out on our difficult days of military service, and I
reckon he's just about the best danged sergeant there is in the
whole danged Air Force!
>   (*Pause.*)
Sir, you really ought to get up off'n his back.

(CAPTAIN *turns slowly to* KING; KING *turns slowly to liquid.*)

CAPTAIN

How long have you been a sergeant?
>   (KING *gives an incomprehensible mumble.*)
Speak up!

KING

Sixteen years, sir.

CAPTAIN

How long do you expect to remain a sergeant?

KING
>   (*Hopefully.*)
Twelve years?

CAPTAIN

You will remain a sergeant for exactly one week. One week! Unless this man completes the entire classification process and is shipped out with the group he came in with. Do you understand? Unless this man is out of here by the end of next week, you will not be in charge of this barracks, you will not be a sergeant; you will in all probability be a permanent latrine orderly. P.L.O.!

KING

(*Saluting weakly.*)

Yes, sir!

(CAPTAIN *returns salute and goes to door. Stops outside latrine doorway, turns and speaks to* WILL.)

CAPTAIN

This is not your fault, Private. You've done a fine job. This is the cleanest latrine I've seen in my entire career.

WILL

Thank you, sir. My aim was to get it just as clean as that operatin' room where they're gettin' ready to cut out your heart.

(*Before* WILL *has finished the above,* KING *has leaped across room and slammed door in* CAPTAIN'S *face. He remains against door, staring at* WILL, *trembling.*)

You forgot to ask him about the transfers.

KING

What happened? What did you do it for?

WILL

Well, I couldn't see no sense in *me* gettin' all the credit.

KING

   (*Coming close to* WILL, *not daring to touch him.*)
Look, Will, we got to get you classified. We got to get you out
of here . . .

WILL

   (*Pause.*)
You don't want me around no more? I thought we was
buddies.

KING

   (*Quickly:*)
It ain't what I want, Will; it's what the Captain wants.
   (*Leading* WILL *out of latrine.*)
Come on, we gotta get you classified in a hurry. There's all kinds
of tests you'll have to take, and people you'll have to talk with.
You'll have to work real hard.

(KING *and* WILL *are now spotlighted downstage, as rest of stage
fades into darkness.*)

WILL

I'll work hard, all right, but I don't know . . . The last time I
took a test was close on to five years ago, and then it was just
one of them tests where you try this fellow's toothpaste for ten
days and see if'n your teeth don't get brighter.
   (*Pause.*)
I failed.

KING
(*Looks desperate. He shows* WILL *his wrist watch.*)
Look, you been admiring this watch of mine, haven't you?

WILL
I sure have! It's the prettiest . . .

KING
If you're ready to ship out by next Saturday like the Captain said—it's yours!

WILL
Mine?

KING
Yours!

WILL
Gol-ly!

KING
So you're going to try your hardest, right?

WILL
Right!

KING
And not waste no time?

WILL
No sir!

KING

Good! Good boy! Now first thing Monday morning we start Classification. You just stay right here and relax, rest your head. I'm going over to the testing area and see if I can . . . uh, borrow some of the tests.

(*He vanishes into the darkness.* WILL *turns to audience.*)

WILL

That Classification was really somethin'. They got this great big buildin' all full of doctors and nurses and officers—all of 'em walkin' around real quickety-quick and not smilin' at nobody. And first thing you knowed, one of 'em was mashin' down your tongue with an ice cream stick! You think I'm makin' this up. It's the truth! One of them fellows was even goin' around poppin' everybody in the knee with a little rubber hammer!

(*Lights fade up on a hallway with three doors marked "Manual Dexterity," "Psychiatrist" and "Oculist."* OFFICERS, INDUCTEES, NURSES *and* DOCTORS *cross back and forth. Type-writers and tabulators can be heard.* WILL *sets about rolling a cigarette.*)

FIRST CORPORAL
    (*Crossing.*)
Hey, you there!
    (WILL *turns.*)
No smoking!
    (*Points to wall sign.*)
Don't you know how to read?

WILL

(*To audience:*)
Good thing Pa ain't around to hear that. Well, anyhow, I did pretty good on it all. The written tests was exactly the same as the ones Sergeant King borrowed, but the only trouble was the Sergeant spent so much time drummin' the answers into me, there was hardly no time left to study the questions they joined up with. So in the tests, the answers was easy, but the questions was real hard. By Friday afternoon, I was down to the last three tests, and Sergeant King said it looked like maybe I might get myself classified for Gunnery School.

(*"Manual Dexterity" door opens.* KING *sticks his head out.*)

KING

Will! Come on!
(WILL *goes up to* KING.)
Corporal's waiting for you.

(*Lights come up in "Manual Dexterity" room and fade out in hallway. An officious little* CORPORAL *stands waiting; a large irregularly shaped link in each hand.*)

SECOND CORPORAL

(*Motions* WILL *into chair.*)
What we do here, Private, is evaluate your manual dexterity. On a time scale in relation to digital-visual coordination.
(*He holds up links.*)
Two irregular steel links . . .
(*He fits them together, a complex job.*)
. . . which can be interconnected . . . thusly.
(*Holds them up, joined, then separates them.*)

I separate them . . .
> (*Joins them again.*)

. . . I join them. It will be your task, Private, when I give the signal, to place the two links in the interconnected relationship I have just demonstrated.

(*He puts a link in each of* WILL'*s hands.* WILL *looks at them confusedly.*)

WILL

I put 'em together?

SECOND CORPORAL

That's right, you "put them together." I'll time you. Three minutes is passing.
> (*Winds stop watch.*)

KING

Whatever you do, don't get nervous.

SECOND CORPORAL

Ready?
> (*Raises watch.*)

Go!

(WILL *slowly touches one link against the other, baffled.* KING *is on top of him.*)

KING

There we go! At-a-boy! Put 'em together!

SECOND CORPORAL

Sergeant! Please. No one ever does it in less than two minutes!
Please! You're not even supposed to be in here!

(*He pulls* KING *away. They move aside, conversing in low tones.*)

KING

No, no. It's okay. You see, I'm rushing him through so he can
catch up with the group he came in with. He's a special case.

SECOND CORPORAL

Well, I'll have to ask you not to speak to him during the actual
testing. It's a difficult problem and requires his full attention.

(*As* KING *and* SECOND CORPORAL *continue their exchange,* WILL
*is busily wrenching open one link, shoving it through its mate and
compressing the pair into something resembling a bowknot.*)

WILL

I'm done.

KING

Stop the watch!

SECOND CORPORAL

Done?
          (*Looking at watch.*)
In fourteen seconds?
          (*Takes links from* WILL.)
He . . . look what he . . . look!
          (*Tries to separate links.*)

KING

He put them together, didn't he?

SECOND CORPORAL

(*Running into hallway.* KING *and* WILL *follow. Lights dim out in room and come up in hallway.*)

Corporal!

KING

Now what are you making a fuss about? You said put 'em together and he—

SECOND CORPORAL

(*To* FIRST CORPORAL *as he enters:*)

Look! Look what he's done, for Pete's sake. How you supposed to mark him on that?

FIRST CORPORAL

You're supposed to be grading this. Can't you do a simple thing like that?

(*Exits.*)

SECOND CORPORAL

(*Calling after him:*)

I'm supposed to mark it down if they put it back together or not and there ain't supposed to be but one way of doing it, and he sure didn't do it that way . . . How you gonna mark a thing like that? And who's gonna pay for these things?

(*To* WILL:*)

Sixteen dollars they cost. If you think I'm gonna pay sixteen lousy dollars . . .

KING

(*Advancing on him, soothingly:*)

Corporal, Corporal . . .

SECOND CORPORAL

Sixteen lousy dollars!

KING

Corporal . . . I'll be *glad* to pay the sixteen lousy dollars.

SECOND CORPORAL

You will?

KING

Sure. If he passed the test . . .

SECOND CORPORAL

But he did it completely wrong. He was supposed to—

KING

(*Taking* CORPORAL'*s arm and leading him* OFFSTAGE.)

Now let's take this logically; you need some money and I need for him to pass the test . . .

(WILL *watches them go. Door of* PSYCHIATRIST'*s office opens and* BEN *emerges.*)

BEN

(*Seeing* WILL.)

Will!

WILL

(*Turning.*)

Ben!

(*They rush to each other and pump hands.*)

BEN

I ain't hardly seen you all day! What you been doing, classifying?

WILL

Yeh!

BEN

Find out where you're going?

WILL

Sergeant King says if I pass the eye test I'll be goin' to Gunnery School!

BEN

That's where I'm going if I pass the eye test!

WILL

How about that—

(*Flips* BEN'*s tie out of his shirt.*)

BEN

(*Suddenly deflated:*)

Yeah. How about that.

WILL

Ben, you ain't *still* sad about not bein' in the Infantry?

BEN

The Captain never even read my letter. I even asked that there psychiatrist.

WILL

What did he say?

BEN

He didn't say nothing. I don't think he understands so good. Looks like I'm stuck with the Air Force.

WILL

But Ben, maybe it's really the Air Force that's the real soldiers and the Infantry that's just the helpers.

BEN

Never.

WILL

What about that movie they showed us, about that airplane that goes up *fifty* thousand feet, and makes the blood boil up inside you and kills you in ten seconds! It's the Air Age, Ben! And the gunner is right up there with the pilot and the bombardier and all the others!

BEN

Yeah! Bombardier! Throws bombs! But who does he throw' em at? The Infantry, that's who!

WILL

And medals! Ooh, the way that fellow took on! You get one for practically everythin' in the Air Force. They even give you one for just bein' there and not doin' nothin' wrong. How about that!

BEN

Wait till my brothers find out. Airman!

(BEN *pulls his cap from his belt and hurls it to the floor. As he does so, a black* LIEUTENANT *is passing by. He stops.*)

LIEUTENANT

Private!

BEN

(Snapping to attention.)

Sir!

LIEUTENANT

That's no way to treat government property.

BEN

Yes, sir!

LIEUTENANT

Pick up your cap, Private.

BEN

Yes, sir.

(Stoops to retrieve cap.)

LIEUTENANT

You shouldn't be loitering here anyhow.

BEN

(Rising quickly and coming to attention again.)

We're being classified, sir.

LIEUTENANT

(*To* will:)

I'm looking for Sergeant King. Do you know him?

WILL

(*Gaping.*)

Sure do . . . He's ourn . . .

LIEUTENANT

Where is he?

WILL

He went down there with a corporal in tow. He's havin' trouble gettin' me classified.

LIEUTENANT

(*Knowingly:*)

Uh-huh.

(*Starting to go.*)

Pick up that cap, Private.

BEN

(*Retrieves cap.*)

Yes, sir.

LIEUTENANT

And let's get that tie tucked in.

(*Exits.*)

BEN

Yes, sir.

(*To* will:)

What's the matter with you? Don't you know enough to stand
at attention and salute an officer?

WILL

(*Still gaping after the* LIEUTENANT.)
You know, he talked whiter than I do.

BEN

Whiter than you do? Listen, he was an officer, that's all!

WILL

And I'll bet he's a good one, too, so snappy and all . . .

BEN

Will, when a man's in uniform, he ain't black or white or yellow or
nothing! You ain't supposed to notice the color of a man in uniform!

WILL

You ain't?

BEN

No sir!

WILL

Ben, you mean . . . when that Lieutenant come over . . . you
didn't notice he was . . . is it all right if I say colored?

BEN

All I saw was a lieutenant, period!

WILL

A colored lieutenant.

BEN

A lieutenant! Can't you understand nothing, Will? The only thing that's important in the service is rank! If a man's an officer, he's higher than you, even if he's green with purple spots!

WILL

Oh, now, Ben . . .

BEN

Rank! That's all! A man in uniform don't see nothing else!

WILL

Well, dang it, Ben . . . I'm a man in uniform all right and the minute he come in here I seen he warn't like us!

BEN

Honest, Will. Sometimes I wonder how come they ever took you in the draft at all!

(KING *and* SECOND CORPORAL *re-enter, both smiling,* KING *pocketing his wallet.* SECOND CORPORAL *exits into "Manual Dexterity" room.*)

KING

Well, it looks like we're just liable to get you classified after all. It goes to show what the Air Force has come down to.

THIRD CORPORAL

(*Entering from* PSYCHIATRIST'S *office with form in hand.*
To KING:)
Is this fellow Whitledge in your group?

BEN

That's me, Corporal.

KING

Yeah—that's him.

THIRD CORPORAL

Psychiatrist says he has a secondary anxiety with inferiority and systematized delusions of persecution.

KING

I ain't surprised.

THIRD CORPORAL

Recommends he be considered for transfer to the Infantry.

BEN

The *Infantry!*

THIRD CORPORAL

Don't get excited. He didn't say you have to.

WILL

That's what Ben's always wantin', Corporal.

BEN

Just what do I have to do?

THIRD CORPORAL

(*Gives* BEN *a form.*)
Here—fill this out.

(*To* KING:)

Soon as he's finished, buck it through to the Colonel for approval.

KING

Okay. If that's what the crazy kid wants.

WILL

How about that, Ben—you made it!

BEN

Just wait till I tell my brothers!

THIRD CORPORAL

(*Holding out another form.*)

Okay, Stockdale—Psychiatrist.

KING

(*Takes form from* CORPORAL, *who exits.*)

Oh Lord. Now Will, listen carefully. The psychiatrist test is one I couldn't get the questions for because there ain't any. The doctor just asks you whatever pops into his head. So keep your wits about you.

WILL

I'll try. Maybe I can get a transfer too, huh, Ben?

KING

He'll just ask you stuff like "What do you dream?"

WILL

Okay.

(*Touches* BEN.)
Maybe he'll give me a transfer too, huh, Ben?

BEN

Yeah, sure . . .

KING

Safest thing, I guess, is to say you never dream at all.

WILL

See you later, Ben.
(*Exits into* PSYCHIATRIST'*s office.*)

KING

No dreams!
(*Begins pacing.*)
Oh, jeez . . .

BEN

Do you think he can?

KING

Can what?

BEN

Get transferred too? Maybe you could talk to the doctor.

KING

Listen! Don't you complicate things.

BEN

I just wish Will was going too. I mean it'd be more fun . . .

KING

Listen, Whitledge, you take care of yourself. *I'll* take care of *him*.

BEN

Okay, okay . . .

(BEN *begins filling out his form as the lights fade out in hallway and fade up in* PSYCHIATRIST*'s office.* PSYCHIATRIST, *a major, signs and stamps a paper before him, then takes form from* WILL, *seated next to desk.* PSYCHIATRIST *looks at form, looks at* WILL. *A moment of silence.*)

WILL

I never have no dreams at all.

PSYCHIATRIST

(*A pause. He looks carefully at* WILL, *looks at form.*)
Where you from, Stockdale?

WILL

Georgia.

PSYCHIATRIST

That's . . . not much of a state, is it?

WILL

Well . . . I don't live all over the state. I just live in this one little place in it.

PSYCHIATRIST

That's where "Tobacco Road" is, Georgia.

WILL

Not around my section.
(*Pause.*)
Maybe you're from a different part than me?

PSYCHIATRIST

I've never been there. What's more I don't think I would ever *want* to go there. What's your reaction to that?

WILL

Well, I don't know.

PSYCHIATRIST

I think I would sooner live in the rottenest pigsty in Alabama or Tennessee than in the fanciest mansion in all of Georgia. What about that?

WILL

Well, sir, I think where you want to live is your business.

PSYCHIATRIST

(*Pause, staring.*)
You don't mind if someone says something bad about Georgia?

WILL

I ain't heared nobody say nothin' bad about Georgia.

PSYCHIATRIST

What do you think I've been saying?

WILL

Well, to tell you the truth, I ain't been able to get too much sense out of it. Don't you know?

PSYCHIATRIST

Watch your step, young man.
(*Pause.*)
We psychiatrists call this attitude of yours "resistance."

WILL

You do?

PSYCHIATRIST

You sense that this interview is a threat to your security. You feel yourself in danger.

WILL

Well, kind of I do. If'n I don't get classified Sergeant King won't give me the wrist watch.
(PSYCHIATRIST *stares at* WILL *uncomprehendingly.*)
He won't! He said I only gets it if I'm classified inside a week.

PSYCHIATRIST

(*Turns forlornly to papers on desk. A bit subdued.*)
You get along all right with your mother?

WILL

No, sir, I can't hardly say that I do—

PSYCHIATRIST

(*Cutting in:*)
She's very strict? Always hovering over you?

                             WILL

No, sir, just the opposite—

                        PSYCHIATRIST

She's never there.

                             WILL

That's right.

                        PSYCHIATRIST

You resent this neglect, don't you?

                             WILL

No, I don't resent nothin'.

                        PSYCHIATRIST
                (*Leaning forward paternally.*)
There's nothing to be ashamed of, son. It's a common situation.
Does she ever beat you?

                             WILL

No!

                        PSYCHIATRIST
                    (*Silkily:*)
So defensive. It's not easy to talk about your mother, is it.

                             WILL

No, sir. She died when I was borned.

                        PSYCHIATRIST
                    (*A long, sick pause.*)
You . . . could have told me that sooner . . .

WILL

(*Looks hang-dog.* PSYCHIATRIST *returns to papers.* WILL
glances up at him.)
Do you hate *your* Mama?
(PSYCHIATRIST'*s head snaps up, glaring.*)
I figgered as how you said it was so common . . .

PSYCHIATRIST

I do not hate my mother.

WILL

I should hope not!
(*Pause.*)
What does she beat you or somethin'?

PSYCHIATRIST

(*Glares again, drums his fingers briefly on table. Steeling
himself, more to self than* WILL:)
This is a transference. You're taking all your stored up antag-
onisms and loosing them in my direction. Transference. It
happens every day . . .

WILL

(*Excited:*)
It does? To the Infantry?

PSYCHIATRIST

(*Aghast:*)
The Infantry?

WILL

You give Ben a transfer. I wish you'd give me one too. I'd sure
love to go along with him.

PSYCHIATRIST

Stop!

     (The pause is a long one this time. Finally PSYCHIATRIST
points at papers.)

There are a few more topics we have to cover. We will not talk
about transfers, we will not talk about my mother. We will only
talk about what *I* want to talk about, do you understand?

WILL

Yes, sir.

PSYCHIATRIST

Now then—your father.
     (Quickly:)
Living?

WILL

Yes, sir.

PSYCHIATRIST

Do you get along with him okay?

WILL

Yes, sir.

PSYCHIATRIST

Does he ever beat you?

WILL

You bet!

PSYCHIATRIST

Hard?

WILL

And how! Boy, there ain't nobody can beat like my Pa can!

PSYCHIATRIST

(*Beaming.*)
So *this* is where the antagonism comes from!
(*Pause.*)
You hate your father, don't you.

WILL

No . . . I got an uncle I hate! Every time he comes out to the house he's always wantin' to rassle with the mule, and the mule gets all wore out, and *he* gets all wore out . . . Well, I don't really *hate* him; I just ain't exactly partial to him.

PSYCHIATRIST

(*Pause.*)
Did I ask you about your uncle?

WILL

I thought you wanted to talk about hatin' people.

PSYCHIATRIST

(*Glares, drums his fingers, retreats to form. Barely audible:*)
Now—girls. How do you like girls?

WILL

What girls is that, sir?

PSYCHIATRIST

Just girls. Just any girls.

WILL

Well, I don't like just any girls. There's one old girl back home
that ain't got hair no longer than a hound-dog's and she's
always—

PSYCHIATRIST

No! Look, when I say girls I don't mean any one specific girl. I
mean girls in general; women, sex! Didn't that father of yours
ever sit down and have a talk with you?

WILL

Sure he did.

PSYCHIATRIST

Well?

WILL

Well what?

PSYCHIATRIST

What did he say?

WILL

(*With a snicker:*)

Well, there was this one about these two travelin' salesmen that
their car breaks down in the middle of this terrible storm—

PSYCHIATRIST

Stop!

WILL

—so they stop at this farmhouse where the farmer has fourteen daughters who was—

PSYCHIATRIST

Stop!

WILL

You heared it already?

PSYCHIATRIST

(*Writing furiously on form.*)

No, I did not hear it already . . .

WILL

Well, what did you stop me for? It's a real knee-slapper. You see, the fourteen daughters is all studyin' to be trombone players and—

PSYCHIATRIST

(*Shoving form at* WILL:)

Here. Go. Good-bye. You're through. You're normal. Good-bye. Go. Go.

WILL

(*Takes form and stands, a bit confused by it all.*)

Sir, if girls is what you want to talk about, you ought to come down to the barracks some night. The younger fellows there is always tellin' spicy stories and all like that.

(*Lights fade out in* PSYCHIATRIST*'s office and come up in hallway.* KING *and* BEN *are as before.* IRVIN *emerges from oculist's office, putting on his dark glasses.* BEN *exits into oculist's office.*)

KING

Irvin! How's the eye test?

IRVIN

A snap.

KING

Listen, I want you to coach Stockdale. He's going in there next.

IRVIN

Now, listen, Sarge . . .

KING

You'll coach him!

(*Door of* PSYCHIATRIST'*s office opens and* WILL *emerges.*)

WILL
            (*Over his shoulder:*)
Excuse me for sayin' it, sir, but I don't think a fellow your age
would be so confused about it all if you went out and *seen* some
girls once in a while.
            (*Closes door.*)

KING
            (*Seizing him.*)
What are you doing? Are you crazy?

WILL

That fellow's in pretty bad shape, Sergeant.
            (*Handing* KING *his form.*)

KING

(*Looking at form.*)

What did he say?

(BEN *comes out of oculist's office.*)

Thank the Lord! Good boy! Normal!

WILL

Hey, Ben. You fill out that transfer yet?

BEN

It's only an application, Will. Don't mean a thing unless the Colonel okays it.

(*Hands application form to* KING.)

WILL

I asked that fellow in there to give me a transfer too, but all he done was squench up his eyes.

(*The black* LIEUTENANT *enters.*)

LIEUTENANT

Sergeant, is your group all through?

KING

Just these two to go and that's the lot.

LIEUTENANT

(*Consulting his clipboard.*)

Names?

BEN

(*Saluting.*)
Whitledge, Benjamin B.

WILL

(*Saluting, outdoing* BEN:)
Will Stockdale, sir!

LIEUTENANT

Make sure they finish today. The ones chosen for Gunnery School will be leaving tomorrow, right after the Colonel's lecture.

KING

Yes, sir.

LIEUTENANT

The Colonel is taking the inspection himself. Thought you might like to know.

KING

Thanks for the tip, sir.

LIEUTENANT

(*To* BEN, WILL *and* IRVIN:)
Good luck, fellows.

WILL

(*Saluting vigorously.*)
Thank you, Lieutenant! It's been real nice bein' here! We'll sure miss y'all!

LIEUTENANT

(*Smiles.*)

Thanks, Private.

(*Salutes and exits.* WILL *looks at* BEN *for approval.*)

KING

(*To* IRVIN:)

Why in hell does the Colonel want to come nosing around? Irvin, you better get back to the section and start slicking up the place.

IRVIN

Me?

BEN

Sergeant, can I take the clean-up detail? I'll do a real good job of it for the Colonel.

WILL

I'll lend you a hand, Ben, soon as I'm through the eye test.

KING

Lord, the eye test.

(*To* IRVIN:)

Tell him all about it. Okay, Whitledge, you're in charge of clean-up.

(*To* WILL:)

Have you been eating them carrots like I told you?

WILL

(*Taking carrot from pocket.*)

Just one more to go.

KING

Eat fast, but chew it well—good for your eyes. And none of them wise cracks to the eye doctor. Just be nice and polite.

IRVIN

(*Crossing to* WILL.)

He'll be polite, all right.

(*Saluting.*)

"Yes, sir. No, sir. Been real nice bein' here, sir!" You're even polite to coloreds, ain't you?

WILL

I don't know what you're talkin' about, Irvin.

IRVIN

That Lieutenant, that's what.

WILL

Was the Lieutenant . . . colored?

(*Glances at* BEN.)

IRVIN

What are you, blind?

WILL

I didn't notice whether he was black or white or what.

(*Glances at* BEN.)

KING

(*Looking at* WILL *with dawning horror.*)

You . . . didn't . . . notice . . .

WILL

I don't notice *no color*. He might've been black or white or yellow or even green with purple dots; it's all the same to me. All I seen was the uniform. I never notice color *nohow*.

(WILL *looks at* BEN; BEN *grins. Door of oculist's office opens and* FIRST CORPORAL *sticks his head out.*)

FIRST CORPORAL

Stockdale! Eye test!

KING

(*Paralyzed.*)
No, no . . . it couldn't be . . .

WILL

See you at the bunk, Ben. We'll clean up good for the Colonel, huh, Ben?

BEN

Yeah. Okay, Will.

(WILL *exits into oculist's office.*)

KING

He's color-blind . . .

IRVIN

I don't know what you're going to do now. Half that test is matching red and green squares.

BEN

Sergeant, could I look at that application a minute?

KING

(*Hands him application.*)

I'm doomed . . .

    (BEN *tears application in half and hands pieces back to*
KING.)

What the hell are you . . .

BEN

(*Starting to exit.*)

Guess I changed my mind.

KING

For Pete's sake, this all started from you wanting to go in the
Infantry!

BEN

(*Gruffly:*)

I changed my mind!

    (*Exits.*)

KING

I get all the nuts! Now what am I going to do with *that* one?
If he's color-blind, Gunnery won't take him, and if they won't
take him, nobody'll take him. I'm going to be a permanent latrine orderly . . .

IRVIN

Yeah . . . looks that way . . . unless . . .

KING

Unless what?

IRVIN

Unless Stockdale gets into some real trouble.

KING

What kind of trouble can he get into? He *makes* trouble.

IRVIN

He could get into plenty of trouble at the Purple Grotto.

KING

(*Horrified:*)

The Purple Grotto?

IRVIN

Sure. We could invite him there . . . you know, to celebrate . . .
you know—a couple of drinks . . .

KING

That's a pretty stinking idea, Irvin. After all, he ain't a bad kid.
I even got to like him in a way . . .

IRVIN

His being a nice kid ain't gonna get the Captain off your back.

KING

(*Pause.*)

Yeah, let him be a nice kid on his own time.

IRVIN

We could take him there tonight . . .

KING

(*Starting to go.*)
I guess we could . . . Yeah, I guess we better . . . Tell you one
thing though, Irvin . . . I'm glad I didn't think of it.

(*They exit. Blackout. Low-down music is heard, and lights come
up on "The Purple Grotto," a sordid den reeking of vice and cor-
ruption.* WILL *sits at a bottle-laden table downstage, looking
about with innocent enjoyment. A* CIGARETTE GIRL *undulates
toward him.*)

CIGARETTE GIRL

Cigars, cigarettes, anything else you want to smoke . . .
        (*Snakes her way around* WILL *to his other side and repeats.*)
Cigars, cigarettes, anything else you want to smoke . . .

WILL

(*Flashing tobacco pouch.*)
Thank you, ma'am, but I roll my own.

(*With a contemptuous sniff,* CIGARETTE GIRL *heads upstage.* KING
and IRVIN *enter, their arms loaded with bottles, their feet a wee
bit rubbery.*)

KING

Here we are, Will. Round two.
        (*Sets bottles on table.*)

WILL

I sure appreciate it. But I don't feel right my glass bein' so much bigger'n yourn.

    (*Holds up enormous brandy balloon.*)

IRVIN

Guest of honor always gets the biggest glass. That's the honor.

    (*Raising glass.*)

To Will.

WILL

Again?

    (KING *quells him with a glance.* WILL *drinks.* KING *and* IRVIN *toss down their shots and watch, fascinated, as* WILL *drains his glass. He sets down empty glass and makes a slight grimace.*)

This here Scotch stuff tastes kind of sharp. I like the other stuff you give me better.

IRVIN

    (*Pouring it for* WILL.)

The rye.

WILL

No, the gin.

(KING *grabs gin bottle and adds it to the rye that* IRVIN *is pouring.*)

KING

How you feeling, Will?

WILL

Fine, fine.

KING

That eye doctor wouldn't tell you nothing, huh?

WILL

Nope. Seemed kind of angry most of the time.

KING

What made you think he was angry?

WILL

Well, he got sort of fussed when I was readin' this here sign they
had on the wall. That was kind of hard at first 'cause they was
right peculiar words like IP and GNXL and BUGLUMP.

IRVIN

You were supposed to read them letters one at a time.

WILL

Didn't make no sense that way neither.

KING

You're not drinking your rye and gin.

WILL

After this one I reckon we ought to be headin' back to Ben at
the barracks. With the Colonel coming the place has got to be
fixed up special.
    (*Drinks, then rises.*)

KING

Now, wait a minute . . .
    (*Gets to his feet—sort of.*)

I promised you my watch, and I'm gonna give you my watch, and we gotta have several, several drinks on that!
(*Unfastens watch strap.*)

WILL

Oh, golly!
(WILL *sits.*)

KING

My mother give it to me . . .
(*He's got it off now. He clears his throat.*)
To Will Stockdale because, because—because I'm proud of him for doing such a good job getting classified and cleaning the latrine and all . . .
(*He hands watch to* WILL *and resumes seat.*)

WILL

Thank you, thank you . . .
(*Starts fastening watch, realizes he should be standing, rises.*)
I—I sure am glad I come into the draft!
(*Snatches up his glass.*)
To Sergeant King! The best danged sergeant in the whole danged Air Force!

(*He drinks.* KING *and* IRVIN, *less eagerly, down their drinks.* WILL *sits, examines watch happily.*)

KING

Will . . . are you absolutely sure you never drank no whiskey before?

WILL

Never no *store* whiskey. Only some ole stuff that my Pa makes.

KING

Stuff that . . .

WILL

Corn likker, kind of. Corn, and grain . . .
          (*Sips his drink.*)
. . . and kerosene . . .

KING AND IRVIN

Kerosene!

WILL

Just a mite. For flavorin'.

(CIGARETTE GIRL *crosses.*)

KING

          (*Despondently:*)
Where we gonna get kerosene?

CIGARETTE GIRL

Cigars, cigarettes, anything else you want to smoke . . .

IRVIN

          (*Thrusting dollar bill into her tray.*)
Here's some lighter fluid . . .

KING

He *wants* kerosene, he *gets* kerosene!

(IRVIN *fires a few squirts of fluid into* WILL*'s glass.* KING *and* IRVIN *sit raptly as* WILL *lifts glass, inspects it, sips, and savors the aftertaste.*)

WILL

It's familiar.
> (KING *and* IRVIN *groan.*)
Hey, there's an Infantry man! Hey, Infantry!

(*A burly* INFANTRY PRIVATE *staggers to their table.*)

INFANTRY

Hi, Jack!

WILL

Have a drink! We're celebratin'!

INFANTRY

(*Pulling up a chair.*)
Thanks a lot. I do not mind if I do.

WILL

(*To* KING *and* IRVIN:)
Let's drink one to the Infantry.

INFANTRY

(*Grabbing* WILL*'s upraised glass.*)
To the Infantry!
> (*He drinks, stiffens, sets glass on table, shakes his head.*)
Smooth . . . Say, I never seen fly-boys so nice to the Infantry.

WILL

Well, heck, this is the Air Age, and you're our helpers, ain't you?

KING and IRVIN

Will, Will . . .

INFANTRY

Your what?

WILL

Our helpers. And don't think we don't appreciate it.

INFANTRY

Listen, you guys got it easier than anybody, even the Navy!

IRVIN

For your information they drill us fifteen miles every day!

INFANTRY

Twenty miles, we drill! When it rains, twenty-five!

KING

Do you have to put up with all the stupid kid officers we do?

IRVIN

And sergeants . . . we got the roughest, toughest, meanest sergeants in the whole service!

INFANTRY

Go on, you don't know what a tough sergeant is till you've been in the Infantry!

IRVIN

Ain't nobody tougher than my sergeant! He's *tough*!

KING

I sure am!

WILL

Now, Sergeant, I wouldn't say that.

KING

I'm a louse, ain't I, Irvin?

IRVIN

Yes, sir, you are.

KING

Thanks, Irvin.

INFANTRY

I don't know, you look like a pretty decent Joe to me.

KING

(*Rising.*)
You take that back!

INFANTRY

All right, I'll bet you five bucks *I'm* a bigger louse than you.
And I'm just a private!

IRVIN

Put up or shut up.
(*Throws money on table.*)

INFANTRY

(*To* KING:)

What's a bigger louse than a louse that'll drink your booze and then punch you in the guts?

IRVIN

Put up or shut up!

INFANTRY

Sure.

(INFANTRY *punches* KING *in the stomach.* KING *doubles up.* IN-FANTRY *turns to* IRVIN, *who violates the Marquess of Queensberry Rules with his right knee. A brawl ensues, in the midst of which* WILL *attempts to disengage* KING.)

WILL

Sergeant, I think we better go home now. Ben's waitin' for me to—

KING

(*Strangling someone.*)

Go on away! You're drunk!

WILL

No I ain't. My fingers is a mite tingly, but—

KING

Go 'way!

(*With bottles flying and a siren wailing, the lights fade out on "The Purple Grotto" as* WILL, *in a pin-spot, reluctantly comes downstage. He addresses the audience.*)

WILL

Well, I finally figgered I better quit bein' a wet blanket and stop spoilin' the Sergeant's fun. So . . . much as I hated to miss the fun myself—you know, quit a party early and the best things happen after you're gone—I went on back to the barracks 'cause I had a lot to do before the Colonel come.

(*An* AIR FORCE POLICEMAN *rushes across.*)

AIR FORCE POLICEMAN

Hey! Which way's that Purple Grotto?

WILL

Right down yonder there.
        (*To audience:*)
There's a thirsty fellow for you! Well, anyhow, I went on back to the barracks and give Ben a hand with the cleanin'. And afterwards, when everyone was asleep, I got me some nails and a board and some wires and I fixed up somethin' special for the Colonel. Then in the mornin', right before inspection, I give it the finishin' touches.

(*Lights come up on barracks set.* WILL *takes a wire-entangled board from within latrine door and stands straightening the wires as* BEN *approaches.*)

BEN

What you been doing in there?

WILL

Fixin' up somethin' special. It ain't every day a Colonel inspects.

BEN

I sure wish the Sergeant was here.

WILL

He'll show up. Sergeant King ain't gonna miss no inspection if he can help it.

BEN

The heck he ain't. Here comes the Captain now—and the Colonel!

WILL

Oh, golly.

BEN

Who's going to report?

WILL

You're in charge.

BEN

Me? Oh!
          (*Rehearsing salute.*)
Barracks ready for inspection, sir. Barracks ready for inspection, sir . . .

WILL

Now mind, when you throw open this door, holler "attention" just as loud as you can!

BEN

          (*Preoccupied.*)
Yeah, yeah . . .

(*Closes latrine door.*)

Barracks ready for inspection, sir. Barracks ready . . .

> (CAPTAIN *and* COLONEL *enter in conversation.* BEN, *between latrine and* KING's *room, keeps rehearsing until officers are upon him. He calls to* INDUCTEES *in back:*)

Ten-shun!

> (*Saluting officers.*)

Barracks ready for inspection, sir!

(OFFICERS, *flinching at his vehemence, return salute.* WILL, *in latrine, is placing the wired board on the floor before commodes, fussing with wires, etc.*)

CAPTAIN

Where's Sergeant King?

BEN

I don't know, sir, but

> (*Saluting.*)

the barracks are ready for inspection, sir!

CAPTAIN

> (*Saluting mechanically.*)

All right, all right . . .

> (*To* COLONEL:)

Sir, before we go any further, I'd like you to take a look at this latrine. There's a man in this barracks whose latrine work is quite surprising.

(BEN *flings open latrine door.*)

BEN

Ten-shun!

(*Up comes* WILL*'s arm in a snappy salute, down stomps his foot, up fly the toilet seats; clattering, banging, quivering at attention.*)

WILL

Latrine ready for inspection, sir!

(OFFICERS *recoil through the door, then peer in again timorously. They enter latrine, hesitantly approach the commodes. The seats waver.* WILL *gives the board a further push and the seats regain their precision.* OFFICERS *turn their dumbfounded gaze at* WILL.)

WILL

Latrine ready for inspection, sir!

CAPTAIN

(*Dazedly returns salute.* WILL *drops his hand.*)
What is . . . the *idea* behind this?

WILL

Welcomin' the Colonel, sir.

CAPTAIN

(*To* COLONEL:)
I'm sorry, sir.

COLONEL

It's all right, Captain . . . I've been welcomed in many ways; with ticker-tape, with waving flags, the women of a French village once threw rosebuds at me . . . But this . . . this . . .

(Shaking his head, he and CAPTAIN *leave latrine and exit into bar-*
racks proper. The clatter of the falling seats speeds them.)

WILL

(*Joining* BEN *outside latrine.*)
They didn't hardly inspect the latrine at all.

*(*KING *comes staggering in, looking back cautiously over his shoul-*
der. He is a bruised and battered wreck, his uniform in shreds. His
stripes are hanging by a thread, literally and figuratively.)

BEN

(*As* KING *totters up:*)
Sergeant!

KING

Lieutenant there . . . almost spotted me . . .

WILL

You all right?

KING

I'm not sure . . .

WILL

Where's Irvin?

KING

The M.P.s got him.

WILL

Golly . . .

COLONEL

(OFFSTAGE:)
Excellent! Excellent!

KING

(*Wide-eyed.*)
The Colonel?
(WILL *nods excitedly.*)

BEN

They inspected the latrine already!

WILL

Watch out for the treadle!

(KING *ducks into latrine.* COLONEL *and* CAPTAIN *reappear.*
CAPTAIN *opens door of* KING'*s room.* COLONEL *pokes his
head in.*)

COLONEL

Excellent! Excellent!
(*To* BEN:)
Were you in charge during your sergeant's absence?

BEN

Yes, sir. Complete charge.

COLONEL

Captain, I think you should make a note of this man's name.

(KING *is examining himself in the mirror.*)

CAPTAIN

Yes indeed, sir. What is it, Private?

BEN

Private Ben Whitledge, sir!

(KING *backs away from mirror to get better look at himself. He steps on the treadle. The seats fly up with a horrendous clatter. As he turns to see what the clatter is he steps off the treadle and the seats crash down again.*)

CAPTAIN
(*When the noise subsides:*)
What was that again?
(*Produces pencil and note pad.*)

BEN

Whitledge, sir. W—H—I—T—

(KING *has been cautiously tiptoeing toward seats to examine them. He steps on the treadle. The seats fly up. As he backs up, they crash down.*)

COLONEL

What in blazes?

CAPTAIN

What's going on in there?

(COLONEL *and* CAPTAIN *move to latrine door.* WILL *blocks it.*)

WILL

Latrine's out of order, sir. You'll have to use the one next door.

(CAPTAIN *gestures* WILL *aside, flings open the door.* KING *retreats to the far corner of the latrine and attempts a salute, but with the hangover and the shock he can't quite make it.*)

CAPTAIN

This is the barracks sergeant!

KING

How are ya, sir . . .

CAPTAIN

All slicked up for inspection!
        (KING *withers. Pause.*)
Explain!

KING

Explain . . . uh . . . mm . . . Well, sir . . . I went to a movie last night. And there were these . . . *eight infantrymen* sitting behind me. And they took to cussing the Air Force, and saying how our officers wasn't as . . . understanding . . . as Infantry officers.

COLONEL

So you fought them. All night long.

KING

Yes sir. It was awful.

CAPTAIN

What was the name of the movie?

KING

The movie . . . ?

CAPTAIN

The movie!

KING

Uh . . . Forward March . . . American Battalion . . . of the Air . . . in the Wild Blue . . . It was a sneak preview.

COLONEL

I don't know how this man ever got *on* my base, Captain, but he certainly isn't going to remain here, corrupting new airmen with his—hideous example. Ship him out!

CAPTAIN

There's a group leaving today for Gunnery School.

COLONEL

Splendid! General Bush can always use another private.

KING

Private?

COLONEL

(*Plucks dangling stripes from* KING's *arms and drops them to the floor.*)

Private!

(KING *clasps his arms as though wounded.* COLONEL *and* CAPTAIN *leave latrine.* BEN *confronts them outside.*)

BEN

That was Whitledge, sir. W—H—I—T—L—

CAPTAIN

Whitledge, eh? This is going on your record, Whitledge! This is going on everybody's record!

(COLONEL *and* CAPTAIN *exit furiously.* WILL *enters latrine.*)

KING

(*Pointing at commodes, flapping his hand.*)
Something special for the Colonel . . .

WILL

(*Nods.*)
You ain't a sergeant no more?

KING

No I ain't a sergeant no more! I'm a private, a forty-five-year-old private!

WILL

Oh, gosh, I—

BEN

(*Coming to door.*)
He's putting it on my record . . .

WILL

Gosh, Ben, I didn't . . .

KING

There's a silver lining to this cloud, by God! You're staying here, but I'm going to Gunnery School, a thousand miles away!

(*Comes out of latrine.* WILL *and* BEN *follow.*)

WILL

Sergeant . . .

KING

Private!

WILL

I ain't stayin' here. I'm goin' to Gunnery School, just like you.

KING

They . . . took you?

WILL

It's right on the bulletin board. It was your helpin' that done it for me.

KING

No . . .

WILL

(*Hesitantly:*)
We're gonna be together.

KING

Now listen, I've had all I can take, you understand? You and him be together; leave me out of it!

WILL

But we're buddies.

KING

Buddies?

WILL

Last night you said you was proud of me . . .

KING

I was drunk! I didn't know what I was saying!

WILL

You give me your watch . . .

KING

I was drunk!

WILL

Not when you set me in charge of this latrine!

KING

Oh, my God!
    (*To* BEN:)
You tell him! Maybe you can get through!

BEN

Cleaning the latrine isn't a good job, Will. It's the worst job there is. It's a punishment job.

WILL

    (*Turns slowly from* BEN *to* KING.)
It is?
    (*Begins unfastening watch strap.*)

KING
(*Uncomfortable now:*)
Now do you understand? There's your buddy. Make some trouble for *him* for a change.
(WILL *holds out the watch.* KING *hesitates, then crosses and snatches it from him. To* BEN:)
You glad now you tore up your transfer?

(*He exits into his room. There is a moment of silence.*)

WILL
You tore up your transfer, Ben?

BEN
(*Inching away.*)
It was just an application, that's all.

WILL
To the Infantry!

BEN
(*Heading for wings. More for himself than for* WILL:)
Nothing would've come of it!

WILL
I didn't know you done that. I'll make it up to you, honest I will. Ben . . .

(BEN *stops, turns, holds himself in check.*)

BEN
I got to go pack for Gunnery School . . .

(He exits. After a moment, WILL *turns downstage, looking at floor. He becomes aware of the audience watching.)*

WILL

I didn't realize . . . honest . . . I was just . . .

(He turns, putting his back toward them. The lights fade slowly.)

CURTAIN

END OF ACT ONE

ACT TWO

WILL

Feels right good to move around after settin' still so long, don't it?

(*Glances at slip of paper.*)

Uh . . . Preacher says that Mrs. Henry Calhoun couldn't find one of her shoes when y'all went out for that orange drink. Would all them around her look under you and if it's there just pass it on back to her? Thank you.

(*Pockets paper.*)

Let's see . . . where was I—oh yeh. Well, the three of us—Ben and Sergeant King and me—we went to Gunnery School together, like the Three Musketeers. Only to be real honest, we warn't really much like the Three Musketeers; it was more like three fellows that two of 'em warn't talkin' with one of 'em any more'n they could help. Anyway, after Gunnery School they put me and Ben on the same flight crew, because they put you accordin' to how you come out in the class, and we was the bottom two. Sergeant King, though, he come out on top. He did. The instructors said they never seen nothin' like it. It was just as if he had copies of the tests before they give them. He done so good that General Bush—he's kind of like the principal of the school—General Bush give him his stripes back and made him his orderly, and an orderly is kind of important; it's like a right-hand man . . . or an assistant . . . or a helper . . . Well, it's really more like a servant is what it is. Everybody said this crew Ben and me was on was the worst one on the base, on account of the officers was all from the bottom of their class too. The other crews had a nickname for our'n, only I can't say it with the ladies here. In fact I don't think I could say it with the *men* here. Ben and me, though, we went on most of the missions; it warn't much trouble and there warn't nothin' else to do anyhow.

      ("Meeting Hall" curtain rises on an airstrip. A medium-sized plane stands ready for take-off, a mounting ladder reaching up into its underbelly.)

Ben was pretty upset about it. You know how he is.

(BEN, *in flying gear, comes striding in from* LEFT.)

BEN

If this ain't the sorriest crew on the whole danged base! We're supposed to take off five minutes ago, and do you know what? Every one of our officers would still be fast asleep if I hadn't gone and shook them awake! What a crew!

WILL

It's just that they ain't used to gettin' up at three in the mornin', Ben.

BEN

All the other planes got off on time except ours. These officers are a disgrace to the Air Force!

WILL

Now, Ben, they ain't so bad. Easy goin', that's all.

BEN

All I know is that if you're going to fly a plane you ought to be awake first. I'm going aboard.

(*He climbs the ladder into the plane.*)

WILL

(*Calling after him:*)

Here's Lieutenant Bridges now, Ben.

(LIEUTENANT BRIDGES *enters sleepily, his parachute at half-mast.* WILL *salutes smartly.*)

Good mornin', Lieutenant Bridges!

BRIDGES

Good morning, Lieutenant Bridges . . .

(*He continues across stage somnambulistically.* WILL *calls after him.*)

WILL

The plane's right here, sir.

(BRIDGES, *without stopping, turns back and drags himself up the ladder and into the plane.*)

That's the pilot. Easy goin' fellow.

(LIEUTENANT GARDELLA *and* LIEUTENANT KENDALL *enter. They pause a few feet onstage and* GARDELLA *helps* KENDALL *adjust his parachute straps.*)

This here is Lieutenant Kendall, the engineer, and Lieutenant Gardella, the co-pilot. Lieutenant Kendall ain't quite got the hang of puttin' on a parachute yet.

(*The pair approach.* WILL *salutes.*)

Good morning, sirs!

KENDALL AND GARDELLA
                    (*Saluting.*)
Good morning . . .

WILL

Lieutenant Gardella.

(GARDELLA *stops.* KENDALL *exits into plane.*)

GARDELLA

Yes?

WILL

Sir, would it be all right if I come up to the front of the plane
for a while and watch what y'all do up there?

GARDELLA

Sorry. Only crew members allowed on board.

WILL

I'm a crew member, sir.

GARDELLA

You are?

WILL

Yes, sir. I been on the crew for close on to a month now. Is it
okay if I come up front and—

GARDELLA

Sure. Sure. Come on up. There ain't much to see though. All
I do is let the wheels up after we take off and let them down
again when we're ready to land.

WILL

That might be nice. Thank you, sir.

GARDELLA

I *knew* I'd seen you *some place.*

(*Exits into plane.* WILL *takes parachute from behind ladder, puts it on during following.*)

WILL

(*To audience:*)

I think he really knowed who I was. It's just the sleep ain't wore off yet. You see, we never had to go up this early before. This here mission is we're supposed to fly to Denver, Colorado, and when we get to Denver, Colorado, we're supposed to turn around and fly back again. That's the biggest mission we got so far. Usually, all they ask is for us to get the plane up off'n the ground and keep it up for half an hour or so without smackin' into nothin'.

(LIEUTENANT COVER *comes scurrying on, his arms loaded with maps, sextants, slide rules, books, etc. He climbs the ladder, muttering a hasty inventory, oblivious of* WILL*'s salute.*)

COVER

Maps . . . sextant . . . slide rule . . . scale . . . dramamine . . . I forgot the——No, here it is.
(*He is gone.*)

WILL

That's Lieutenant Cover, the navigator. He's the serious one of the bunch.

(*Glances at his wrist watch but he doesn't have one. Rubs wrist.*)
Well, I guess I'll just get on the—

(SERGEANT KING *and two* MECHANICS *enter.* KING *wears a staff armband and carries a clipboard. Engines rev up as* MECHANICS *busy themselves underneath the plane.*)

KING

(*To* MECHANICS:)
Get this one off and we can all go back to sleep.

WILL

Hey, look at you! An armband and a writin' board and everythin'!

KING

All right, get this plane off on the double.

WILL

We can't. Everyone ain't here yet. The radio operator and the front gunner—

KING

You heard me, get moving!

WILL

How come we're goin' up so early?

KING

To break the sound barrier. You gotta sneak up on it when nobody's looking.

(GENERAL BUSH *enters.*)

BUSH

Oh, there you are, Sergeant. Is this the last of them?

KING

Yes, General.

BUSH

Fine. That does it for tonight. Don't disturb me unless there's a big emergency. Breakfast a little later than usual, I think . . .

KING

Yes, sir. What about your eggs, sir?

BUSH

My eggs? What eggs?

KING

For breakfast. Poached or scrambled?

BUSH

Scrambled, I think . . . nice and loose. No, no . . . poached.

KING

Yes, sir, poached.

BUSH

Poached. I feel like poached.

WILL

Scrambled is tastier, sir. Especially with chitlins.

KING

Get on that plane!

BUSH

Chitlins?

WILL

Yes, sir, at home we always have scrambled eggs with chitlins.

BUSH

Poached!
          (*Exits.*)

KING

Yes, sir!
          (*To* WILL:)
Can't you keep your mouth shut? Scrambled with chitlins!

WILL

A bit of red pepper helps.

KING

Get on that plane!

WILL

          (*Climbing ladder.*)
Sure, Sergeant.

VOICE ON P.A.

Sergeant King! Sergeant King! Report to General Bush immediately.
          (*Incredulous:*)
With chitlins?

BLACKOUT

(*The roar of the engines grows louder. Clouds are seen, and running lights blinking in a rhythmic pattern. Lights come up on a cross-section of the plane in flight. In front,* BRIDGES *and* GARDELLA *are seated at the controls, asleep. Behind them,* KENDALL *sits by his needles and gauges, asleep. Farther back,* COVER *is at his work table, frantically operating six instruments at once. Toward the rear of the plane,* BEN *sits reading a comic book.* WILL *is peering at the audience from the tail blister. After a moment the sound of the engines fades low and* WILL *moves forward. He crouches beside* BEN.)

WILL

I got my penknife. Want to play mumbly-peg?

BEN

That's a kid's game.
> (*Turns a page of his comic book.*)

WILL

We could play for money.
> (*No comment from* BEN.)
Well, I guess I'll go see what they do up front.

BEN

We're supposed to stay at our stations.

WILL

I asked Lieutenant Gardella. He said it was all right. Want to come along?

(BEN *shakes his head.* WILL *hesitates, then moves forward.* COVER *is working like a man possessed—marking charts, measuring, drawing circles, searching for instruments and papers.* WILL *watches him, fascinated.*)

COVER
(*Talking to himself:*)
Compass, compass . . . ah . . . mmm . . . now . . . scale. Where's the . . .
(*Snaps his fingers.*)
Ruler, ruler . . .
(WILL *hands it to him.*)
Ah . . . there . . .
(*Copying data from various sheets of paper onto central sheet.*)
Ground speed . . . mmm . . . air speed . . . mmm . . . wind direction—Wind direction, wind direction . . .

(*Searches furiously through papers.* WILL, *behind him, licks his forefinger and holds it up. He taps* COVER.)

WILL
Wind's comin' from that way, sir.
(*Points forward.*)

COVER
(*Turning.*)
Dead ahead?

WILL
Yes, sir.

COVER

(*Returning to charts.*)

Then something's wrong with the compass. We're supposed to
be . . . that couldn't . . .

(*He is beginning to get a bit desperate.* WILL *watches him
for a moment, then heads forward.*)

Now wait a minute, let's start all over again. If we took off at
0315 . . .

WILL

(*Stepping over* KENDALL's *outstretched legs.*)

Excuse me, sir . . .

(*He comes up behind* BRIDGES *and* GARDELLA, *who are
slumped over the steering wheels.*)

Howdy, sirs!

(*They sit bolt upright and whirl around in their chairs.*)

GARDELLA

It's all right, George; he's one of the crew.

BRIDGES

Lord! Don't come sneaking up on people, fella.

WILL

Sorry, sir. Just wanted to watch what y'all do up here.

(*Pause.* BRIDGES *and* GARDELLA *resume their sleeping positions.*)

BRIDGES

Automatic pilot.

> WILL

You already let up the wheels?

> GARDELLA

Hell, yes.

> WILL

Shucks.

> BRIDGES

What do y'all do in back?

> WILL

Oh, nothin' much. I mostly look out the blister and sweep up a little.
> (*Pause. Apprehensively:*)
You don't have to guide this here thing?

> BRIDGES

Automatic. Everything's automatic. Every little ole thing.

> GARDELLA

You come back when we're ready to land and you can watch me let down the wheels.

> BRIDGES

It's a real spectacle.

> GARDELLA

I do it all with one hand.

WILL

Well, thank you, sir. Guess I'll go look out the blister some.
>(*Pause.*)
Good night.
>(*He heads for the rear of the plane, stepping over* KEND-
>ALL's *legs . . .*)
Excuse me, sir.
>(*. . . and stopping behind* COVER, *who is staring straight
>ahead with a stoned expression, his hands flat on the work
>table.*)

COVER

We're off our course.

WILL

We are?

COVER

If we're heading straight into a south wind then we can't be
going west, can we?
>(WILL *licks his finger and holds it up.*)
Are they in contact with the base up there?

WILL

Well, no . . .

COVER

>(*Putting on earphones.*)
What the hell *are* they doing?

WILL

Well, sir, you might say they're kind of sleepin'.

COVER

Sleeping! Navigator to pilot, navigator to pilot. Over.

> (BRIDGES *lifts one hand and pulls down earphones with-*
> *out opening his eyes. He holds one phone to ear.*)

Navigator to pilot, navigator to pilot. Over.

BRIDGES

Pilot to navigator. Fred, I wish you wouldn't call me once we're off the ground. Over.

COVER

I just thought you might like to know that we're heading for Mexico, that's all. Over.

BRIDGES

Now Fred, everything is automatic and you know it. Every time we go off on a mission you start fussing with those maps and things, and all you do is confuse everybody. Over.

COVER

Well, for your information we got a south wind and we're heading straight into it and we're supposed to be going west. Over.

BRIDGES

> (*Extends his toe and does something with the instrument*
> *panel.*)

All right. I just moved us up ninety degrees. Are you happy? Over and out.

> (*Hangs up earphones.*)

COVER

I don't see why you guys should get to sleep when I have to work like a dog back here. None of *my* instruments are automatic and they're pretty damn complicated, let me tell you. Over. Navigator to pilot, navigator to . . . Damn!
(*Hangs up earphones.*)
Sometimes I think he doesn't take a serious attitude.

WILL

I noticed that.

COVER

Now let's see . . . moved us up ninety degrees . . . wind from the south . . . flying since 0315 hours . . .

(WILL *retreats toward rear of plane.*)

BEN

(*Not looking up from comic book.*)
Taking an awful long time to get to Denver, Colorado. What are they doing up there?

WILL

Oh, you'd be right proud of them, Ben! They're workin' real hard; navigatin' and steerin' and engineerin' and all.

BEN

Yeah, I'll bet.

WILL

They're about as good a crew as you can find, when they're sober like this.

(*Lights fade, engine sound rises, clouds and running lights are seen. After a moment, interior lights come up again.* BEN *is sleeping,* WILL *is sweeping,* COVER *is shouting frantically into his microphone.*)

COVER

Navigator to pilot, navigator to pilot, over! Navigator to pilot, navigator to pilot!

BRIDGES
(*Snatching earphones.*)
Fred, what the hell's the matter with you?

COVER

We're over the Gulf of Mexico, you idiot!

BRIDGES

Now, Fred, how can we be over the Gulf of Mexico when there's a city below us half the size of New York?

COVER

You want to come back here and check the maps? I figured our position by dead reckoning and we're smack dab in the middle of the Gulf of Mexico!

BRIDGES

Well, by God, I can see, can't I? I can look right out the window and *see*, can't I?

KENDALL
(*Taking earphones, partially awake.*)
Engineer to pilot. Are we lost again?

COVER

No, Kendall, we know exactly where we are. Smack dab in the middle of the Gulf of Mexico.

BRIDGES

There ain't any towns in the middle of the Gulf of Mexico!

GARDELLA

Maybe we're across the Gulf already.

COVER

You stay out of this, Gardella!

KENDALL

(*A bit surprised.*)
Hey, fellows. Number two engine is dead.

GARDELLA AND COVER

Oh Lord!

BRIDGES

Prepare for landing!

COVER

This is *not* a seaplane!

BRIDGES

Cover, will you please look out the ever-loving window. What do you think that is down there?

GARDELLA

Wait a minute, wait a minute! That gunner fellow said he was going to watch from the blister . . . Co-pilot to rear gunner, co-pilot to rear gunner, over. Co-pilot to rear gunner . . .

(*A red light blinks in rear of plane.* WILL *goes to it, takes earphones.*)

WILL

Howdy. Over.

GARDELLA

Hey, you seen anything below that might've been a body of water?

WILL

No sir, I ain't seen nothin'. I been sweepin' up.

BRIDGES

What the hell's the radio operator doing? Pilot to radio operator, pilot to radio operator, over.

GARDELLA

Co-pilot to radio operator. Over.

COVER

Navigator to radio operator, over.

WILL

Rear gunner to everybody. Radio operator missed the plane. Over.

OFFICERS

Oh, no!

BRIDGES

Listen, rear gunner, get on the radio and see if you can find out
where we are. This is an emergency. Over.

WILL

It is?

COVER

(*Tossing aside earphones, gathering up maps.*)
We know *exactly* where we are!
(*Storms toward the front of plane.*)

WILL

Hey, sir, you ought to give the job to the other gunner! I reckon
he'd be just about the best danged radio operator in the whole
danged Air Force!

BRIDGES

(*Over him:*)
All right, get him on it.

WILL

(*Going right on:*)
He's a real smart fellow and right military-like. His whole family
been—

BRIDGES

ALL RIGHT! Just get *somebody* on the damn radio! Over and out!

WILL

Roger!
(*Hangs up earphones, drops broom and goes to* BEN.)

COVER
(*Thrusting maps over* BRIDGES*'s shoulder.*)
You want to see the map? Here's the Gulf of Mexico right here!

(BRIDGES *pushes him away.*)

WILL
(*Shaking* BEN *gently.*)
Ben? Hey, Ben. Wake up, Ben.

BEN
What . . .

WILL
It's an emergency! We're lost and Lieutenant Bridges wants you
to be the radio operator and find out where we are! It's up to
you to save the plane and us and everythin'!

BEN
Me?

WILL
They heared what a good soldier you was.
          (*Drags* BEN *to his feet and leads him to radio equipment.*)

BEN
Me? . . . Oh golly . . . oh Lord . . .

WILL
(*Picks up pamphlet, looks at it.*)
Here's some instructions . . .

BEN
(*Sitting at equipment.*)
Good. Read them off. I'll operate and you'll be my assistant.
(*Puts on earphones.*)

WILL
Assistant? Yes, sir!

(*He opens pamphlet, while* BEN *straightens his jacket, sitting proudly erect.*)

KENDALL
Watch out! Those are mountains there!

GARDELLA
Pull up! Pull up! *Pull up!*

BRIDGES
How do you pull up with only one engine, Mr. Rickenbacker?

GARDELLA
You're the pilot, Mr. Lindbergh.

COVER
There aren't any mountains on the map . . .

WILL
(*Reading with difficulty.*)
Con-grat-u-lations. As an Air Force radio operator yours is one of the most important jobs in—

BEN
Skip that part. Get to the instructions.

WILL

Yes, sir.

> (*Turns several pages, skimming them as he does so. Reads
> again:*)

Important notice. The taxpayers of the United States paid their
hard-earned—

BEN

The instructions! How to operate it.

WILL

> (*Turns several more pages, which brings him to the end of
> the pamphlet. Shows* BEN.)

Just half a page.

> (*Squints, reads:*)

One. Turn the power switch to the on position.

BEN

Here, this one. This is it.

> (*Pause.*)

Here goes . . .

> (*Turns switch. Lights appear on equipment.*)

Hey . . .

WILL

How about that!

BRIDGES

Pilot to radio operator. You getting anything back there?
Over.

BEN
(*As baritone as he can get.*)
Radio operator to pilot, sir! Roger! Wilco! We're working on it.
Over! How about that?

WILL
Pretty good! Two. Turn . . . turn . . . O-S-C-I-L-L-A-T-O-R . . .

BEN
Oscillator.

WILL
Turn—what-you-just-said—control knob to tran . . . tran . . .
T-R-A-N-S—

BEN
(*Taking off earphones, rising.*)
Here. You operate, I'll read.
(*Gives* WILL *earphones, takes pamphlet.*)

WILL
But they give you the job, Ben!

BEN
Go on! I got to think of the good of the outfit!

(WILL *sits, puts on earphones. During following* BEN *strips off parachute, up-ends it beside* WILL *and sits on it. He reads with less
difficulty than* WILL.)

BEN
Two. Turn oscillator control knob—I think that's the big one
there—to transmission frequency desired.

WILL

(*Turns knob.*)
What frequency we desire?

BEN

Oh . . . I'll leave it up to you.

WILL

(*Makes careful adjustment.*)
All righty . . .

BEN

Three. Adjust knob B so as to obtain minimum impedance.

WILL

(*Pause.*)
Ben, listen, we got a little radio on the porch back home, and
when it won't start, Pa spits in the back of it and whomps it a
good one. Works every time.
 (BEN *shrugs noncommittally.* WILL *leans over radio, spits*
 in the back of it and whomps it a good one. A red bulb
 on top lights up.)
There y'are! She's workin'!
 (*Picking up microphone.*)
Hello? Hello? I don't hear nothin'.

BEN

You got to keep saying it over and over again until somebody
picks up your signal.

WILL

Hello? Hello? Hello?

BRIDGES

I told you I'd find an airport!

GARDELLA, KENDALL AND COVER

That's a drive-in movie! Pull up!

(Lights begin to fade, light on WILL *and* BEN *going last.)*

WILL

Hello? Hello?

BEN

If you get somebody, be careful what you say. They might be the enemy.

WILL

What enemy?

BEN

I don't know, but be careful.

WILL

Hello? Hello?
　　(Spits at microphone.)
Anybody out there? Hello?

———

(Fade-out complete. Lights come up on a sandbagged bunker at extreme right of stage. GENERAL POLLARD, *the ramrod type of officer, stands scanning the horizon with powerful binoculars. His aide, a* LIEUTENANT, *is seated at a bank of radio, telephone and*

radar equipment. A SENATOR *approaches from right, where the*
bunker appears to extend.)

SENATOR

Did you just hear an airplane?

POLLARD

An airplane? You're joking, Senator.

SENATOR

No, no, I'm perfectly serious.

POLLARD

My dear Senator, a plane couldn't conceivably slip in here unless
they had Lindbergh for pilot and Rickenbacker for co-pilot.
Ha, ha, ha. When General Pollard is in charge of an operation,
safety is the prime consideration. You can mention that in your
report to your Committee if you'd like.

SENATOR

I could have sworn I heard engines . . .

POLLARD

(*Ushering the* SENATOR OFFSTAGE RIGHT.)
The desert plays strange tricks on the ear. Auditory mirages,
so to speak.

LIEUTENANT

Excuse me, sir, but I'm getting a very odd signal here. Listen . . .

RADIO

Tphhh . . . tphhh . . . tphhh . . . tphhh . . .

POLLARD

Hmmm, that *is* odd . . . Sounds like somebody spitting.

BEN'S VOICE

(*Heard through* LIEUTENANT's *radio set-up.*)
Okay, Will. Try again.

WILL'S VOICE

(*Through radio.*)
Yes, sir. Hello? Hello? Anybody there? Hello?

POLLARD

(*Seizing* LIEUTENANT's *microphone.*)
Hello.

WILL'S VOICE

Hello?

POLLARD

Hello!

WILL'S VOICE

HOWDY! Ben, I got somebody!

POLLARD

Who are you? Where are you?

WILL'S VOICE

Ben, he wants to know who we are.

POLLARD

Answer me, dammit. Who the hell are you?

WILL'S VOICE

He talks like an American, Ben.

POLLARD

Who are you?

WILL'S VOICE

Ben says, first who are you?

POLLARD

This is Command Post, "Operation Prometheus." Are you in . . .
an airplane?

WILL'S VOICE

Sure are!

POLLARD

Oh Lord . . .

LIEUTENANT

I've got them on the PPI scope, sir! They're heading straight
for the tower!

POLLARD

Oh my God!

WILL'S VOICE

Is this the Gulf of Mexico?

POLLARD

No, you idiot!
        (*To* LIEUTENANT.)
Send word to stop the detonator!

LIEUTENANT

It's too late, sir! Zero minus three!

WILL'S VOICE

Where'd you say we was?

POLLARD

You're right over Yucca Flats! Now listen to me, you turn that plane around and go right back where you came from! This minute!

LIEUTENANT

(*Pointing to radarscope.*)
There they are! See? Straight toward the tower!

WILL'S VOICE

Ben says sorry, our orders come from General Bush. Gotta do like he says.

POLLARD

Eugene Bush?

WILL'S VOICE

Our Commandin' General. Short fellow with a mustache.

POLLARD

I might have known. Get a line through to that idiot! I'll kill him for this!
(LIEUTENANT *picks up the telephone, ad libs putting through of call.* POLLARD *speaks into microphone again:*)
All right now, I don't care what Ben says or what Eugene Bush said. I'm a General too, in the U.S. Infantry—

WILL'S VOICE

The Infantry?

POLLARD

Yes! I'm ordering you to turn that plane around this instant!
You're heading straight into . . . Hello? Hello? Oh God, I lost
them!
>   (*He twirls radio dials furiously.* SENATOR *enters from*
>   *right.*)
Hello? Hello?

SENATOR

Has something gone wrong?

POLLARD

No, no, no! Everything's fine. Lieutenant, help the Senator into
his ear plugs and blinders.
>   (LIEUTENANT *does so and through the rest of the scene*
>   *the* SENATOR, *now deaf, smiles benignly in anticipation.*)
Where's Bush? Where is he?

LIEUTENANT

I've put the call through, sir.
>   (*Looks at watch.*)
Zero minus two.

POLLARD

>   (*Taking telephone.*)
Hello? Hello? Hello? Hello?

(*At the other side of the stage, lights come up on a corner of* BUSH's
office. KING *stands behind desk, telephone in hand.* BUSH *enters.*)

KING

(*Overlapping* POLLARD:)
Hello? Hello? Hello?—Here he is now, sir!

(BUSH *grabs phone from* KING.)

BUSH

Bush here.

POLLARD

Eugene? This is Vernon Pollard!

BUSH

Vernon! How are you, old boy?

POLLARD

You've sabotaged my operation, you miserable idiot! You were ordered to send your planes as far away as you could, and one of them is right here!

BUSH

I sent them away, Vernon! I sent them to Denver!

POLLARD

I don't care where you sent them! What's wrong with your communication?

BUSH

What's wrong with your security measures?

POLLARD

Shut up and listen! I'm trying to re-establish radio contact. What kind of idiot radio operators did you *put* in those planes?

BUSH

(*To* KING.)
What kind of idiot radio operators did you *put* in those planes?

POLLARD

I'll skin you for this, Eugene.

LIEUTENANT

Sir, I've got that signal again!

POLLARD

Hold it! Don't move, Eugene!

RADIO

Tphhhh . . . tphhhh . . . tphhhh . . . tphhhh . . .

WILL'S VOICE

(*Still through radio.*)
Hello? Hello?

POLLARD

(*Seizing* LIEUTENANT'*s microphone.*)
Hello! Listen! Here's your General Bush!

WILL'S VOICE

He's got General Bush there, Ben!

POLLARD

(*Into phone.*)
Eugene, I'm putting the telephone next to the microphone. Tell this idiot to turn back!
(*He holds telephone and microphone together.*)

BUSH

Hello? Who is this?

WILL'S VOICE

Private Stockdale, sir.

BUSH

This is General Bush, Stockdale.

KING

Stockdale!
(*Starts for door.*)

BUSH

Don't move, King! Tell your pilot to reverse course immediately, Stockdale. You're in extreme danger.

WILL'S VOICE

Roger, sir! Wilco.
(*Pause.*)
Ben says how do we know you're General Bush?

BUSH

What? I can't go up there and identify myself!

KING

(*Frantically:*)
Tell him Sergeant King will give him his watch!

BUSH

What?

KING

It's the only way, sir!

BUSH

Sergeant King will give you his watch!

WILL'S VOICE

He will!

BUSH

I *think* so . . .

WILL'S VOICE

That's good enough for me! Ben, tell Lieutenant Bridges to reverse course!

LIEUTENANT

(*Over this.*)
Twenty seconds, sir!

POLLARD

(*Looking at radarscope.*)
They're turning. There they go. They're still turning! They're heading for the tower again!
(*Drops mike, raises telephone.*)

LIEUTENANT

Ten seconds! Nine . . . eight . . . seven . . . six . . . five . . . four . . . three . . . two . . . one . . . *zero!*

(*During count-down, simultaneously:*)

POLLARD

It's all your fault, Eugene! You've never forgiven me for those hazings back at the Point. For thirty years you've been out to get me and now you've wrecked my career!

BUSH

(*To* KING:)

It's all your fault, you blundering idiot! How in the name of Creation did you let that plane get off the ground without a radio operator?

(*As* LIEUTENANT *reaches zero, both* GENERALS' *tirades are cut short by a blinding flash of light and a thunderous explosion. The stage blacks out.*)

———

(*Pre-dawn sky.* WILL *descends into view swaying from a parachute. He holds* BEN *by the scruff of the neck.*)

BEN

Pull to the left! Pull to the right!

WILL

Hold still, Ben.

BEN

What did you do it for? You snatched me right out of the plane! What did you do it for?

WILL

Well, I knowed you done took off your parachute. Heck, you'da done the same for me.

BEN

I wouldn't! Our post was the tail of the plane and nobody told us to quit it!

WILL

But the tail was on fire, Ben. Our post was quittin' us.

BEN

Do you know what we are now?

WILL

We're alive . . .

BEN

We are deserters! Deserters!

WILL

Stop wrigglin', Ben. *Please.*

BEN

Here's the first lick of danger and you snatch me away from it!
(*Folds arms belligerently.*)
I'd rather be a dead hero than a live deserter.

WILL

(*Pause. Stubbornly:*)
I ain't gonna drop you, no matter *what* you say.

BEN

(*Sullenly:*)
Out in the middle of no place . . . take us *weeks* to get back to the base. Can't even see where we are . . .

WILL

Sun'll be up in a few minutes, Ben. Don't worry.
(*Pause. Conversationally:*)
It's always darkest before the dawn.

(BEN *squirms disgustedly, putting an end to the talk.* WILL *looks at audience, gives an uncomprehending shrug. Lights fade out.*)

———

(*A spotlight appears on* GENERAL BUSH, *standing before a microphone, downstage near portal. He reads from a sheet of paper.*)

BUSH

"Ten days ago, in 'Operation Prometheus,' the power of the atom bomb was challenged by a band of battle-hardened air aces. When General Pollard and I planned this shining symbol of man's unconquerability we had no idea that the newspapers would give it so very much publicity. To these brave volunteers I award the Air Medal for valor beyond the call of duty: Lieutenants Bridges, Gardella, Kendall and Cover." How does it sound, King?

(KING, *wearing earphones, sticks his head out from behind portal.*)

KING

Very sincere, sir.

BUSH

I just hope I don't choke on their names. When this whole thing quiets down I'm sending those men to Iceland.

KING

Ready to hear the playback?

BUSH

Wait, there's more.
(KING *disappears.*)
"Two did not return. In the shattered tail of the plane, all that
remained were two charred helmets and a handful of dust. I ask
you now to rise as I award these medals posthumously to the
gallant heroes who gave the last measure of devotion, Privates
Stackpole and Whitehead."

KING

(*Appearing again.*)
Stockdale and Whitledge, sir.

BUSH

(*Squinting at script:*)
"Stockdale and Whitledge . . ." This is where the bugler plays
Taps, right?

KING

Yes, sir. And the flags go to half-mast.

BUSH

Be sure that second bugler is stationed up in the hills to play
the echo.

KING

I'll check on it, sir.
(*Martial music is heard.*)
I'll just rewind the tape and give you the playback.

BUSH

There isn't time. The band has started.

(*Lights come up on* BUSH's *office and anteroom.*)

LIEUTENANT ABEL

(*In office, holding* BUSH's *jacket.*)
General Bush! Only five minutes, sir!

(BUSH *goes* UPSTAGE *into office.* KING *takes microphone and exits
into wings. In office* CAPTAIN CHARLES *is crouching by the radio,
busily brushing the visor of* BUSH's *garrison cap.* LIEUTENANT BAKER
is looking out the window with a pair of binoculars. BUSH *slips
into the jacket which* ABEL *is holding for him.*)

BUSH

(*To* CHARLES.)
Brush, man, brush! That's genuine leather!
(*To* ABEL.)
Watch the sleeve there . . .

BAKER

The grandstands are full, sir!

BUSH

You're darn right they are! Those men are on duty. All leaves
were cancelled today.
(*Mumbling from radio.*)
What? What did he say?

CHARLES

Senator Hawk and Senator Winkle are in the reviewing stand!

BUSH

Good, Good! Baker, bring the car around!

BAKER

Yes, sir.

(*Exits.*)

BUSH

Abel, check on those reporters!

ABEL

Yes, sir.

(*Exits. More mumbling from radio.*)

BUSH

What was that? What did he say?

CHARLES

General Pollard just came in!

BUSH

(*Snatching cap from* CHARLES.)

Shut that off!

(CHARLES *turns off radio and hurries out.* BUSH *dons cap,
unfurls speech, rehearses:*)

Two did not return . . .

(BEN *and* WILL *come into the anteroom.*)

Two did *not* return . . .

(BEN *moves closer to dividing door, which is open.* WILL *follows.*)

BEN

Excuse me, sir, I—

BUSH

Your uniform is *filthy*, boy!

BEN

I know, sir. We hitchhiked some but we had to walk a lot and—

BUSH

You know? And do you know what day this is?

BEN

Saturday, sir. I wanted to—

BUSH

The proudest day in the history of this base, that's all! People have come from miles around—generals, senators—to do homage to two enlisted men, your brothers-in-arms, and you don't even have enough courtesy and respect to put on a decent uniform!

BEN

Sir, please, I want to turn myself in.

WILL

(*Over him:*)
He didn't jump, sir! I pulled him out!

BAKER

(*At the door.*)
The car is ready, sir.

BUSH

What squadron are you in?

BEN

The Ninth Squadron, sir.

BUSH

The Ninth! Stackpole and Whitehead's own outfit . . . !

WILL AND BEN

(*Coming to attention and saluting.*)
Stockdale and Whitledge, sir!

BUSH

Well, whoever they were. By God, you're going to stay right
here until I finish the ceremony and then we'll see if we can put
a little decency and esprit de corps into you! I don't want our
visitors to get even a *glimpse* of you! Dirty uniforms, today of
all days!

(*He exits.* WILL *and* BEN *look at each other, drop salutes.*)

WILL

Well, we turned ourselves in. I *think* . . .

BEN

Yeah, wait till he finds out that besides wearing dirty uniforms,
we're deserters.

(BEN *stalks into anteroom.* WILL *follows, closing connecting door.* BEN
sits on bench, grimly snaps up a copy of Time *from adjacent table.*)

WILL

I told him I pulled you out, Ben. I'll tell him again . . .

BEN

Aww . . .

(BEN *riffles pages of magazine gloomily.* WILL, *watching uneasily, sits beside him.* KING *enters office, whistling "Flow Gently, Sweet Afton." He flicks radio on, and martial music is heard.* KING *sits at* GENERAL's *desk. In anteroom,* WILL *is watching* BEN's *black mood with concern.*)

WILL

Say, Ben, did I ever tell you the story about the turkey that got in with a coopful of chickens?

BEN

I don't want to hear it . . .

WILL

You'll enjoy it, Ben . . . You see, this turkey got in with these chickens—

BEN

I don't want to hear it.

WILL

It's a right good story, Ben.

BEN

Don't you understand, we'll probably be shot!

WILL

Well, then, you don't hear it now, you're likely never to hear it.

BEN

(*Rising, magazine in hand.*)

Oh!

WILL

What's the matter, Ben?

BEN

Lieutenant Bridges on the cover.

WILL

I wish you'd look!

VOICE ON RADIO

(*As music fades:*)

General Bush has just taken his place on the reviewing stand . . . and now the four Lieutenants who are to receive the Air Medal are bravely mounting the platform.

(KING *is removing his shoes, putting them beside desk.*)

BEN

(*Looking from magazine to radio.*)

The Lieutenants are getting medals! They're heroes!

WILL

Gol-ly!

BEN

If we'd stayed on the plane, we would be heroes!

VOICE ON RADIO

It's a solemn moment, ladies and gentlemen; the many visiting dignitaries standing at attention, the flags at half-mast in honor of the two men who gave their lives in "Operation Prometheus," Privates Stockdale and Whitledge . . .

WILL AND BEN

Stockdale and Whitledge?

VOICE ON RADIO

Yes, Stockdale and Whitledge! Names that will live as long as men are free!

(*Martial music comes up again.*)

WILL

We *are* heroes, Ben!

BEN

But we ain't dead!

WILL

Well, that makes it even better, don't it?

BEN

They think we're heroes and we're a couple of rotten no-good deserters . . .

WILL

Golly, will they be surprised!

(KING *rises, crosses office.*)

BEN

They'll kill us, that's what they'll do! They'll kill us!

(KING *opens anteroom door, takes magazine from table, closes door, heads back for desk. He stops, looks back at closed door, shakes his head vigorously and continues to desk.*)

WILL

Come on, Ben. They'll be real glad we're alive, you'll see.
> (WILL *goes to connecting door, opens it.* BEN *follows.* KING *has his feet up on the desk and the magazine held open before his face.* WILL *and* BEN *enter office.*)

Howdy, Sergeant!

BEN

> (*Saluting.*)

Private Ben Whitledge reporting for duty after an unforeseen delay, sir!

WILL

I'll bet you never expected to see us again, but here we are!

KING

> (*Slowly lowering magazine.*)

No . . . No . . . No . . .

WILL

Didn't I tell you he'd be surprised, Ben?

KING

Why—ain't—you—dead?

(BEN *remains at petrified attention.*)

WILL

No excuse, sir!

KING

You ain't dead . . . You ain't dead . . .

WILL

Well, I had my parachute on.

KING

. . . and I'm the one who identified your remains . . . Two charred helmets and a pile of dust . . . they're having a ceremony down there . . .

BUSH

(*On radio:*)
Ten days ago, in "Operation Prometheus," the power of the atom bomb was challenged by a band of battle-hardened air aces. When General Pollard and I planned this shining symbol of man's unconquerability, we had no idea—

WILL

(*Over the above, pointing to radio:*)
Is that the General? Is he gonna give us medals?

KING

The General . . . !
(*Flings himself at radio, shuts it off, beats on it.*)
Oh, God! Oh, my God!

WILL

Now that ain't no way to act, Sergeant. Here Ben and me is
alive and you—

KING
(*Pushing them into anteroom.*)
Medals! He's giving you medals!
(*Slamming door on* WILL *and* BEN, *he rushes from the
office.*)
Lieutenant! Lieutenant!

BEN

We'll be shot. We'll be shot!

WILL
(*Leading* BEN *to the bench.*)
No, it's just that he's kind of surprised right now. Later on, they'll
be right happy we're here, you'll see.

(KING *and* ABEL *come running into office.*)

ABEL

What?
(KING, *nodding, points to door.* ABEL *throws it open.* BEN
snaps to attention.)
No . . . No, no . . . Don't move, do you understand, don't move!
(*He slams door, then flings it open again.*)
Don't move or I'll have you shot!
(*He slams door again.* BEN *wilts.* ABEL *grabs* KING.)
You get over to the reviewing stand on the double and tell
the General to stop the proceedings. There's radio and televi-
sion and newsreel cameras there, and if he gives posthumous

medals to two men who are standing right here in his own office he'll be the laughing stock of the whole country! Step on it!

(KING *runs.* ABEL *flings connecting door open.* BEN *snaps to attention.*)

Stay away from the windows, you understand? Stay away from the doors! Just don't move! And if anybody comes in here you tell them you're John Jones and Jack Smith, you got that?

WILL

Yes, sir!

(ABEL *slams door and mops his brow.* BEN *collapses.*)

BEN

They're gonna kill us . . . they're gonna kill us . . .

WILL

(*Taking up* Time *and fanning* BEN *with it.*)
No they ain't. Breathe deep.

(CHARLES *bursts into office.*)

CHARLES

(*To* ABEL:)
What the hell's going on here? Sergeant King just jumped an Air Policeman and stole his motorcycle.

ABEL

The two men who are getting the posthumous medals . . . they're inside.

CHARLES

The medals?

ABEL

The men.

CHARLES

You're drunk.

ABEL

Go ahead, look!

CHARLES

(*Opens connecting door slowly. Peers in.* WILL *turns from his fanning.*)

Who are you?

WILL

I'm John Jones and this here is Jack Smith.

CHARLES

(*Slams door.*)

Listen, Jim, if you're trying to pull my leg, it'll be the last time, because joking about the dead is carrying it just a little too far.

ABEL

Dead? That's them, right there! That idiot gave those names because I told them to! They're the ones; Sergeant King identified them.

CHARLES

I'm beginning to think that doesn't mean too much! *He identified them once before, didn't he?*

ABEL

(*Snatching newspaper from desk.*)

Here's their pictures! You want more proof?

CHARLES

Lord. Lordy Lord . . .

(WILL *stops fanning, looks at back of magazine.*)

WILL

Lieutenant Gardella don't really smoke Camels, does he?

(WILL *resumes fanning.* KING *runs into office.*)

ABEL

Well? Did you stop him in time?

KING

Sir, I reported to the General and informed him as to the situation and advised him that under the very unusual circumstances, as it has been found out that contrary to all Intelligence reports to the contrary, he desist . . .

ABEL

In English, damn it! Had he already presented the medals or not?

KING

Yes sir, he had.

ABEL

Lord!

(*Runs from office.*)

CHARLES

Lordy Lord. What did he say?

KING

He said that—

BUSH

(*A fearful bellow from* OFFSTAGE.)
I'll court-martial everybody in the whole damn Air Force!

KING

That's what he said, sir.

(BUSH, *livid, bursts into office.* BAKER *follows him.*)

BUSH

Where are they? Where are they? Where are the two privates
who hold my career in the palm of their hands?

CHARLES

In there, sir.

(*Points to door.* BUSH *flings it open and steps into anteroom.* BEN
and WILL *come to attention and salute.*)

BUSH

You two!

WILL

Yes, sir. We got back here as quick as we could.
        (*Pause.* BUSH *stares.*)
And we sure do appreciate you givin' us medals and all and
settin' the flags at half-mast.

(WILL *shakes* BUSH*'s hand.* BUSH *winces sickly.*)

And I got the whole thing figgered out, sir. I have. You see, before all the excitement started in the plane up there, I was cleanin' and sweepin' in the back. Well, you know that handful of dust Sergeant King was talkin' about?

(BUSH *nods dumbly.*)

That's what it was, a handful of dust. If I'da knowed y'all was gonna think it was *us*, I'da swept it under a seat or somethin'! Well, anyhow, what it all comes down to is, we ain't dead!

(BUSH *totters back into office, closing the door.* WILL *lowers* BEN*'s saluting arm and resumes fanning him.* BUSH *stares at* KING.)

BUSH

Ten minutes ago, in front of half the brass in the continental United States, I awarded the Air Medal to a pile of dust. Do you know what this is going to do to me, Sergeant King, when this story gets out?

KING

Sir, I didn't know that they were—

BUSH

For thirty-two years I've been building a reputation! For dignity, for responsibility, for coolness in the crisis and clear-thinking in the clutch! Tomorrow I will probably be known throughout the entire Pentagon as "Old Dustpan!"

KING

Sir, there were these two charred helmets and this—

BUSH

I am not interested in how you *knew* these men in there were dead, Sergeant King! You are responsible for this whole mess!

KING

(*Saluting rapidly.*)

Yes, sir! Yes, sir!

ABEL

(*Entering office.*)

The reporters, sir! They're on their way over. They want to know why you ran out in the middle of Taps.

BUSH

Stall them! Keep them away! Show them the new gymnasium!

(ABEL *exits.*)

I've got to get those men off my base. If anybody sees them—if anybody hears them—

KING

You could transfer them to another base, sir—

BUSH

Shut up! . . . What? Of course!

(*To* CHARLES.)

Go down to the basement and get as many DD-613 forms as you can lay your hands on.

CHARLES

You mean DAF 39-J, don't you, sir?

BUSH

I mean DD-613!

(CHARLES *exits.* BUSH *calls after him:*)

Well, if you find any DAF 39-J's . . .

(*To* BAKER:)

You. Go get a car and bring it around back. Quietly. See if you can find one of those old jobs, with window shades.

BAKER

Yes, sir!

(*Exits.*)

BUSH

You!

KING

(*Saluting, heading for door.*)

Yes, sir!

BUSH

The phone. Get through to General Hooper, down in Texas. See if he's got room for a couple of new privates on his base. Bright, hardworking boys.

KING

Yes, sir.

(*Goes to phone.*)

BUSH

But first get those miserable men in here!

KING

Yes, sir.

(*Heads for anteroom.*)

BUSH

And put your shoes on!

KING

Yes, sir.

(*Snatches shoes from floor, opens anteroom door and beckons* WILL
and BEN *into office.* KING *returns to telephone.* WILL *and* BEN *enter
office hesitantly.* BUSH *draws himself up, glares at them, then melts
into a department-store-Santa-Claus chuckle.*)

BUSH

Ha-ha-ha-ho-ho-ho. Well, it looks like we've had a little mix-up,
boys, doesn't it?

WILL

Yes sir, it sure do.

BUSH

It sure do, all right, ha-ha-ha-ho-ho. But I guess we can straighten
it out, can't we? You can straighten most things out if everybody
co-operates. That's all it takes, just a little cooperation isn't that
so? Ha-ha-ha.

BEN

(*Through chattering teeth.*)
Yes, sir, yes, sir, yes, sir, yes, sir . . .

BUSH

Well, I'm mighty glad to hear you feel that way about it, because if you didn't there could be all kinds of trouble! You boys could even get court-martialed and you wouldn't like that, would you? Ha-ha-ha. No sir, that's the reason we're—

BEN

Give it to us, sir! We deserve it!

BUSH

No, no, no, we're just going to co-operate and everything will—

BEN

We deserted when we should've stuck to our posts!

BUSH

Well, accidents will happen, and sometimes—

BEN

Throw the book at us, sir!

BUSH

(*To* WILL.)
What's the matter with *him?*

WILL

He's worryin' he ain't dead.

BUSH

Oh, for pity's sake!

BEN

I plead guilty, sir. There was no excuse, sir.

ABEL

(*Entering.*)

The reporters, sir. They've seen the gymnasium and they still
want to see *you*.

BUSH

Oh, no . . .

BEN

I'll make a full confession, sir!

BUSH

No! Don't let them in. Tell them I'm sick. Tell them I've gone
home.

(ABEL *exits.*)

BAKER

(*Entering through anteroom.*)

I've got the car, sir.

BUSH

Good! Good! Get rid of this idiot!

BEN

(*As* BAKER *hustles him out.*)

The Universal Code of Military Justice says that a soldier who
deserts his post should be tried by court-martial!

BUSH

(*Calling after them.*)

Lock him in!

WILL

Sir, listen—

BUSH

Get into that car out there.

WILL

Sir, listen, I don't want you to give Ben no punishment. It's my fault he warn't killed, not his'n.

BUSH

Now *look*, nobody's going to punish anybody! I'm just going to transfer the two of you to another air base, that's all! Now will you please get into that car?

WILL

(*Snapping his fingers.*)

Sir, as long as you're fixin' to transfer us, couldn't it please be into the Infantry?

BUSH

No, no! I said I wasn't going to punish you and I meant it!

WILL

But it's where we *want* to go, sir!

BUSH

Out of the question! Airmen can *not* transfer into the Infantry.

Now if you don't get into that car before someone sees you, so help me Hannah, I'm going to have you court-martialed!

WILL

(*Starts to go, then stops.*)
Excuse me for sayin' it, sir, but if you done that a whole lot of people would see me, wouldn't they?

BUSH

What! . . .
(*Dazed, turns slowly to* KING. *Softly:*)
Every bit of this is your fault, Sergeant. If you hadn't sent that plane up with this nincompoop at the radio—

KING

(*Rising, covering mouthpiece of phone.*)
Me, sir? *My* fault! Now look, sir—

BUSH

Stockdale, be reasonable! I'll find an air base right near your home! That would make you happy, wouldn't it?

WILL

I'm sorry, sir, but if Ben and me can't go into the Infantry I reckon we're better off staying right here.

KING

Will, what do you want to upset the General for? The Infantry's murder. Believe me.

WILL

Ben had a chance to go and he tore it up. You know that.

KING

I'll give you back the watch, Will.

BUSH

I'll give you mine too.

WILL

I'm sorry, sir. The Infantry's what we want.

(BUSH *and* KING *look at each other.* KING *becomes conscious of phone in his hand, hangs up.* ABEL *enters.*)

ABEL

The reporters are *here*, sir.

BUSH

You're asking the impossible, Stockdale! It would take an Act of Congress! Absolutely impossible!

(*Blackout—except for a spot on* WILL. *He grins, comes* DOWNSTAGE *and addresses audience.*)

WILL

Now *you* know, when you put your mind to it there ain't *nothin'* impossible. General Bush, he got them reporters in there and told 'em all about how it was such a proud day in the history of the base and all like that, and then the reporters left and him and Sergeant King let me out of the closet . . . And then General Pollard come over and him and General Bush talked some . . . argued, you might say . . . well, what it was was cussin'. All I said to General Pollard was "Howdy" and he knowed who I was right off. He did. Then he left and the next thing you know, me and Sergeant King and General Bush was all pilin' into this great big car. With window shades. And did we drive! Till after dark and then some. And all the time General Bush kept mumblin' to hisself. After a while I made out what he was mumblin'. He was sayin' over and over again, "Where there's a will, there's a way." I asked him to stop, 'cause it's right embarrassin' to hear someone praisin' you like that. Well, finally we was done drivin', and I could tell by the smell of the pines and the sound of the frogs we was out in the woods. Just then the moon come up and things commenced to happen.

(*Spot on* WILL *blacks out, and lights dim up on a clearing in the woods. The rear end of an* AIR FORCE *sedan projects onstage* RIGHT. *There is a tent* UPSTAGE, *with its side rolled up. Within the tent, a* CORPORAL *sits typing by lantern light.* WILL *steps back into the scene and watches as* KING *gives orders to a line of armed* SENTRIES.)

KING

All right, have you got it straight now? Challenge everybody. The password is "Nightmare." If they don't give it, *shoot!* Okay— sentries, take your posts. On the double!

(SENTRIES *trot off in various directions.* BUSH *enters, followed by* ABEL, BAKER *and* CHARLES, *who go into tent.*)

BUSH

Are you sure we've got the whole area surrounded?

KING

I think so, sir. Tell you the truth, I've never done anything like this before.

BUSH

Do you think I have? Guns. Passwords . . .

WILL

It sure is excitin', ain't it?

BUSH

Look, you just stand over there and let me handle this. Please!
(*To* KING:)
Where's General Pollard?

KING

On his way, sir.

BUSH

Are the forms ready for him to sign?

KING

The corporal's working on them, sir.

(*An approaching car is heard from the* LEFT.)

BUSH

Well, speed him up! That must be Pollard's car now.

KING

Yes, sir.
(*Goes to tent.*)

SENTRY

(OFFSTAGE:)
Halt! Give the password!

(*Silence, then a volley of shots ring out.*)

BUSH

Great Scott, they've shot Pollard!

POLLARD
(OFFSTAGE:)
Eugene! Tell these idiots to stop shooting! It's me! Vernon!

(*Another shot.*)

BUSH

Give the password!

POLLARD
(OFFSTAGE:)
I've forgotten the damn thing.

BUSH

Nightmare!

WILL

Nightmare!

(*Another shot.*)

POLLARD
(OFFSTAGE:)
Nightmare, goddammit!
        (*He storms into the clearing, brandishing a shooting stick.*)
Look here, Eugene, you're carrying this thing just a little too far!

BUSH

I'm sorry, Vernon, the sentries are as nervous as I am.

(*There is loud hammering from the trunk of the sedan.* BUSH *and* POLLARD *throw up their arms.*)

BUSH AND POLLARD

Nightmare!

BUSH

It's the other dead hero, Vernon. The talkative one. I hid him in the trunk for total security.

WILL

Ben's in the trunk?

(*More hammering.*)

BUSH

All right, Stockdale. Get the keys and let him out.

(WILL *goes around car for keys.*)

POLLARD

Listen, Eugene, we could both get into a hell of a lot of trouble, pulling a deal like this.

BUSH

We are in trouble, Vernon. Clear up to our pensions. Now come on, sign those papers.

(*They go up to tent.* WILL *unlocks trunk of car, raises lid.* BEN *sticks his head out, peers around.*)

WILL

Howdy, Ben!

BEN

I knew it . . . they got us out in no-man's land . . .

WILL

(*Helping him out.*)
Come on . . . here you go . . .

BEN

Good-bye, Will.

WILL

We just now got here, Ben.

BEN

And we ain't never going back. Will, I know you didn't do it on purpose and I know there wasn't no meanness behind it.
(*Extends hand.*)
I forgive you.

WILL

(*Shaking hands.*)
You mean we're buddies again?

BEN

For a little while . . .

KING

(*Coming down from tent.*)
All right, Whitledge, you're first. Sentry! Take him inside. See that he signs everything in triplicate.

(*A* SENTRY *drags* BEN *up to the tent.*)

BEN

'Bye, Will.

WILL

'Bye, Ben.
(*To* KING:)
Golly, is he gonna be surprised!

KING

We can say good-bye too, Will.

WILL

I'm sure gonna miss you, Sergeant!

KING

Me too. I could hardly type your transfers for the tears in my eyes.

WILL

You know—everyone's all the time sayin' how sergeants is mean and tough, so I'm right glad you was my first one. You showed me different.

KING

Thanks, Will.
(*They shake hands.* WILL *looks at* KING'*s watch.*)
Okay, I'm going to give you the watch anyway. Here. Go on, take it.

WILL

Gee, I never held that against you . . .

KING
(*Backing away.*)
We're square now. I don't owe you nothing; you don't owe me
nothing. We're square.

(BUSH *and* POLLARD *come down from tent.*)

BUSH
King, what's the matter with that Whitledge? He keeps saying
he's sorry he has only one life to give for his country.

(KING *makes crazy sign, goes up to tent.*)

WILL
He figgers you brought us here to get shot, sir.

BUSH AND POLLARD
Shot?
(*They look at each other speculatively.*)

BUSH
Ridiculous . . . All these witnesses, Vernon . . .
(POLLARD *returns to tent.* BUSH *flourishes a clipboard.*)
All right, Stockdale, I've just got a couple of letters for you to
sign and then we'll be through with this mess. This one is to
your folks, saying that you're on a very important secret mis-
sion, and this one certifies that you've never heard of "Operation
Prometheus" and have never been on my base in your entire
life. Sign here.
(*Shoves pen at* WILL.)

WILL

But if we never heard of "Operation Whatchamacallit," then we don't get no medals, do we?

BUSH

Medals! Of course not! Sign here . . .

WILL

Ben sets a lot of stock in medals and all like that.

BUSH

Now look—you just sign these letters! You're going into the Infantry; what more do you want?

WILL

But if we don't sign, then we're still dead—and Ben's medal will be sent to his folks and he could just go home and pick it up, couldn't he?

BUSH

Well, yes . . . well, no! . . . well . . .

WILL

Looks to me like we're *best* off just stayin' dead!

BUSH

You can't *do* that! All right, all right.
(*Detaches a ribbon from his jacket.*)
Here's a ribbon. Now sign.

WILL

This way is okay for me, sir, but couldn't you do it up right for Ben?

BUSH

Do it up—

WILL

You know, give him a real medal, not just a little ribbon. And everybody standin' up stifflike and you sayin' a whole lot of words.

BUSH

You want me to *present* a medal . . . out here in the woods . . . in the middle of the night?

WILL

That's right! We'll get everybody standin' up over there, and we could turn some of the cars around so their lights is shinin'! Maybe we can get some music on the radio! Hey, driver, could you turn that car around!
(*Runs* OFFSTAGE RIGHT.)

BUSH

No! No! I don't have any medals!

POLLARD

(*Coming down from tent.*)
How long is this going to take, Eugene?

BUSH

(*Calling after* WILL.)
I didn't bring any medals!

POLLARD

I want to get to bed.

BUSH

(*Turning to the be-medaled* POLLARD.)

I don't have any med— Ohhh . . . !

POLLARD

What are you staring at?

BUSH

Vernon . . . old man . . . I wonder if you could give me . . . one of your . . . medals?

POLLARD

What?

BUSH

Just one, Vernon! You've got so many of them!

POLLARD

What are you talking about, Eugene?

BUSH

Stockdale wants a medal!

POLLARD

To hell with him!

BUSH

No! Vernon, if you give me one of yours . . . I'll give you *two* of mine. I swear I will.

POLLARD

But these medals are sewn on!

BUSH

Sewn?

(WILL *re-enters, approaches them.*)

POLLARD

Yes, dammit!

BUSH

(*To* WILL, *pleadingly:*)
His medals are *sewn* on . . .

WILL

I got my mumbly-peg knife.
(*Producing it.*)

BUSH

(*Handing* POLLARD *the knife.*)
A small one, Vernon . . . Please . . .

POLLARD

(*Snatching knife.*)
I'll do this in private, if you don't mind!

(POLLARD *storms off into the trees. From the* RIGHT, *a pair of
headlight beams swing around, and an orchestra playing "Goody,
Goody" is heard.*)

BUSH

There's nothing else you can think of at the moment, is there,
Stockdale? You do understand why we don't have a brass band,
don't you?

WILL

I wouldn't worry about it none. This'll do fine. I'll just get the fellows lined up. Hey, Corporal!

(CORPORAL *comes out of tent.* WILL *salutes.*)

Howdy. Would you please go over there and stand up at attention, real smart-like.

CORPORAL

Do what?

BUSH

Just do as you're told! On the double!

WILL

Captain, could you and the Lieutenants come out here a minute, please?

(CHARLES, BAKER *and* ABEL *emerge from tent.* WILL *salutes.*)

Howdy. Would you fellows go over there with the Corporal and stand up at attention, please?

THREE OFFICERS

DO WHAT?

BUSH

Get over there! You ought to know enough to obey orders by now!

(POLLARD *storms back on, the front of his jacket slashed and torn. He thrusts a medal at* BUSH.)

POLLARD

I've been blackmailed, I've been shanghaied, I've been shot at,
and now I've been robbed.

WILL

Boy, Ben's gonna pop his shirt when *both* you Generals snap
to attention!

POLLARD

DO WHAT?

BUSH

Vernon, please . . .

POLLARD

Never! Not on your life!
      (*Flips open his shooting stick and sits on it.*)

BUSH

I'll stand at attention! I'll stand on my head! Please sign!

WILL

      (*Taking pen.*)
Clean forgot! Last name first, first name, middle name last?

BUSH

Just your regular signature.
      (SENTRIES *enter.*)
You men get over there with the others!

(SENTRIES *join group standing at attention.*)

WILL

I'll go fetch Ben.

(WILL *exits into tent as* KING *emerges, a sheaf of papers in his hand.*)

BUSH

King, have you got those orders?

KING

Yes, sir.

BUSH

(*Calling to tent.*)
All right, dammit, come out and get it!

WILL

(*Leading* BEN *out.*)
Go ahead, Ben. Strut right up to the General and he's gonna give you somethin'.

BEN

I know. Good-bye, Will.

BUSH

King . . .

KING

(*Reading:*)
"The following enlisted men are hereby relieved of duty and removed from the records of Major General Eugene Bush, and transferred to the command of Major General Vernon I. Pollard, U.S. Army, Infantry."

BEN

What?

WILL

We're in the Infantry, Ben.

BEN

The Infantry?

WILL

You finally made it, Ben.

BEN

Oh, no . . . oh, golly . . . oh . . .

KING

(*Crossing and handing papers to them.*)
Private Benjamin B. Whitledge . . . Private Will Stockdale . . .
So long, boys. It's been swell knowing you!

WILL AND BEN

So long, Sergeant.

KING

Wish I could go along with you, but that's life!

WILL

(*To* BUSH.)
Gee, couldn't he, sir? Go along with us?

BUSH

Brilliant idea, Stockdale! Vernon?

POLLARD

Wonderful!

KING

No, no, no—

WILL

(*Throwing his arm around* KING'*s shoulder.*)
We're still gonna be together!

BEN

In the Infantry!

KING

What happened?

BUSH

Detail, atten-shun!

POLLARD

(*Sitting with his arms folded.*)
Damned if I'll stand at attention!

VOICE ON RADIO

. . . broadcasting on 1200 kilocycles. Good night.

(*Drum roll.*)

BUSH

It gives me great pleasure to award this medal which through a regrettable error was previously awarded posthumously, to Private Benjamin B. Whitledge, U.S. Army, Infantry.

(Band on radio plays "The Star-Spangled Banner." POLLARD *leaps to attention and salutes.* BEN *marches up to* BUSH *to receive his medal.* WILL *comes downstage and addresses audience as "Meeting Hall" curtain falls and the scene behind it slowly fades out.)*

WILL

Everythin' come out as good as Tony and the Pony, didn't it? Well, that's how I got my ribbon and Ben got his medal, and how us Three Musketeers wound up in the Infantry after all. I want to thank y'all for bein' such good listeners and not leavin' the hall no more'n you had to. Mrs. Calhoun got her shoe back? Good. Well, I guess I better quit now, because—
  (Looks carefully at watch.)
—Mickey Mouse got his hands way up to goin' home time! Good night! Good night!
  (He runs off into the wings.)

CURTAIN

THE END

GENERAL
SEEGER

INTRODUCTION

(GENERAL SEEGER)

Several years after writing this volume's *Notebook Warrior*, and his dual TV and stage adaptations of *No Time For Sergeants*, Ira Levin returned to the military (so to speak) with *General Seeger*—the last of his three works set in the armed forces. While those earlier military outings were in the first instance youthfully earnest, and in the second strictly comedic, here the outlook is starker, and more worldly-wise.

Seeger is pure classical drama—a Greek tragedy in khaki. Was the general's son, in whose name an impressive new building is to be dedicated, a rightful hero? Or is the life Seeger has built for himself blind to the larger truths that surround it? Over the course of a single sun-streaked day, he'll conduct his own personal inquest to uncover the truth.

Levin was often ahead of the curve in examining social concerns that hadn't yet entered the mainstream, such as the incursion of computers and surveillance technology into our daily lives (*This Perfect Day* and *Sliver*), the ethical and practical implications of cloning (*The Boys from Brazil*), and the backlash against feminism (*The Stepford Wives*). Here, he was examining the "Military-PR complex" some fifteen years before the series of acclaimed works known collectively as *Friendly Fire* captured the nation's attention; here too is a tale centered on the possible cover-up of a soldier's true manner of death—and a parent desperately seeking the truth.

As critical as *Seeger* may appear to be of the military, Levin saw its issues as applying to the members of any large organization, explaining: *"It is about people who accept any way of life without questioning it. A general might be like that, but so could many other people—a corporation officer, a man in a political party."*

As with the earlier-written *Notebook Warrior*, there's a decidedly autobiographical thread present in *Seeger*. You may note that the play's unnamed corporal (who serves as something of a one-man Greek chorus) has a backstory that's remarkably close to Levin's own (as detailed in the introduction to *Notebook Warrior*): drafted into the army at war's end, a few improbable months at Radar School, attachment to his base's *Public Information Office* . . .

The idea for the play came to its author while he was stationed in Fort Monmouth, New Jersey's own Public Information Office. One day, the base's commanding general passed by Levin's office door, when the young writer was suddenly struck by the realization that behind the uniform was a flesh-and-blood human being. That set Levin thinking about the possible personal history of someone in that position. (Though beyond the above, what's on offer here is a tale of pure fiction).

It's difficult to consider *Seeger* outside the context of Levin's other military works, and his own service. After having acted as something of a pitch-man for the Army with the praiseful *Notebook Warrior* (and the subsequent training films he was tasked with writing)—then adapting the jocular *No Time For Sergeants*, Levin was perhaps seeking to balance the scales a bit, and provide a more frank and sober inspection of some of the realities of life in the military, beyond what those earlier, more rose-tinted portrayals conveyed.

To that end, *General Seeger's* title character seems to provide a more solemn counterpart to *No Time For Sergeants'* farcical *Sergeant King*. And, while both works employ scenarios touching on the legitimacy of posthumous honors, this was previously done to comic effect; here the ramifications are real—and weighty. As it happens, both works' lead characters share not only the same first name, but the same *initials* as well—here, William (J.) Seeger, and in *Sergeants*, Will Stockdale.

Seeger also shares a feature with Levin's earlier *Notebook Warrior*—a father who confuses his own worldly interests with those of his son, both having named their boys *juniors*—iterations of themselves, furtherings of their own egos. Levin's somewhat strained relations with his own father—who'd harbored hopes he'd enter the family business—may have partly informed that dynamic (though Levin appears to have reconciled those feelings by the time of his later, warmly-rendered stage play *Cantorial*).

General Seeger was directed by the actor George C. Scott, who chose Levin's drama as the inaugural production of Scott's newly formed *Theatre of Michigan Company* which was, uniquely, financed through the sale of three-dollar shares to the local citizenry. Scott would become the show's *star* as well, after veteran actor William Bendix quit the role of Seeger in frustration over continued changes which Scott continued to request from Levin, which Bendix deemed unneeded. Lest anyone think physical combat is purely the army's domain, when Levin refused one such change, Scott literally tried to hurl him down the grand staircase of Detroit's *Shubert Theatre*. "He didn't succeed, though; I was holding on too tightly to the bannister," Levin recounted.

The *Windsor Star* termed *Seeger* "society-shattering," praising the play's "human touches of wit with wisdom," while the *Detroit Free Press* deemed it "authoritative and moving." The Broadway reaction to *Seeger* was less glowing; underlying some of the response seemed to be a genuine discomfort at seeing the military critiqued, as well as the play's portrayal of the press as unquestioning mouthpieces.

However you slice it, *General Seeger* and the remaining two legs of Ira Levin's military *triad (Notebook Warrior* and *No Time For Sergeants)* provide a unique window into their author's own experience in uniform, both as a youthful draftee, then later a more seasoned, contemplative observer—his own Seeger-like *review.* And also, we hope, some thought-provoking and entertaining reading.

Nicholas Levin
New York
March 2025

GENERAL SEEGER

William Bendix (3rd from left) and company of General Seeger (Credit: Friedman-Abeles Studio)

William Bendix and Ann Harding in *General Seeger* (Credit: Friedman-Abeles Studio)

To
FLORA ROBERTS

GENERAL SEEGER was presented by the Theatre of Michigan Company and Theodore Mann at the Lyceum Theatre in New York City on February 28, 1962. It was staged by George C. Scott; lighting was by Ralph Holmes; costumes by Noel Taylor; and setting by Gerald Parker. The cast, in order of appearance, was as follows:

A CORPORAL............................. Roscoe Lee Browne
A WOMAN.................................Dolores Sutton
CAPTAIN PECK.........................Gerald Richards
CAPTAIN THIBAUDEAU.................... Paul Stevens
LT. COLONEL BONNEY .... Lonny Chapman
MAJOR GENERAL VOHS.....................John Leslie
BOYD MCKAY.........................Tim O'Connor
MAJOR GENERAL SEEGER .... George C. Scott
RENA SEEGER .... Ann Harding

REPORTERS, PHOTOGRAPHERS
Charles Dierkop, J. Nathan French, Elaine Hyman, John O'Leary, Loree Marks, Thomas Maxwell, Martin Priest, Tom Signorelli, Frank Simpson

COLOR GUARDS ....Johnny Cosgrove, Matt Bennett

CHARACTERS

A CORPORAL
A WOMAN
CAPTAIN PECK
CAPTAIN THIBAUDEAU
LIEUTENANT COLONEL BONNEY
MAJOR GENERAL VOHS

Boyd McKay

Major General Seeger

Rena Seeger

Reporters

Photographers

A Private

The action takes place on an Army post in one of the New England states, in the office of the Commanding General. The time is peacetime; a Saturday in a recent July.

There are two acts.

The characters in this play, including those who hold existing military or civilian offices, are fictional and not intended to represent specific persons, living or dead.

Occasional minor license has been taken with military procedure and terminology.

I. L.

SETTING

An Army post in one of the New England states. The Commanding General's office and a portion of the anteroom.

A cyclorama. UPSTAGE CENTER, a broad walnut executive desk with occupant's and visitor's chairs of maroon leather. An American flag stands UPSTAGE LEFT of the desk; a red flag with two white stars (the official flag of a Major General) stands UPSTAGE RIGHT of it. Suspended in space behind the occupant's chair hangs a large gilt-framed painting of a hearty young Army lieutenant standing at ease and smiling directly into the eyes of the observer. The top of the portrait hangs higher than the eagles of the flanking flags.

The imaginary RIGHT wall of the office is marked by a free-standing window and, farther DOWNSTAGE, a maroon leather couch flanked by ashstands. The window has a Venetian blind, blue drapes, and an air-conditioning unit mounted in its lower section. The imaginary LEFT wall of the office is marked by a free-standing pair of walnut double doors and, farther DOWNSTAGE, a slat-backed chair and a walnut table. The double doors, which open outward, are symmetrically opposed to the window unit at RIGHT. There should be two or three chairs in addition to those already mentioned.

The anteroom section is at extreme LEFT, quite narrow. Adjacent to the slat-backed chair and walnut table (on the other side of the imaginary wall) stands a small secretarial desk, facing UPSTAGE. Below it, a posture-back swivel chair. The imaginary LEFT wall of the anteroom is marked by a free-standing single door which opens inward and, DOWNSTAGE, a visitors' settee and a gray steel filing cabinet.

There is a telephone on the secretarial desk and two on the executive desk, although only one is used in the course of the play.

ACT ONE

SCENE: Darkness and silence. Out of the distance, faintly, comes the sound of a field drum, rat-a-tat-tatting a half-time marching cadence. It grows louder, approaching, and louder still, reverberant, tightening the hearer's stomach, and then it turns away, fading into the distance again . . .

AT RISE: The curtain rises slowly. The set stands empty against the bright summer blueness of the cyclorama. The window blind is closed, a shaft of sunlight strikes against it from the wings and filters through to suffuse the office with a limpid morning half-light. The double doors to the anteroom are opened, the single anteroom door is closed. The drum dies out.

The single door opens and a CORPORAL enters. He is twenty-four. About his left arm is pinned a white cloth band with the initials P.I.O. stencilled in black. He carries his cap and a clipboard filled with varicolored papers. Seeing that no one is about, he walks into the office. He stands for a moment, fanning himself once or twice with the clipboard, and then goes to the window and studies the controls of the air-conditioning unit. He turns it on, adjusts it, feels the air-flow. He opens the blind and glances at what lies below, squinting against the sunlight. Then he turns, comes DOWNSTAGE and addresses the audience.

CORPORAL

Welcome to the theater, ladies and gentlemen. The name of the play is *General Seeger. Seeger*, please; not *SeeGAR.*

(*Tucks his cap into his belt.*)

A number of years ago my trick knee maliciously untricked itself and I was drafted into the Army. The most recent war had ended, and so, after Basic Training and a few improbable months at Radar School, I found myself at Fort Nameless, in one of the New England states, a corporal attached to the Public Information Office.

(*Indicates his armband.*)

The P.I.O. This armband, by the way, is my own handiwork. I'm quite proud of its official appearance. If you know a boy who's been drafted, tell him to make an armband. Sergeants fall back in awe, lieutenants are disquieted, even captains and majors talk gently to the man with an armband. Any initials; it makes no difference. This is the Commanding General's office, on the second floor of Headquarters Building. It's twenty past ten on Saturday morning, July twelfth, and throughout the post those without armbands are readying themselves for a parade. High brass has come here today, to attend the dedication of a shiny new building. It stands at the far end of the post, near the barracks where the trainees are billeted. It's a recreation center for the enlisted men, and a beautiful one, although it kills me to admit it. There are two lounges, a cafeteria, a library, a music room, a gymnasium, and a blue Olympic swimming pool, all housed under a flying wing of white concrete miraculously poised on vertical sheets of pale green glass. That sterling description comes easy; we chaps in P.I.O. have sent it out this week to every newspaper and magazine from Abbeville, Alabama, to Zion, Illinois. In peacetime, in a democracy, an army travels not on its stomach, but on its favorable publicity. And so . . . at three this afternoon, Himself, Our Leader—

(*A gesture at the desk behind him.*)

—Major General William J. Seeger, known to the troops as Eager-Seeger or Cigar Butt, will unveil a bronze plaque mounted on the portal of the new recreation center. An element of human interest creeps in at this point, and constitutes the real reason reporters and photographers have come here today; for the building is to be dedicated, not to some unrelated hero of long-ago battles, but to a man much—

WOMAN

(*Cutting in on "battles."*)

Excuse me.

(*A* WOMAN *is standing in the double doorway. She is in her early thirties, slim, neatly dressed, tense. She carries a purse and a small blue satchel with a white wing printed on it.*)

Is this General Seeger's office?

CORPORAL

Yes, ma'am.

WOMAN

He isn't here?

CORPORAL

No, ma'am. Are you a reporter?

WOMAN

No, I'm—not.

CORPORAL

The General will be here in ten minutes or so. Would you like to wait?

WOMAN
(*Retreating toward visitors' settee.*)
Yes. Thank you. I'll wait . . .

CORPORAL
You can sit in here if you'd like. The air-conditioning doesn't
make it out there.

WOMAN
Oh, thank you.
(*Entering office uncertainly.*)
It's terribly hot, isn't it?

CORPORAL
Ninety-two, and still rising.
(*To the audience.*)
Here is the play, ladies and gentlemen. This woman begins it.

WOMAN
It's supposed to go up past ninety-five . . .

(*Before the desk, she stands looking up at the portrait behind it.*
CORPORAL *moves* UPSTAGE.)

CORPORAL
That's the General's son. A first lieutenant. He's dead now.

WOMAN
He smiled as though he intended to live forever . . .

CORPORAL
Thirty-one years . . . The new building today is being dedicated

in his honor. He gave his life to save a couple of lame-brained enlisted men.

WOMAN

(*Moving away* RIGHT.)
Are you the General's orderly?

CORPORAL

No, I'm with the Public Information Office. Have you an appointment with the General?

WOMAN

No, I haven't. He knows me, though. He'll see me.
(*She sits on the couch* DOWNSTAGE RIGHT, *putting her purse and satchel beside her.* CORPORAL *has observed her tension, studies her. She feels his eyes.*)
Is this building always so deathly quiet?

CORPORAL

Saturday isn't a regular duty day.

WOMAN

(*An ill-at-ease pause.*)
If you have any work to take care of, please don't let me interfere.

CORPORAL

(*Crosses* UPSTAGE *to* RIGHT *of desk.*)
I'm just waiting for the chief of my office. We have a press meeting here in a few minutes.

WOMAN

(*With a caustic edge:*)
And the General will make a little speech to the reporters.

CORPORAL

(*Registering her inflection. Sits on back of chair,* DOWN-
STAGE RIGHT *of desk.*)

Yes, ma'am. Judging from that bag, you came here by airplane.

WOMAN

(*Studying her* RIGHT *hand.*)

Corporal, may I ask you a hypothetical question?

CORPORAL

Yes, ma'am.

WOMAN

(*With a forced flippancy.*)

My hands, you have noticed no doubt, are trembling. If I were
to take a small bottle of whiskey from this bag and draw off,
say, a quarter-inch of its contents, would you think me—an
alcoholic?

CORPORAL

(*Pause.*)

Maybe. Or you might be a woman under some . . . unusual
tension, for whom a drink would be . . . wise medicine. I don't
think I'd form a fixed opinion either way.

WOMAN

That's fair enough, Corporal . . . Let's make the question *un*-
hypothetical . . .

(*Unzips satchel and takes out a pint bottle with a cap that
serves as a drinking cup.*)

CORPORAL
(*Starting* LEFT.)
I'll get a glass.

WOMAN
(*Stopping him at* CENTER STAGE.)
Don't bother; the top of the bottle does the trick.
(*Pouring.*)
This is a Saint Christopher's bottle; the patron saint of travelers.
(*Holding up bottle.*)
You see? It's almost full. If I were an alcoholic it would be almost
empty, wouldn't it? I bought it yesterday afternoon.

CORPORAL
(*Smiling.*)
You're not an alcoholic.

WOMAN
(*She looks at him.*)
Thank you. I don't want to be.
(*Sips, then offers bottle.*)
Are you?

CORPORAL
No. No, thanks.
(WOMAN *sips again.* CORPORAL *moves* RIGHT *to window,*
watches her from this new perspective.)
Have you traveled far?

WOMAN
From San Francisco to New York, from New York to Boston,
from Boston to here.

CORPORAL

To see the ceremonies today?

WOMAN

No, I've seen enough of military ceremonies. They leave me quite cold. In fact you might say they freeze me to death.
(*She sips again.*)

CORPORAL

(*Crossing* DOWNSTAGE *of chair* DOWNSTAGE RIGHT *of desk.*)
You flew all this way just to see the General?

WOMAN

Yes.
(*Caps the bottle, her tension not visibly diminished.*)

CORPORAL

You're a relative of his?

WOMAN

Everything you say is a question, Corporal.

(*She puts bottle in satchel, zips it closed. Voices are heard* OFFSTAGE LEFT.)

CORPORAL

I'm sorry. I didn't mean to be rude.

WOMAN

It's all right. You weren't, really. People are coming.
(CORPORAL *moves to* CENTER STAGE.)
Let me stay in here, please.

(CORPORAL *looks at her for a moment. She meets his gaze effort-fully. He turns to doorway and then to audience.*)

CORPORAL

Captain Peck, the chief of the Public Information Office, fol-lowed by reporters and photographers.

(CAPTAIN PECK *enters, the professional greeter's smile lingering on his face. He is 36, likeable, a bit hasty and nervous on this spe-cial day.*)

PECK

Ah, here you are.

CORPORAL

Morning, sir.

PECK

Do you have all the info sheets?
        (CORPORAL *shows clipboard in answer.*)
Good.
        (*The first of the* REPORTERS *and* PHOTOGRAPHERS *are entering.*)
Right in here, gentlemen, ladies . . .
        (*Seeing the* WOMAN.)
Are you with the press, Miss?

WOMAN

        (*Taking cigarette from purse.*)
No, I'm not.

PECK

(*Turning quickly to door.*)

Come right in! I'm afraid there aren't going to be enough seats.
Quite frankly, we weren't expecting such a fine turnout!

(REPORTERS *and* PHOTOGRAPHERS *enter. There are seven or eight
in all, two of them women. Two of the men carry cameras. Some
of them take seats immediately, others drift about the room.*)

FIRST REPORTER

(*A woman, indicating portrait.*)

Isn't this Lieutenant Seeger?

PECK

Yes. Yes, it is.

SECOND REPORTER

(*A man, looking out window. To another* REPORTER
near him.)

I'll tell you, I'd just as soon watch the parade from up here.

THIRD REPORTER

Can we take any seats?

PECK

(*Indicating seats near desk.*)

Well, I think we'd better leave those . . .

FIRST REPORTER

(*To the* WOMAN.)

May I?

WOMAN

Oh, yes.

(WOMAN *takes her satchel and purse from couch, puts satchel on floor* DOWNSTAGE RIGHT. FIRST REPORTER *sits next to* WOMAN.)

SECOND REPORTER

(*Still at window.*)
Will we be out in the sun or do we get to sit under the awning there?

PECK

Oh, you'll be under the awning. All the guests . . .

FOURTH REPORTER

Is that Lieutenant Seeger?

(CORPORAL *has gone* LEFT *into anteroom and now brings swivel chair into office, offering it to a* REPORTER *near door.*)

PECK

Yes, it is. Please, if you'll all take whatever seats you can find . . . Leaving those, please. We're only going to be here for a few minutes. I'm sorry there aren't enough seats for all of you, but quite frankly we weren't expecting such a fine turnout.

> (REPORTERS *and* PHOTOGRAPHERS *have now grouped themselves about the office, most sitting, a few standing, one sitting on* UPSTAGE *arm of couch.* CORPORAL *is crouching on his haunches* DOWNSTAGE LEFT. PECK *stands* CENTER STAGE. WOMAN *is smoking, as are a few of the* REPORTERS.)

Now, then . . . The Corporal here has some information sheets that he's going to give you.

> (CORPORAL *rises and begins distributing typed and sta-*
> *pled papers to the* REPORTERS. PECK *glances at a card he*
> *holds in his palm.*)

These sheets contain a little data on General Seeger and our special guests, including official titles and correct spelling of names. The sheets also include some interesting facts and figures on the Recreation Center and a short biography of *Lieutenant* Seeger. Now . . . there is one change. One of our special guests, Lieutenant General Del Ruth, the First Army Commander, is unable to be here today. To represent him he has sent Major General Ernest C. Vohs—that's V-O-H-S; Vohs—whose official title is Deputy Commanding General of the First Army.

> (*Several* REPORTERS *are jotting this down.*)

Deputy . . . Commanding General . . . of the First Army . . .

(CORPORAL *has just given information sheets to* FIRST REPORTER *and is crossing* LEFT, *away from couch.*)

WOMAN

May I have one of those?

(CORPORAL *turns, hesitates a beat, crosses* RIGHT *and gives* WOMAN *information sheets.*)

SECOND REPORTER

Why did General Del Ruth cancel?

WOMAN

Thank you.

PECK

I honestly don't know. He just sent a wire saying he couldn't make it and that Vohs was coming instead. Duties, I suppose.

(*During the following,* WOMAN *studies information sheets and* CORPORAL *resumes his crouching position* DOWN-STAGE LEFT.)

Now as I said, we'll only be in here a few minutes. General Seeger will introduce you to our special guests, and he also wanted the chance to say a few informal words to you before the official proceedings begin. The parade will take place in half an hour on the field down below; that's eleven o'clock. The luncheon is twelve to two-thirty at the Officers Club—there'll be cars to transport you—and the dedication of the Recreation Center will begin promptly at three and should only take fifteen or twenty minutes. Afterwards there'll be a tour of the building.

(*Another reference to his notes.*)

Oh, one final point. This meeting here is informal, as I said, and General Seeger has asked that there be no taking of photographs. You can take all the pictures you want later in the day, and our own photographers' prints will also be made available to you.

(*Glances at his watch, then* OFFSTAGE LEFT.)

Let's see now . . . If any of you, after touring the Recreation Center, should want to visit other parts of the post—the Ordnance School or the training battalions—we'll be more than happy to—Ah!

(CAPTAIN THIBAUDEAU *has entered quickly during the final words of the above. He nods at* PECK *from the doorway and exits again.*)

That was General Seeger's aide. They're coming now. Gentlemen, ladies . . .

(*Everyone rises except the* WOMAN. *She folds her information sheets precisely. Others face the doorway.* BOYD MCKAY, MAJOR GENERAL VOHS, LIEUTENANT COLONEL BONNEY, MAJOR GENERAL SEEGER, RENA SEEGER *and* CAPTAIN THIBAUDEAU *enter. They group themselves before the desk.* THIBAUDEAU *remaining* UPSTAGE LEFT. *Cyclo-rama has become a warm yellow-gold.*)

Ladies and gentlemen: General Seeger. General: the reporters.

(PECK *steps aside* UPSTAGE RIGHT.)

SEEGER

Thank you, Captain. And thank you all for coming here today. I am so—very, very pleased . . . Sit down, please. Sit . . .

(REPORTERS *and* PHOTOGRAPHERS *who were sitting resume their seats.* SEEGER *watches them, flushed with pride and happiness impossible for him to conceal. He is 57; a strong, forceful man. The* WOMAN, *at the* DOWNSTAGE *end of the couch, is sitting turned well toward the front, partially shielding her face with the folded information sheets in her* UPSTAGE *hand.*)

I'd like to introduce three honored visitors. This is Mr. Boyd McKay, ladies and gentlemen, the Assistant Secretary of the Army.

(MCKAY *nods, smiles. He is in his early fifties, immaculately dressed, cool, reserved.*)

And Major General Vohs, the Deputy Commanding General of the First Army . . .

(VOHS *is in his late fifties, white-haired, warm, with an air of judicial dignity.*)

Lieutenant Colonel Bonney, of the Weapons Testing Center at Fort Colleran, Oklahoma. Colonel Bonney was Lieutenant Seeger's senior officer at the time of his death.

(BONNEY *is in his mid-forties, looking more like a doctor than a military man. There is a faint aura of unease about him.*)

And this is my wife, ladies and gentlemen.

RENA

Thank you all for coming here . . .

> (RENA *is 54; nervous, anxious-eyed. She is trying to appear as happy as* SEEGER, *but she is not. Her eyes seldom leave him.*)

SEEGER

Gentlemen, would you sit for a minute or two, please? I want to say something to these people, and to you, too.

> (MCKAY, VOHS *and* BONNEY *take seats.* RENA *looks about uncertainly.* THIBAUDEAU *moves a chair toward her, she takes it gratefully.* SEEGER, *before the desk, waits until all are settled. A feeling of gravity clouds over his earlier exuberance.*)

This afternoon I'm going to make a formal speech dedicating our new Recreation Center to the memory of First Lieutenant William J. Seeger, Junior, and when I do, I'm not going to say anything at all about Lieutenant Seeger being my son. A military ceremony isn't the place for bringing up personal relationships. Higher authorities put me in command of this post, and a building went up, and now higher authorities have decided who gets the honor of the dedication; *personal* relationships are—irrelevant. It wouldn't be honest, though, for me to go through the whole day pretending that the relationship didn't exist, because today of all days it's—very much in my mind, and I know it's in some of your minds, too. So I want to say a few words now *in*formally; not as Commanding General Seeger, just as Lieutenant Bill Seeger's father. It's a—terrible thing when a man lives longer than his own son. It's—backwards, reversed. You expect a son to go on beyond you. You give him your name, junior . . . it's as if you're trying to make a *chain*. And when the link you put forward in front of you gets broken, well—that's the end of the chain, right there. When the son dies, the father dies, too. All right. It's sad.

But we've each got a death coming to us sooner or later, and the finest way a man can meet his death, it seems to me, isn't to be ambushed by it, to have it spring out at him from an accident or an illness. No, the finest way is to face it squarely, with awareness, for a purpose. To die *for* something instead of to die *of* something. Bill saw those two boys in front of that grenade, he didn't have to run in and do what he did. He could have stayed outside that door and *no one in this whole wide world would have reproached him or said he failed in any way to do his military duty or his human duty!* Bill didn't see it that way. He chose to save those boys, at the almost certain cost of his own life. He risked, and *gave* his life, for his belief; that an officer's first responsibility is the men beneath him. Sixteen months ago . . . I wouldn't be a father if I weren't still—brokenhearted today . . . But I wouldn't be a soldier if I weren't *proud* today, too. I'm proud that First Army and the Chief Ordnance Officer and the Secretary of the Army have chosen to honor Bill in the way they have; I'm proud that you people are interested enough to come here and write stories and take pictures; and I'm proud most of all that Bill died *for* something and not *of* something; that he added another thread of honor to——this uniform woven of honor that we wear.

     (*Silence. The* WOMAN *stands. Everyone stares at her.*)
Helena . . . ? Helena!

RENA

Helena!

(SEEGER *and* RENA *go hastily to the* WOMAN. SEEGER *embraces her.*)

SEEGER

Where did you come from? How did you know?
     (*Kisses her on the cheek.*)

RENA

We didn't know where to write you, Helena . . .

WOMAN

(*Impassively, as* RENA *kisses her.*)
I flew in from San Francisco . . .

SEEGER

(*Still holding her hand.*)
This is wonderful! We wanted you here!

RENA

San Francisco?

SEEGER

(*Turning beamingly to the others in the room.*)
Gentlemen—Oh—this day gets better every minute! This is
Helena, Bill's wife, my daughter-in- . . .

WOMAN

(*On "wife."*)
Widow. His widow.

SEEGER

Yes, widow. Helena. My daughter-in-law!
          (*There are general murmurs of interest and approval.* COR-
          PORAL *rises from his crouching position, surprised.*)
How did you know about this?

HELENA

Your photograph was in the newspapers yesterday.

SEEGER

The *San Francisco* newspapers?

RENA

Why didn't you tell us that you were coming?

SEEGER

You brought the baby, didn't you? Where is he now? You'll stay
with—

HELENA

(*Overlapping.*)
I did not bring him. I left him with a friend.

SEEGER

Oh, no, Helena! You should have brought him!

RENA

(*A nervous laugh.*)
Why have you made such a surprise of this? There are tele-
phones . . .

SEEGER

Come. Come meet everybody . . .

(*He draws* HELENA UPSTAGE CENTER. MCKAY, VOHS, *and* BONNEY
rise. CORPORAL *crouches again.*)

RENA

Springing up from nowhere . . .

SEEGER

Helena, this is Mr. McKay, the Assistant Secretary of the Army.

MCKAY

How do you do, Mrs. Seeger.

HELENA

How do you do.

(MCKAY *anticipates a handshake, but* HELENA *does not offer one.*)

MCKAY

It's a—pleasure to meet you.

HELENA

Thank you.

SEEGER

Major General Vohs . . .

VOHS

Mrs. Seeger . . .

HELENA

General.

SEEGER

Lieutenant Colonel Bonney . . .

BONNEY

How do you do, Mrs. Seeger.

HELENA

I remember you from Fort Colleran.

SEEGER

The Colonel was Bill's senior officer.

BONNEY

(*An uneasy smile.*)
We met at the Christmas party, and at General Ramey's once
or twice.

HELENA

You were Major Bonney then.

BONNEY

That's right.

HELENA

Congratulations on your promotion.

BONNEY

Thank you, Mrs. Seeger.

SEEGER

Oh, and, Helena—Come here, Dick—Helena, this is Dick Thibaudeau, my aide. Dick was with Bill at the Point!

THIBAUDEAU

How do you do, Mrs. Seeger.

HELENA

How do you do, Captain.

(THIBAUDEAU *is holding out his hand.* HELENA *has not offered
her hand to any of the others. Now* THIBAUDEAU *waits, smiling*

kindly. He is 33, warm and engaging. HELENA *finds herself obliged to give her hand.)*

THIBAUDEAU

(*Holding* HELENA'*s hand throughout.*)
I was a year ahead of Bill, and got to know him fairly well. That's why the General chose me as his aide.

SEEGER

He plays good golf; that's why I chose him!

THIBAUDEAU

Did Bill ever mention me to you?

HELENA

I don't recall—

THIBAUDEAU

I've mentioned him often, to many people. I wish he and I had served together after the Point. Knowing him is—one of my best memories.

HELENA

Thank you, Captain. You're kind.

THIBAUDEAU

Not kind; only truthful.

HELENA

Thank you . . .

(THIBAUDEAU *releases her hand.*)

SEEGER

Have you seen the building, Helena? The Recreation Center?

HELENA

No, I haven't.

SEEGER

Oh, wait till you do! It's the best in the whole damn Army! Bill's face would have lighted up like a Christmas tree! It's got a—

FOURTH REPORTER

General Seeger—

SEEGER

Yes? I'm sorry; I've ignored all of you. I *am* sorry.

FOURTH REPORTER

Sir, the Captain said before that you wanted no photos taken in here, but I wonder if we could have just one, of you and your wife and your daughter-in-law standing in front of the Lieutenant's portrait?

SEEGER

Yes, yes, of course! That would be a shot I'd like to have for myself! Rena, step in close here.

HELENA
(*Softly, under the above line:*)
No, no . . .

SEEGER

Helena, come in a bit.

HELENA

I don't want this . . .

SEEGER

It will only take a moment. Will this be all right?

FIRST PHOTOGRAPHER

It would be better if you were all behind the desk, right up
against—

HELENA

No. No pictures. No.

RENA

If she doesn't want to, Will . . .

SEEGER

(*Over* RENA's *line:*)
Helena, it will only take a moment. We'll just do the one, and
that—

HELENA

No! No pictures!
(*An embarrassed silence.*)

THIBAUDEAU

Sir, I think it's time everyone . . .

SEEGER

Yes. Yes. I'm sorry, gentlemen, but—Later on we'll pose for
photos.
(*His momentary confusion washes away.*)

Pose you clean out of flashbulbs! Captain Peck, would you take the press people down to the field?

PECK

Yes, sir.

SEEGER

Thank you all very much! I hope I'll get a chance to chat with each one of you at the luncheon!

>   (HELENA *has turned away and moves tensely* LEFT. RENA
>   *stands near, watching her with nervous concern.*)

Dick, will you take Mr. McKay and General Vohs down to the platform? And Colonel Bonney?

THIBAUDEAU

Yes, sir.

PECK

>   (*To* REPORTERS *and* PHOTOGRAPHERS.)

Right this way, please, ladies and gentlemen . . .

SEEGER

>   (*To* MCKAY, VOHS *and* BONNEY, *over* PECK*'s line.*)

Some of my staff officers are waiting to meet you by the reviewing platform. I hope you don't mind if I stay behind a minute or two. It's been a long time since we've seen Helena.

VOHS

Of course we don't mind.

MCKAY

She's under a good deal of strain . . .

SEEGER

She's fine, sir. It's just—the traveling, and the excitement of all this. She's fine! Dick, we'll be down in a few minutes.

THIBAUDEAU

Yes, sir.

(*Turning aside.*)

Corporal, stay in the anteroom. Knock on the door in five minutes.

CORPORAL

Yes, sir.

MCKAY

I think it's a wise decision you've made, not to mention the father-son relationship this afternoon. People know without our pointing to it.

SEEGER

It would have made the ceremony smaller somehow. The Army should stay impersonal, bigger than fathers and sons.

VOHS

Those things you said were quite moving, Seeger.

SEEGER

Thank you, General Vohs. Thank you. I said what I felt.

VOHS

You said it well.

THIBAUDEAU

Gentlemen . . . The elevator at the end of the hall should be waiting for us.

(RENA *reaches out and tentatively touches* HELENA*'s arm. An unhur-
ried general exodus has begun,* REPORTERS *and* PHOTOGRAPHERS,
PECK, BONNEY, MCKAY, VOHS *and* THIBAUDEAU. *Their conversations create an indistinct murmuring background.* CORPORAL *puts
his clipboard on vacated swivel chair and pushes chair* DOWNSTAGE.
Lights in office dim to half as exodus continues. CORPORAL, DOWN-
STAGE LEFT, *stands behind swivel chair, leaning on the back of it.*)

CORPORAL

Generals are men built on spring-steel armatures. They move
more briskly than the rest of us; come clicketing into a room
willing to shake any man's hand, earnestly trying not to be
proud. Their eyes have the glitter that our eyes win only after
a drink or two; they're high on happiness. But their ears lean
away, listening; for a twig-snap or a gun-bolt's click. Generals
are men forever aware of an enemy. Generals' wives live carefully
behind their teacups. They switch on sociability like a dining
room chandelier, and talk of everything except pain. Their hats
have flowers and their gloves are white. Generals' wives always
look as though it's Mothers' Day.

(*During the following, he draws the swivel chair* UPSTAGE
into its original position below the anteroom desk.)

We corporals, watching, give nicknames to generals; Eager-Seeger,
Cigar Butt; it's a way we have of pretending superiority. But we
call a general the *Old Man*, too, which means that we feel a piece
of our Father in him, and recognize and confirm the power in
his bearing.

(*Putting clipboard on desk, sitting in the chair with his
back toward the imaginary wall.*)

Who *is* old Seeger, we wonder. If Captain Thibaudeau hadn't
told me to stay, I would have stayed anyway. And listened with
both my ears.

(*The lights dim on* CORPORAL *and rise to full in the office.* THI-
BAUDEAU, *the last to leave, is in the anteroom, about to draw closed
the double doors.* HELENA *stands* RIGHT *of desk, looking up at the portrait.* SEEGER *faces the doors.* RENA *is between the two, looking from
one to the other. The cyclorama is blue, shot with a streak of red.*)

THIBAUDEAU

The Corporal from P.I.O. is out here, sir. I told him to knock
in five minutes.

SEEGER

Fine, Dick, fine! Thank you!
   (THIBAUDEAU *closes double doors and exits from ante-
   room.*)
Boy, boy, boy, boy, boy! What a day! What a day! What a day!
Let me cool off for a minute! Let me grab myself a smoke!
   (*Unbuttoning jacket.*)
Only the sun is against us!

RENA

We mustn't stay here too long . . .

SEEGER

   (*Taking off jacket.*)
Oh, have I got a surprise for *you!* Have I got news! How's that
for a portrait, Helena? Isn't that Bill in the breathing flesh? Had
it copied from a snapshot—you know the one. Why didn't you
want to pose for that photo? That would have been a great one
to have; the three of us and Bill behind us.
   (*Going* UPSTAGE *around desk.*)
It's wonderful that you're here; like putting the final piece in a
jigsaw puzzle! Only the baby; he ought to be here, too.

HELENA

He's a little too young to appreciate speeches.

SEEGER

(*Draping jacket on back of desk chair.*)
You should have brought him, his father being honored . . .
Someday he'll ask you why he wasn't here.

RENA

(*A beat, then quickly making conversation.*)
Is he with someone reliable?

HELENA

A woman I work with. She's had two of her own.

RENA

Tell us about him. Did you bring any pictures?

HELENA

(*Crosses LEFT of desk.*)
No.

SEEGER

(*Taking cigar from humidor on desk.*)
Now why on earth didn't you? In that one you sent from Tulsa
he looked like just *any* baby; I want to see one where he looks
like a Seeger! Hey, General Vohs liked what I said! Did you hear
him? "Quite moving," he called it. He's a fine-looking man, isn't
he? Reminds me of a judge or a—I'm *glad* now that General
Del Ruth cancelled out on us! I *am!* Too big a big shot to leave
his Governors Island!
(*Lights cigar.*)

RENA

Helena, are you doing that accounting work again?

HELENA

It's economic research. Yes, I am.

RENA

I forget . . . Have you found a nice place to live?

SEEGER

Listen, I'm holding in a piece of news and I'm going to burst if I don't sing it out! McKay, the Assistant Secretary—and that cold way of his, that's part of being a good executive; underneath he's warm and friendly—well, driving over here from the Guest House, he told me as plain as could be that when the next promotion list comes out—this second star of mine will be made permanent!

RENA

Oh, Will! Oh, thank God!

SEEGER

Major General. *Permanent!* That's five more years for certain! I'll be sixty-two before they boot me out!

RENA

(*Going to him, embracing, kissing him.*)
Oh, Will, I'm so happy for you, darling! For both of us! I knew it would happen! I knew! He's been so worried about being retired! I told you not to worry!

SEEGER

(*Holding* RENA *in his arms.*)
"It's a wonderful day," I said, and he said, "I think you'll be
having another wonderful day when the new list is published!"
Isn't that telling me plain?

RENA

I knew they wouldn't let go of you!

SEEGER

Five more years! You bet I was worried! Five more years!

HELENA

(*Crossing* DOWNSTAGE.)
Congratulations, Major General. Permanent.

(*Her sardonic tone hangs in the air.* RENA *kisses* SEEGER'*s cheek, as
though to distract him.*)

RENA

Oh, Will! Will . . .

SEEGER

What's wrong, Helena? Are you angry? Because you weren't invited here? How could we invite you when we didn't know where
you were? It's you who put this—hole between us.

RENA

She's here now; there's no point in discussing it . . .

SEEGER

(*Freeing himself of* RENA.)
No, no, we have to discuss it sooner or later.

HELENA

I'm not angry because I wasn't invited.

SEEGER

Why did you just—vanish from Tulsa that way? We wrote you, wrote to people at the Fort . . .

HELENA

You didn't think I would spend the rest of my life at Colleran, did you? I stayed there to have Billy, and then I left.

SEEGER

Why San Francisco? Why not here or New York; that was your home.

HELENA

I chose to go west.

SEEGER

But why didn't you let us know where you were? Rena has been making excuses for you all year, but now—I don't believe them . . . Why didn't you write?
> (HELENA *turns away*.)

You and Billy are our family, Helena, and we're yours. To cut us apart this way . . .

(RENA *steps* DOWNSTAGE.)

HELENA

Bill was the only connection between us.

RENA

(*Turning* RIGHT.)

We should go . . .

SEEGER

(*To* RENA:)

Plenty of time.

(*To* HELENA:)

Then don't we owe it to Bill to *keep* the connection, now that he's gone? Rena and I never got to know you as well as we wanted, but that was because of my duty in Europe. It was going to be different when I got here; you know that. I was going to have Bill reassigned; you would have been in one of those houses right up on the Circle . . .

RENA

Tell me, please, where is the sense in bringing up the past and what-would-have-been?

SEEGER

Rena, will you stop interrupting every time I open my mouth? You are as nervous today as—

HELENA

(*Cutting in on "nervous":*)

Oh, yes, General, you were going to have Bill reassigned!

(*A beat. There is a challenge in her tone that disquiets* SEEGER.)

RENA

Will . . .

SEEGER

You're right; the past is—past! You're here now, Helena, and that's what counts. This day has brought us together again and we're going to stay together! We're going to write to each other and visit, see that little Billy-Boy—I *wish* you'd brought a picture of him! Do you know why Rena is so on edge? Because this is the first time she has been out of the house before five P.M. in more than a month! This woman is a television fan! She has sold her soul to that seventeen-inch screen! Sits in the living room all day in an old green bathrobe with the blinds pulled down; pretty soon they're going to give her one of those Academy Awards for just watching! It's Saturday, Rena! Relax! You're not missing any of your quiz shows or dancing teen-agers!

RENA

Please . . .

SEEGER

I'm teasing, Rena, I'm teasing!

HELENA

Whose idea was this ceremony today?

SEEGER

Idea? Why, it was no one's idea! It's a tradition; an important building is dedicated to a hero; that's Army tradition.

HELENA

Who chose Bill for the dedication?

SEEGER

(*A beat.*)

McKay, General Del Ruth. The Chief Ordnance Officer, the Secretary. The same men who decided to build the building in the first place. Decisions like that come from higher up, way high up.

HELENA

How did those men choose Bill?

SEEGER

Well . . . a list of names was submitted to them. Possible candidates . . . This is an Ordnance post; they wanted someone in Ordnance. The building is for enlisted men; they wanted either an enlisted man or an officer who had performed some outstanding deed for enlisted men.

HELENA

Who put Bill's name on the list?

SEEGER

Well, *I* did. There's nothing against regulations in that. Because I'm in command doesn't mean my son should be disqualified from an honor.

RENA

Will didn't try to influence them; *they* made the decision . . .

SEEGER

Right, and you can bet your life they bent over backwards to be impartial! Army honors are weighed out as carefully as gold! They chose Bill on his merits, not as any favor to me.

HELENA

I am wasting my talents plotting population curves. I ought to be a mystic. I can pick up a newspaper, read a paragraph, look at a smiling picture, and say, "This is all happening because he *planned* it to happen! A celebration day for General Seeger!"

SEEGER

For me? For Bill, Helena! My God, you sound as though you don't *want* him to be honored! Wait till you see that building! A million and a half dollars of the best facilities an army ever gave its men! There's a swimming pool that's the biggest in the whole state! There are handball courts and a basketball court that Bill would have given his eyeteeth to play on! There's a library with—

HELENA

(*Cutting in on "play on":*)

Bill was not an athlete! He did not take after you in that respect.

SEEGER

Oh, no, Helena, you're wrong there. Remember, Rena, when we were at Chaffee, the basketball? No, no, it was Fort Leavenworth, Command School—

(*To* HELENA:)

Fort Leavenworth. There was a basketball hoop on the side of our garage, and Bill was out there every evening before dinner for a solid hour, practicing foul-shots. No stopping him.

(*To* RENA:)

How old was he? Twelve? Thirteen?

HELENA

There were tournaments for the officers' children. He practiced because if he played badly you would be short with him for a week or two. You remember what you want to remember; you forget what you want to forget.

RENA

Will . . .

SEEGER

What do you mean? I was never short with him. He *liked* basketball. He liked handball, too, and tennis. He was a *fine* athlete. We played handball every Saturday afternoon for two—

HELENA

(*Cutting in on "every":*)

He liked those sports because he was afraid not to like them, for fear *you* wouldn't like *him*.

SEEGER

That's crazy! You think I don't know what Bill liked? Just show me another father and son—

HELENA

(*Overlapping, starting on "liked":*)

That's exactly what I think! Did you ever *ask* what he liked? All that counted was what *you* liked, what *you* wanted, what *you*—

SEEGER

(*Overlapping, starting on "all":*)

What? I didn't have to ask; I *knew* what he liked! He and I were—

RENA

(*Cutting both of them off:*)

Stop it! He's dead! Stop! He's dead . . . . What difference does

it make what he liked or didn't like? He's dead. Stop talking
about him . . .

(*A pause.*)

HELENA

There speaks the mother. What kind of mother are you, Rena?
This is your *son* we're talking about, *not some dead horse lying
in the gutter!*

SEEGER

Shut up that kind of talk.

HELENA

(*Turning to* SEEGER.)

Don't you give orders to me, General! I haven't joined the Army!
Major General . . . Permanent . . . Do you know what part of
your speech I loved best? Do you know what part made me *most*
proud to be a member of your family? "When the son dies, the
father dies, too." Oh, there is a line! There is a noble line!

(*Seeger turns* RIGHT.)

What son? What father? You're not dead! Bill is under the grass
at Arlington, what was left of him, but you're here, standing,
with your shoulders full of stars and your head full of speeches,
smoking cigars and posing for photographs! *Who* died when
Bill died? She? Oh, no, *she* died when she was born! *I died when
Bill died! I died!*

(*Pointing at her eyes.*)

Have I slept one night in sixteen months?

(*A pause.*)

SEEGER

(*Turning to* HELENA.)

Why have you come here? This is a day for—pride and happiness, and you've brought hatred.

HELENA

For you; for him, love. I've come here to stop this.

SEEGER

To stop what?

HELENA

This whole day; your parade, your luncheon, your dedication.

SEEGER

Am I—awake?

RENA

Leave her, Will.

HELENA

A memorial of this kind will spin Bill in his grave like a stick in a whirlpool. He detested you and he despised your Army. For thirty-one years you held his arms in your bully's grip and pushed him where you pleased. He's dead now; today you let go.

(*A pause.*)

RENA

Listen to me, Will. She's speaking from spite. She didn't know Bill as well as—

SEEGER

(*Interrupting on "didn't," not turning from* HELENA.)
Be quiet, Rena.

RENA

No, I won't be quiet. A mother knows her son better than his
wife ever—

SEEGER

(*Turning now, on "wife".*)
Quiet, damn it!
(*Turns to* HELENA *again.*)

RENA

(*Softly.*)
Oh, dear God . . .
(*She sinks into chair,* UPSTAGE RIGHT.)

SEEGER

I pushed him, did I?

HELENA

From the day he was born; into games, into races, into the Point,
into a career that was a prison cell. You had a simple trick of
turning your back on him. He could never say "no" to it. You
robbed him young of that word.

SEEGER

(*Crossing to* LEFT *of* HELENA.)
You make me sick, every one of your generation. "Hands off"—
that should be the policy, eh? Mustn't tamper with the tender
children; "father" is a dirty word! What was the awful sin of
your father, a little drinking now and then?

HELENA

Backwards, General; a little sobriety now and then. Let's leave *my* happy childhood out of this.

SEEGER

(*Loses temper.*)

Well, try childhood the way I had it. Try it with *no* father and *no* mother, in a God-damned orphanage where nobody even cares enough to give you a *slap* once in a while, let alone a kiss! Try it that way and maybe you'll change your mind a little! What do you think a father's for? To sit back and ignore a boy? Let him feel his own way, as though nobody'd ever lived and learned before him? Maybe I was wrong to buy Bill a bicycle! Maybe I should have let him invent the wheel himself!

(*Crosses* RIGHT, *paces.*)

Sure, I pushed him! You bet I did! I pushed him where he belonged, and he was happy! Games and races? We celebrated more times than we hung up crepe, I can tell you that! The Point? We celebrated there, too; eighteenth man in a class of four hundred and nine!

HELENA

And he belonged there and was happy? Oh, ho, ho! Get a ouija board and ask Bill's ghost about West Point! They spotted him for The Outsider the minute he stepped through those gates. Ask him about the jolly cadets with the picturesque nicknames; Froggy and Boots and Candy-Bar. Ask him about the jolly hazings dished out to The Outsider, because Froggy and Boots and so on were *Insiders, Army!* Sadists, they were . . .

SEEGER

Oh, don't give me that crap about the hazings! Dick Thibaudeau

got the same treatment and laughs about it! Every man who's
been to the—

HELENA

(*Cutting in on "who's":*)
Dick Thibaudeau was there because he wanted to be there!

SEEGER

(*Crossing* DOWNSTAGE *to* HELENA.)
And so was Bill! Not at first maybe, I'll grant you that, but after
a while . . . It's the only foundation for an Army career! These
would be three stars, not two, if I'd been at the Point! Bill knew
how important it was.

HELENA

Maybe you didn't hear me before. Bill despised the Army. He
didn't *want* an Army career.

SEEGER

(*Crosses* RIGHT *to chair, sits.*)
You're out of your mind. I know what he wanted. He was
my son . . .

HELENA

You never knew what he wanted, nor did you care! He was a link
to you—you said it yourself in that lovely speech of yours—a
link in a chain, to be shaped and hammered and pounded,
not a person to be cared for, to be loved. Did you ever try to
see a quarter of an inch behind that strapped-on smile of his?
Don't tell me you did, General, because I'll call you a liar to
your face!

RENA

(*Rises, crosses* DOWNSTAGE *to* LEFT *of* HELENA.)
How dare you! How dare you speak to this man this way! You
think you have all—

SEEGER

(*Cutting in on "think":*)
All right, Rena . . .

RENA

No! You let me speak now, Will! You let me speak! You think
you have all the truth laid out in front of you; well you haven't,
Helena. I know things that—We were on the ship coming back
from Europe when Bill—when the awful cable—they handed
it to us . . . You think Will didn't care . . . He cried, Helena.

SEEGER

(*Rises, crosses to window* RIGHT.)
Oh, Rena . . .

RENA

He cried! With his face in my lap, he cried so hard that soon I
wasn't crying for Bill any more but for *him*, because I thought
his heart was going to break in two!

SEEGER

Oh, for . . .

RENA

And there's more truth than *that* you don't know about; times
when Bill was sick and he took *leave time* to stay home and sit
with him! Years when we were scraping along on captain's pay

and he spent half of it on toys he'd promised Bill! So don't you ever dare say again that he didn't love him! You don't know *everything!* You *think* you do, but you don't!

(*A pause.*)

SEEGER

That's from watching television.

(RENA *stands motionless, her eyes closed tight.*)

RENA

Will, oh, Will, there are moments when I hate you so much!

(*A pause.*)

HELENA

Were you crying for Bill or for yourself?

SEEGER

(*Crossing* UPSTAGE *behind desk.*)
Are you coming to the parade, Helena?

HELENA

Listen to me, General! Don't be fooled by that soft "A" on the end of my name. I tacked that on for style after I won the Battle of the Bronx. I'm Helen Riker; I'm a gutter-fighter from 'way back, and I tell you now to stop these ceremonies. Don't force me to use all my ammunition, because I'll blow this room sky-high. Bill wanted no dedication. Stop these ceremonies.

(*SOUND: A marching band sneaks in very softly in the distance, bugles, field drums, bass drum and cymbals.*)

RENA

What kind of threats are you making? What do you mean, ammunition?

SEEGER

(*Taking up jacket.*)
She doesn't mean anything.

HELENA

He didn't want his name on Army buildings!

(THIBAUDEAU *comes briskly into the anteroom, followed by a* PRIVATE *in parade uniform.*)

SEEGER

(*Thrusting his arms into his jacket.*)
She's talking, that's all. We've listened to her long enough. Just talk. If you don't want to see your husband being paid one of the highest tributes the Army can pay a man, then you can just stay—

THIBAUDEAU

I told you to knock, Corporal.

CORPORAL

(*Rising.*)
I was just about to, sir.

THIBAUDEAU

(*Rapping on double door.*)
Sir! It's Thibaudeau.

HELENA

I'm not bluffing, General! I did not fly here because I like flying.

(SEEGER *looks at her uncertainly for a moment, his jacket still un-buttoned.* THIBAUDEAU *raps again.*)

THIBAUDEAU

Sir?

SEEGER

Come in, Dick!

(THIBAUDEAU *enters,* PRIVATE *follows.*)

THIBAUDEAU

The Corporal should have knocked, sir. The troops have left the six hundred area. They'll be here in a few minutes.

(*He signals* PRIVATE *to* GENERAL*'s flag,* RIGHT *of desk. During following,* PRIVATE *takes flag from stand and exits* LEFT *with it.*)

SEEGER

Right, right . . .

THIBAUDEAU

McKay, Vohs and Bonney are already on the platform.

SEEGER
(*Rubbing his bands indecisively.*)
Plenty of time . . .

THIBAUDEAU

I arranged a place on the platform for Mrs. Seeger.
          (*Indicating* HELENA.)

SEEGER

She won't be there. She isn't feeling well.

THIBAUDEAU

Oh—I'm sorry. I carry a small infirmary of aspirins and sedatives . . .

HELENA

No, thank you, Captain.
          (*Sits coldly in a chair* DOWNSTAGE RIGHT *of desk.*)

SEEGER

Dick, will you take my wife downstairs?

THIBAUDEAU

Yes, sir.

RENA

Aren't you—?

SEEGER

I want to speak to Helena for a minute. Go along with
Dick.

RENA

I want to stay here.

SEEGER

Go with Dick, Rena. I want to speak to her alone.

THIBAUDEAU

There's really not much time, sir.

SEEGER

I'll be down. Don't worry.

RENA

Will, I don't want you to—

SEEGER

(*Cutting her off on "want":*)
Do as I tell you, Rena!

RENA

(*Pause.*)
Handbag . . .
(*Goes* UPSTAGE *to desk.*)

SEEGER

(*To* THIBAUDEAU:)
I'll join you on the platform. Don't worry.

(*Lights dim to half in office and come up full on* CORPORAL. *During the following,* RENA *takes handbag from desk and exits with* THIBAUDEAU. SEEGER *closes double doors and remains facing them.*)

CORPORAL

Do you hear the band? It's half a mile away, marching toward us through the gray, deserted barracks of the post. Bugles, field drums, a bass drum and cymbals. Nine companies march behind and thirteen more wait along the way, marking time, ready to affix themselves to the parade's growing body. Twenty-two companies in all; two hundred men in each; four thousand four hundred men marching ten abreast; boots, cartridge belts, helmets, rifles. Closer they will come, watched by KP's on a smoke-break, and by a furious dog from somewhere, and by the children of the post; quiet children, already tutored in re-spect. Some of these will put a midgets' tail to the parade, their feet in sneakers keeping careful time with the feet in boots. Straight toward the side of this building the parade will march, and then column left by companies onto the field below. The shoulders of the men will be numb under the weight of their rifles; their helmets will be ovens, the sweatbands dripping, teasing their faces. "Eyes right!" Two hundred heads will snap right, and two hundred more, and two hundred more, and two hundred more—and each of the four thousand four hundred men will see for an eye-flick, on the reviewing stand, General Seeger, perspiring no less than they, his arm locked in perpet-ual salute, motionless as an arm of steel or stone, as the arm of a statue; "Man Saluting."

(Lights dim on CORPORAL *and come up full in the office. The red streak on the cyclorama, having swollen imperceptibly through-out the preceding scene, is now a wide gash across the blueness, still swelling.* SEEGER *turns from the double doors to face* HELENA, *seated* CENTER RIGHT. *During this scene the sound of the distant band grows slowly, steadily louder.)*

SEEGER

You think you understood Bill, but you didn't, and you don't understand me, either. Marrying you was—wrong for him. I don't mean that as criticism of *you*, Helena; you're an admira-ble woman and I'm fond of you, whether or not you believe I am. But it's wrong for Army to marry away from Army. Rena, now; her father was a battalion commander on the post where I made first lieutenant. She understands things about me and about Bill that you'll never understand; things we feel . . .

HELENA

"Army." You make it sound like a religion.

SEEGER

I do; I guess I do. You know the joke line, "He found a home in the Army"? That's *me*, Helena . . . You don't know what it's like to begin your life in a foundling home. No roots, nobody behind you; not even a real name, but one some social worker *made up* for you . . . Who are you? Where do you come from? Where are you going? You're more alone than—anyone on earth. Make your own bed when you're six years old. You haven't even got God, because it's a no-denomination service and they're going to let you *choose* your god when you're old enough! How can you really believe when it's up to you to choose!

(*Crosses* UPSTAGE *of desk.*)

The day I was eighteen I ran away and joined up. The Army assigned me a serial number, Helena, that was *me* and nobody else! They put—a *path* in front of me; "Go up through those ranks!" They gave me fathers, my officers, and they gave me gods, too, the highest brass, the McKays and the General Del Ruths. *System* they gave me!—you get an order, you obey the order; you get the first stripe, the second . . . When you come into a new post, you check the bulletin board and you know where you stand!

(*Buttons a few buttons of his jacket.*)

I *had* to pass it on to Bill! You find something good, you pass it on; that's what parents are for! I'm a Christian. I raised him Christian; you don't call me a bully for that, do you? I'm

American; I raised him American; is that being a bully? You know what he wanted to do? Did he tell you *that?* Seventeen years old he comes to me, he wants to finish high school and go away to the oil fields in Texas, work in the oil fields! "Are you afraid you won't do well at the Point?" "No, Papa, I just want to work in the oil fields." Was I supposed to say yes to that? Some book he'd read about drilling for oil . . . When he came to his senses he would have been too old for the Point, and without the Point he would have got no higher than I am now; commanding the class B training camps, or pushing supplies up for the generals with *four* stars and their faces on the front pages! I wanted him to go higher than me! That's progress! That's human! I know I did something risky. I'm not as dumb as you think I am. If a man hasn't got some soldier in him, you can't force him to *be* a soldier, and it's wrong trying. I know that. *Plenty* of nights I laid awake, wondering if I was hurting Bill more than I was helping him . . . Now I'm going to tell you something, Helena. Yes, I cried on that ship when I got the news—not as much as Rena said, but I cried, and for Bill, not for me—but *after* I cried, Helena, afterwards . . . I stretched out, and I went to sleep! And I slept well that night, and I've slept well ever since. Because the way Bill died told me I'd been *right*. Suppose he *was* unhappy for a week or two at the Point! Suppose he *did* have a few days when he thought he'd like to be an oil man, or a doctor, or a—barber or a plumber! The end is what counts! And the end is that he was a *soldier*, or he would have let those men die without risking his own skin to save them! And if he was that much of a soldier at the end, then there was some soldier in him at the beginning, too, and I was *right* in everything I did with him! You said before he detested me. I don't think he did, but if he did, then maybe that's the price of being a good father. The mother is soft, and she gets the love; the father is hard, and he gets hatred. But it's the father who makes the son a man. Well, I made Bill more than a man; I made him a soldier, a gallant soldier! That's not me talking now, that's a bronze plaque on a million-and-a-half dollar building! "First Lieutenant William J. Seeger, Junior; a gallant soldier and an exemplary officer." Those words have come down from the very top of the Army; and they speak louder and clearer and will last a thousand years longer than anything you've said this morning!

> (*Completing buttoning of his jacket.*)

HELENA

Blind . . . Blind . . . Blind man . . . You see what you want to see; you hear what you want to hear . . .

> (*Rising.*)

Blind man, your plaque is mistaken!

> (SEEGER *takes cap from desk, starts for door.*)

He *wasn't* a gallant soldier! He was sick and despairing, miserable at Colleran and at every post before Colleran!

> (SEEGER *stops, turns to face* HELENA *angrily.*)

He *wasn't* an exemplary officer! He kept a bottle in his desk and another under the edge of the mattress! Drinks pinned him together and kept him walking; drinks, and you pushing him!

SEEGER

> (*Going toward her as if to strike her.*)

Liar! You filthy God-damned liar! I'll slam that—

HELENA

He didn't give his life to save enlisted men!

> (SEEGER's *upraised arm freezes.*)

He gave his life because he could no longer bear to keep it!

Because you and your Army had grabbed onto it so tight that
giving it was his only way to get free!

SEEGER

What are you saying?

HELENA

(*Stepping towards him.*)

Suicide! He committed suicide! How big do I have to paint it to
pull open your eyes? He committed suicide! You blind man . . .
(*SOUND: The band, no more than a block away now,
yields to the field drums. They rip out a hard, rasping
beat, repetitive, increasingly loud. The cyclorama is now
almost entirely red.*)
Fathers and gods, those men who stood here? He saw them clear,
and he *envied* your blindness! A path you gave him? Broken glass
to nowhere! He chose the short cut.

SEEGER

(*Turning to door.*)

It couldn't be . . .

HELENA

(*Near tears.*)

It was! It was! And still you won't let go! Still you're bullying him!

SEEGER

There were—witnesses . . . A roomful . . .

HELENA

I am the witness! *I saw his heart!*

SEEGER

(*Turning towards her.*)

You're—You—There was—*whiskey* on your breath when I kissed you before! There's whiskey in what you're saying now! You're—a bitter, vengeful woman, who's made—a career of her widowhood!

(*Crossing* LEFT *to door.*)

Corporal!

(CORPORAL *rises.*)

Is he still there?

(*Pulls open one wing of double doors.*)

Corporal!

CORPORAL

Yes, sir!

SEEGER

Come in here! Bitter, vengeful . . .

(CORPORAL *enters office.*)

HELENA

No, no . . . It's for *his* sake . . . !

SEEGER

(*Has taken a key ring from his pocket and is detaching a key. To* CORPORAL.)

I'm giving you a key. Key to this door. You lock it behind me and you don't unlock it until I come back. She doesn't get out; nobody else gets in. You understand that?

(*Gives key to* CORPORAL.)

CORPORAL

Yes, sir.

SEEGER

You lock it behind me. And she doesn't go near that window.

CORPORAL

Yes, sir.

(*A beat.* SEEGER, *meeting* HELENA*'s gaze, puts on his cap.*)

HELENA

All right, General, you *have* your parade! Stand in the sun and salute your Army! Three cheers for gods, and systems, and straight paths, and uniforms woven of honor! But I swear to you—I swear by his body in that box at Arlington—you'll dedicate no building this afternoon. I swear that.

(*SOUND: The drums stop. A respite of silence.*)

SEEGER

You don't believe in *anything*, that's your trouble. And you want everyone else to be as poisoned as you are. Bill was a fine soldier in a fine army. He was proud and he was happy.

HELENA

Go to your parade, blind man!

(*SOUND: An explosion of brass and percussion. The band is directly below the window, blasting out a strident, deafening march.* SEEGER *wheels and quickly exits.* CORPORAL *closes the double doors, locks them. Cyclorama is entirely red, with sun-glints from the brass instruments chasing across it.* CORPORAL *turns to face* HELENA. *She stands* CENTER RIGHT, *her hands clapped over her ears against the din.* SOUND: *Under the crashing of the band, the thud of marching feet.*)

VOICE

(*Shouting below.*)
Column left . . . HAR!

(HELENA *is crying now, no longer able to sustain her armor of hardness.* CORPORAL *moves a step toward her, tucking the key into his breast pocket.* HELENA'*s body shakes with sobs. She collapses into the chair* CENTER RIGHT. *There is only the sight of her crying, the sound of it is buried under the bugles and the drums and the cymbals.* CORPORAL *is drawn slowly toward her.*)

ANOTHER VOICE

Column left . . . HAR!

(CORPORAL *stands near* HELENA, *watching her with compassion. He reaches out and touches her shoulder in an ineffectual soothing gesture. He looks at the audience.* THE CURTAIN FALLS.)

END OF ACT ONE

ACT TWO

AT RISE: *The band can still be heard, stationed now at the far end of the parade field. The cyclorama is a blanched noon-day blue.* HELENA *is seated as before, no longer crying, a handkerchief balled in her hands.* CORPORAL *lounges against* SEEGER*'s desk, smoking a cigarette, watching* HELENA. *He crosses to the window, peers out through the slats of the blind.*

CORPORAL

Oop, there goes number six.
> (*A downward swing of his forearm, accompanied by a sibilant sound-effect.*)

Sssssssssseeeeeeep—Pww!

HELENA

How many men have to pass out before they end the parade?

CORPORAL

Well, there are two ambulances that haven't even opened their doors yet.
> (*Turning from the window.*)

Don't worry; of the six men who have dropped so far, maybe one was genuine. The other five are just getting excused from future parades.

(HELENA *is silent.* CORPORAL *returns to* CENTER.)
Why don't you take a little drink, Mrs. Seeger . . .
(HELENA *shakes her head.*)
He's finished inspecting them; they're moving out now.
(HELENA *smooths the handkerchief and holds it out.* COR-
PORAL *takes it, holds it for a moment, then puts it in his
pocket.*)
Would you like to talk about your husband? I would like to
listen.

HELENA

You heard from out there?

CORPORAL

Almost everything.

(*A pause.* CORPORAL *sits against the edge of the desk, crushing out
his cigarette in ashtray.* HELENA *looks at her hands. SOUND:
The music of the band diminishes and grows distant during the
following speech.*)

HELENA

My husband . . . was a man who . . . held himself in contempt.
The Army sickened him, but he sickened himself more, because
he couldn't leave the Army any more than a tree can leave the
ground. His father had rooted him too deeply; in the uniform,
the tradition, the manliness, the honor . . . He hated himself for
not ripping away the uniform, but secretly and more sharply,
I think he hated himself . . . for not *loving* the uniform . . .
But, oh, the face of him! That ringmaster smile! Two drinks
at a party and he could tell a joke in a way that would make a
statue laugh; twinkle an eye so that every woman in the room

went soft and boneless. Three drinks and he fell silent. Four, and I would edge toward our coats, because with five and six he sometimes began to—shiver, like a child in the dark . . . Did you offer me a cigarette before?

      (CORPORAL *rises, taking a pack of cigarettes from his pocket.*)

He picked me up in Rockefeller Plaza. He was on leave. My handbag spilled and he chased my rolling compact, in the best tradition of romantic movies.

      (CORPORAL *offers her a cigarette.*)

Thank you.

      (CORPORAL *strikes a match, holds it for her.*)

Five years ago. His uniform fooled me. That's the double feature.

      (CORPORAL *sits on a nearby chair.*)

I thought I had finally found someone stronger than I had had to be. It was a short honeymoon, though. Loving him was pushing a log uphill. His reasoning was simple; he was contemptible, therefore I, who said I loved him, was either a liar or a fool. I said it loud! With my heart! He turned to— other women, who made no claim of loving. Or who proved to him, perhaps, beyond a doubt, how truly contemptible he was . . . Well, I am not a saint. Compassion and understanding I had, but selfishness came stronger. Toward the end I found myself . . . beginning to share his contempt. No more I-love-you's. I think I might have left him, if not for the baby on its way . . . I owe him this one deed today; to put the knife in that father of his.

CORPORAL

Do you believe that somewhere . . . he's watching you?

(*A pause.*)

HELENA

I owe him this.

(*A pause, and then an imperative knock at the door,* LEFT.)

SEEGER

Corporal.
        (CORPORAL *rises, looking at* HELENA, *then goes to door,*
        taking key from pocket. HELENA *rises.* SEEGER *knocks again.*)
Corporal. It's General Seeger.

(CORPORAL *looks back at* HELENA.)

HELENA

Unlock it.

(CORPORAL *unlocks the door and opens it.* SEEGER *enters, remov-*
ing his cap. His face is running with perspiration. His eyes go to
HELENA *firmly and with authority. SOUND: The band is now*
far away, but still faintly audible.)

CORPORAL

Sir.

(SEEGER *turns.* CORPORAL *gives him the key.*)

SEEGER

Thank you.

(*A beat.* CORPORAL *exits* LEFT *into anteroom, stands facing office.*
SEEGER *puts cap on desk and wipes face with handkerchief, his eyes*
on HELENA *again. She meets them unflinchingly.*)

HELENA

What was the final score? How many men passed out?

(SEEGER *does not answer. He has regained the certainty which he
lost before leaving for the parade.* THIBAUDEAU, *cap in hand, enters
anteroom and continues into office, followed by* PRIVATE *carrying*
SEEGER*'s flag.* THIBAUDEAU *stands waiting* CENTER LEFT. PRIVATE
places flag in stand LEFT *of desk.*)

THIBAUDEAU

I hope you're feeling better, Mrs. Seeger.

HELENA

(*Extinguishing cigarette.*)
I am.

(PRIVATE *steps back, salutes flag.*)

THIBAUDEAU

You missed a very smart parade. Very smart.
(PRIVATE *exits* LEFT.)
Or did you watch from the window?

SEEGER

Close the door, please.

(THIBAUDEAU *closes the door,* LEFT. CORPORAL *sits in swivel chair,
facing office.* SEEGER, *unbuttoning jacket moves* UPSTAGE RIGHT.)

HELENA

What's happening here?

SEEGER

Sit down, Dick.

(THIBAUDEAU *takes a seat* CENTER LEFT. SEEGER, *by the air-conditioning unit, flaps the sides of his jacket against his sweat-stained shirt.*)

HELENA

What is this?

SEEGER

Dick, I'd like you to tell my daughter-in-law what you told me. On the platform.

THIBAUDEAU

Yes, sir. Well, the General asked me if I thought that Bill—Lieutenant Seeger—if I thought that he was ever unhappy at the Point, and I said, quite the contrary; he was one of the most—*contented* men there. He was extremely popular, both with his classmates and with the men in the classes above him, and though he did his full job of studying, he still found time to participate in just about every activity available. And not only participate, but help organize. He had a great natural flair for leadership.

SEEGER

And those bull-sessions . . .

THIBAUDEAU

Yes. He and I had a number of bull-sessions where he said more than once that he could have kicked himself for not wanting to come to the Point originally. We mapped out the careers that we hoped were ahead of us, and Bill thanked

his lucky stars that the General had put some sense into his
head.

(HELENA *watches* THIBAUDEAU *blankly.* SEEGER *is looking from one
to the other, doing his best not to show his satisfaction and relief.
SOUND: The band is gone now. Complete silence.*)

SEEGER

I suppose he was a *bit* unhappy at the beginning . . .

THIBAUDEAU

Of course he was. Good Lord, everyone is. Except maybe the
men who've been to a military prep school. You come into
this whole new world of discipline and regulations . . . It takes
two or three weeks until you're oriented. After that, though—
well, there just isn't any better education *anywhere*, military or
non-military. That's *my* belief, and it was Bill's, too.

(*A pause.* SEEGER *moves towards desk.* THIBAUDEAU *sits forward,
ready to rise.*)

SEEGER

Thank you very much, Dick. You go along to the Club now,
and I'll be over in a few minutes. Tell Mr.—

HELENA
(*On* "minutes":)
Were you a close friend of my husband, Captain?

THIBAUDEAU

Yes, I was. As I told you before, knowing him is one of my best
memories.

HELENA

If you and he were such close friends, how do you account for the fact that he never mentioned you to me?

THIBAUDEAU

Perhaps you forgot.

HELENA

I'm not a forgetter.

THIBAUDEAU

I wasn't his *closest* friend, Mrs. Seeger. That was a fellow named Holly, or Holliday.

HELENA

Holland.

THIBAUDEAU

Holland; yes, that's right.
(*Sitting back in chair.*)
But I was a *close* friend of Bill's nonetheless. If he never mentioned me, well then, I'm probably not as memorable a person as he was.

(SEEGER *smiles, takes a cigar from humidor.*)

HELENA

You said before that you were a year ahead of Bill at the Point.

THIBAUDEAU

That's right.

HELENA

But still you accepted him as a close friend?

THIBAUDEAU

He was popular beyond his own class, as I also said. There was this flair for leadership. He had a—an aura of—*belonging*. It was *he* who accepted *me*.

(*A pause.* SEEGER *lights his cigar.*)

HELENA

Captain, wasn't my husband subjected to unusual hazing at the Point?

THIBAUDEAU

Hazing is part of the Point, Mrs. Seeger. Outsiders exaggerate its significance by about three thousand per cent.

HELENA

I said *unusual* hazing.

THIBAUDEAU

No, he wasn't subjected to unusual hazing.

SEEGER

I didn't think you were going to be cross-examined. I'm sorry.

HELENA

Bill told me that during his first few months at the Point he expressed criticism of its procedures and of military training in general, and as a result of this he was subjected to *barbaric hazing* until the day he became an upperclassman!

SEEGER

(*On "until":*)

Barbaric!

THIBAUDEAU

That is not true. It just isn't true, Mrs. Seeger.

HELENA

Then why did he lie to me, perhaps you can tell me that. Because either he lied or you are lying now.

(*Crosses* DOWNSTAGE LEFT *a beat.*)

SEEGER

Or you're lying, Helena.

THIBAUDEAU

(HELENA *crosses* DOWNSTAGE RIGHT.)

Sir, I don't think anybody's lying. Mrs. Seeger, I told *my* wife about some of the hazings *I* received, and I frankly confess I made them sound a heck of a lot worse than they were, just as I've exaggerated some of my combat experiences to her; because when I do, she goes all big-eyed, and starts clucking over me, and it makes me feel like—Paul Bunyan or somebody! I think maybe that's what Bill did with you.

HELENA

The hazings that Bill described did not make him a hero to me. *Shall I list some of the obscenities?*

SEEGER

(*Crosses* DOWNSTAGE RIGHT *of desk.*)

Now, damn it, that's enough! Those hazings are regulated!

THIBAUDEAU

That's the truth, Mrs. Seeger.

SEEGER

That's the U.S. Military Academy, part of the Army, not a—
trade school full of leather-jacket hoodlums!

HELENA

How would *you* know, you with your visitor's pass!

(*A pause.*)

SEEGER

I wasn't lucky enough to attend the Point, but I know that when
you speak of obscenities and barbaric hazings, you are wrong.
Dead wrong. I know that.
          (*Crosses* UPSTAGE *of desk, looks out window,* CENTER
     STAGE. *A beat.*)

HELENA

Froggy, and Boots, and Candy-Bar. Did you know those men?

(*A beat.*)

THIBAUDEAU

Yes, I did.

HELENA

Am I dead wrong?

THIBAUDEAU

They never went after Bill, Mrs. Seeger.

SEEGER

(*Crosses* DOWNSTAGE RIGHT *of desk.*)

Who? What men?

HELENA

Leather-jacket hoodlums!

SEEGER

What . . . ?

THIBAUDEAU

Sir, the Point gets a cross-section of men, just as any school does. I don't necessarily mean a social cross-section, but a psychological one. They do a more careful job than other schools of sifting out the undesirables, but still, now and then one is bound to slip through.

SEEGER

Well, of course, yes, there's bound to be a bad apple somewhere in the basket. Of course . . .

THIBAUDEAU

When Bill and I were there, there *was* this *very small group* of men who were—pretty disturbed emotionally, and the custom of hazing *did* provide them with—an easy outlet for their disturbances. They made some of the plebes do things that went far beyond the usual bracings and push-ups, and I guess there's no doubt that they were a group of—sick men. Bill was never one of their targets, though; they went after the fellows who were—well, misfits in one way or another. I suppose they justified themselves as—"guardians of the Army's purity."

HELENA

They went after Bill.

THIBAUDEAU

No, ma'am, they did not.

SEEGER

Nobody reported these men?

THIBAUDEAU

Well, sir, you know . . . At that age, reporting someone, it—it hardly seems at all like being a soldier. The authorities found them out, though; don't you worry about that. Not a one of them is in the Army today. The ringleader, the one called Candy-Bar, he was expelled from the Point in his final year.

HELENA

They went after Bill.

SEEGER

Are you—sure that they didn't? When I think there's even a *chance* that . . .

THIBAUDEAU

Yes, sir, I am sure. It was very well known just which men they were badgering. Half a dozen—misfits, as I said. Complainers, fellows who rode the sick-book . . .

HELENA

Do you think I pulled those names out of the air? Bill told me about them! Froggy and Boots and—

THIBAUDEAU

(*On "Boots":*)

And he said they badgered *him?*

HELENA

Tormented him! Endlessly!

(*To* SEEGER.)

I am not lying!

(*A pause.* SEEGER *looks anxiously towards* THIBAUDEAU.)

THIBAUDEAU

(SEEGER *crosses* UPSTAGE *of desk.*)

Mrs. Seeger, I'm going to say something presumptuous, and I hope you won't take offense at it. I'm interested in psychology. I read every book I can on the subject, and though I'm not an authority, I'm not a dabbler, either. It seems to me that when a person, a woman particularly, suffers the kind of loss that you've suffered, she's apt to look around and choose a scapegoat to strike out at. I think you've chosen the Point. I guess you feel that if Bill hadn't gone into the Army he'd still be alive, and so you're saying that he was unhappy at the Point, that he was against military procedure, that he was singled out for unusual hazing . . . It's not true, Mrs. Seeger. Obviously Bill told you about Candy-Bar and the others, but I can't believe he told you they bothered *him*, because what reason would he have had for lying to you?

HELENA

I am imagining things, then . . .

THIBAUDEAU

No, I think what you're doing is simply—deflecting some of

the grief of Bill's death. But you seem to me a strong enough woman to accept reality without the—well, it's a neurotic shield you're carrying around—forgive me, please—and the sooner you put it down, the sooner the grief will go away. Everything I said about Bill at the Point was true. He was the last man those fellows would have gone after. He *belonged*.

(*A pause.* HELENA *turns away.*)

SEEGER

Thank you. Thank you, Dick, very much.

THIBAUDEAU

(*Rises.*)

I'd better get over to the Club and make sure McKay and Vohs are getting the good liquor.

SEEGER

(*Smiling.*)

And cover for me; tell them I'll be there in five minutes.

HELENA

(*Quietly, still facing away.*)

How did you get to be the General's aide, Captain? By saying things about Bill that he enjoyed hearing?

(*A pause.*)

SEEGER

I choose my aide on the basis of his record, and Captain Thibaudeau has one of the finest records of any young officer on this post. His friendship with Bill had nothing to do with my decision. Your remark is an insult to him. And to me, too.

HELENA

(*Turning.*)

I am not carrying a neurotic shield . . .

THIBAUDEAU

If you believe I've been speaking to please the General and stay his aide, Mrs. Seeger, I think you ought to know that I've been after him for two months to relieve me of this duty.

SEEGER

Right! He has!

THIBAUDEAU

I've cleared the path for an assignment at a post near New Orleans, where my family is and where my wife and I could live a most agreeable life. At the moment, to displease the General would be to my distinct advantage. He'd release me a great deal more readily. Sir . . .

(*Turns and goes towards door,* LEFT.)

HELENA

Captain!

(THIBAUDEAU, *near the door, stops and turns.*)

That "very small group" of "emotionally disturbed men" who "guarded the Army's purity"; were you by any chance one of them?

(*A pause.*)

SEEGER

(*Looks at* HELENA.)

What?

THIBAUDEAU

I most certainly was not.

SEEGER

I'm sorry, Dick. You'd better go now.

HELENA

I thought you might be. Your name is French, isn't it? Thibaudeau?

THIBAUDEAU

Yes.

HELENA

A man with a French name might be nicknamed "Froggy,"
mightn't he? French. Frog. Froggy.
(*A pause.*)

THIBAUDEAU

I had no nickname at the Point. Except Dick, that is. I never ad-
ministered any hazings beyond the usual bracings and push-ups.
I never hazed Bill at all. He was my friend. We *all* liked him.
Very much.
(*A pause.*)

HELENA

You keep reading those psychology books, Captain. I hope you
find whatever it is you're looking for.
(*A beat.*)

THIBAUDEAU

I'll be at the Club, sir.

(THIBAUDEAU *turns, opens the door, and exits, closing the door after
him.* CORPORAL *rises as* THIBAUDEAU *passes through anteroom,
then resumes seat in swivel chair.* SEEGER *turns slowly to* HELENA.)

HELENA

You chose your aide poorly, General.

SEEGER

You think that—he was . . . ?

HELENA

Your fine young officer has disease inside of him. Give him that release he wants; he might stand you at attention and torture it out of you!

SEEGER

You heard him deny the nickname!

HELENA

That butter-mouth could deny anything you—

SEEGER

(*Cutting in on "deny":*)
No, no, I—I know him! More than an aide! His record is— No, I won't believe it. There's no evidence, only your—spite and your malice.

HELENA

This is your day for not believing, isn't it. Bill killed himself, and that aide with the glowing record bears part of the blame. Part of it. A *small* part . . .
(*A beat.*)

SEEGER

Bill was not unhappy . . .

HELENA

On the word of that impartial, disinterested witness? That Galahad?

(*A beat.* SEEGER *takes up his telephone with forced decisiveness.*)

SEEGER

All right, we'll *get* an impartial witness in here. We'll get the final, rock-bottom truth in here!
        (*Into phone:*)
Officers Club.

HELENA

Who?

SEEGER

Colonel Bonney. Bill's chief. He was there that morning, and saw with his own two eyes. Will *his* word cut ground with you? I'll humor this—*nightmare* of yours, and rout it, and enjoy my luncheon . . .

(RENA *enters anteroom,* LEFT. CORPORAL *rises.*)

RENA

Is the General inside?

SEEGER	CORPORAL
There are two lines at the Club; try the other. This is General Seeger, and it's important.	Yes, ma'am.

(*Without knocking,* RENA *opens the office door and enters. A beat.* SEEGER *hangs up the telephone.* RENA *closes the door behind her.* CORPORAL *resumes seat. A pause.*)

SEEGER

I told you to go with General Vohs and Mr. McKay.

RENA

I did, and when we got there, your car didn't come. Why are you back here?

SEEGER

I want you at the Club, Rena, to stand in for me. I have to— stay here a little while.

RENA

Why? What has she done? What has she said to you?

SEEGER

Nothing. Nothing at all . . .
     (*A beat.*)

RENA

What did you tell him, Helena?

SEEGER

Nothing, Rena!

HELENA

Bill committed suicide!

(*A pause.*)

RENA

You—*believe* her?

SEEGER

No.

RENA

(*Step* UPSTAGE, *towards* SEEGER.)

You were so—pale when you came on the platform . . .

(*To* HELENA.)

Have you any—proof to back up this—lie, this *hateful, fantastic lie!*

HELENA

The proof of knowing Bill, of having seen his misery, of having heard him speak suicide a dozen times.

RENA

That's not proof . . . That's—nothing! Nothing!

(*To* SEEGER.)

Why do you stay here?

(*To* HELENA.)

Go home. Go home and leave us alone! You come here with lies . . .

(HELENA *doesn't move.* RENA *turns to* SEEGER.)

Why do you still stay here? The telephone was in your hand . . .

SEEGER

I'm going to have Colonel Bonney come over . . .

RENA

Why . . . ?

SEEGER

To hear about that morning from his lips. For her. So that we can—*settle* this.

RENA

Settle . . . ? There's nothing *to* settle. You don't believe her. She has no proof. Only . . . bitterness . . . Bitterness and anger!
(*To* HELENA.)
Bitterness!

HELENA

(*Step* UPSTAGE RIGHT.)
"A neurotic shield" is the phrase we're using today.

(*A beat.*)

RENA

Will, don't . . . Don't do this. They're—expecting you at the Club. The drinks are being served and soon they'll be going into the dining room. You come back there with me. Now.

HELENA

Why don't you want him to call Bonney?

RENA

Because this day has been all planned and you want to upset it and you don't care how you do it!

HELENA

(*Turning to* RENA.)
What are you afraid of?

RENA

Nothing! Nothing! I just *don't* want Will worried and upset for
no good reason! It's pointless, calling people over; we've seen
the official reports . . .

HELENA

What are you hiding, Rena? How much do you know?

RENA

I'm not hiding anything! Go home! You've come here with lies!

SEEGER

Rena—

RENA

Come to the Club, Will!

SEEGER

Rena . . . if there's something you know, that you haven't told
me, for God's sake . . . *tell me now.*

RENA

No. I don't know anything! I was on the ship, the same as you!
I read the same cable, the same reports when we landed, the
same letter from General Ramey . . .

SEEGER

Rena—

RENA

Will, please, as a favor to me, come to the Club where you're
supposed to be. Don't let her spoil things. Everyone is waiting

for you. On the patio, with music . . . If it were true, wouldn't General Ramey have known? Wouldn't the records have said so? If you listen to her you're doubting the records, you're doubting General Ramey . . .

(*A beat.*)

HELENA

Call Colonel Bonney.

RENA

Will . . . please . . .

(*A beat.*)

SEEGER

I have to settle this, Rena . . . I can't go to the Club, and drink, and shake hands . . .
 (*A pause. Hesitantly he picks up the telephone.*)
Officers Club.

(*A pause.*)

RENA

She's making it up.

(*A pause.*)

SEEGER

This is General Seeger, Sergeant. Would you get Lieutenant Colonel Bonney to the phone. Bonney. He's probably out on the patio with the other guests.

(*A pause.* SEEGER, RENA *and* HELENA *look at one another. The lights dim almost to blackness, and come up full on* CORPORAL.)

CORPORAL
(*Turning to audience.*)

Colonel Bonney, the impartial witness, the rock-bottom truth . . . The ride from the Officers Club takes eight minutes; we'll contract it to one, or less than one.

(*Rises, steps* DOWNSTAGE *to edge of stage.*)

Before, at the parade, Seeger inspected the troops. They heightened to attention by companies, and he, standing in the back of a slow-driving jeep, returned the salute of each company commander. That was mere formal inspection; there are closer, more searching ones, where a button unbuttoned can kill a weekend pass. Inspection in the Army is no less important than inspection outside the Army, where too sharp a lapel can kill a promotion, or too low a gown can kill a reputation. Now Seeger's begun a still closer inspection, searching behind the uniform. Doubt has been thrown on the Captain, his aide; we await the Lieutenant Colonel, and Seeger calls this the end, the rock-bottom. But inspection, once begun, is a rolling locomotive. I remember in basic a maniac sergeant who brandished a filthy towel and cried "Whose towel is this? The blankety-blank runs twice around the field!" And the towel, of course, was his own, and he ran twice around the field. Well *once* around the field, and then he forgave himself.

(*Looks* OFFSTAGE LEFT.)

And here is the Colonel . . .

(*Lights come up in office.* SEEGER *is sitting behind the desk, wiping his palms with a handkerchief. His jacket is draped over the back of his chair.* HELENA *stands* DOWNSTAGE RIGHT, *smoking, her back to the desk.* RENA *sits* UPSTAGE LEFT, *watching* SEEGER. *The cyclorama is a deeper blue than before.* BONNEY *enters the anteroom.*)

BONNEY

Lieutenant Colonel Bonney to see General Seeger.

CORPORAL

Yes, sir.

(CORPORAL *goes to door, knocks.* HELENA *turns.*)

SEEGER

Come in.

(CORPORAL *opens door.*)

CORPORAL

Sir, Colonel Bonney is here.

(*A beat.* SEEGER *pockets handkerchief.*)

SEEGER

Ask him to come in.

(CORPORAL *withdraws.*)

CORPORAL
(*To* BONNEY:)

Sir . . .

(BONNEY *enters office and stands guardedly just within door.*
SEEGER *rises.*)

BONNEY

General. Mrs. Seeger.
          (*To* HELENA.)
Mrs. Seeger . . .

(HELENA *extinguishes her cigarette, acknowledging the greeting with a nod, her eyes on* BONNEY. CORPORAL *closes the door.*)

SEEGER

I'm sorry to have taken you away from the—Club, Colonel Bonney.
          (BONNEY *is silent.*)
Will you take a seat, please?
          (CORPORAL *eases into swivel chair.* BONNEY *advances to* CENTER STAGE, *pulls visitor's chair to* DOWNSTAGE LEFT *of desk, sits.* SEEGER *sits.* HELENA *sits* DOWNSTAGE RIGHT *on couch.*)
Colonel, I would like you to describe—in detail—my son's death.

(*A pause.*)

BONNEY

May I ask why?

SEEGER

I would rather not answer that now.

(*A beat.*)

BONNEY

But—I've told this story half a dozen times; surely you've all seen transcripts of the record.

SEEGER

I would like you to tell it again, please.

(*A beat.*)

BONNEY

The details may not be exact . . .

HELENA

After half a dozen tellings?

BONNEY

Sixteen months ago, Mrs. Seeger. That's a long time . . .
          (*A pause.* BONNEY *tries to sound factual and dispassion-
          ate in his narration, but strain is evident throughout.*)
We were running a series of tests on a hand grenade with an
aluminum-alloy casing. The tests were conducted in a concrete-
walled room lined with hanging lead sheets. The lead caught the
fragments and we were able to chart their pattern and velocity.

SEEGER

The grenades were detonated . . .

BONNEY

By an arm-and-clamp device attached to a steel table in the
center of the room. A grenade would be mounted on the arm,
clamped, and then unpinned. The clamp kept the firing lever
from springing until it was released by push-button from the
control room.

SEEGER

Where was the control room?

BONNEY

Thirty, forty feet down the corridor.

SEEGER

But you could see into the testing room.

BONNEY

We had two shielded television cameras there, on a closed circuit to monitors in the control room. One gave us a close-up
of the steel table with the arm-and-clamp device, and the other
gave a full view of the entire room.

SEEGER

A *clear* view?

BONNEY

Absolutely clear.
          (SEEGER *glances at* HELENA. *She shifts noncommittally.*)
It was the first test of that morning. Lieutenant Seeger was in the
control room, along with me and Lieutenant Parisi, the other
officer on the project. The enlisted men were—

SEEGER

     (*On "enlisted."*)
There were other officers present, though, when Bill—at the
actual time he—

BONNEY

No, just Parisi and I.

(*A beat.*)

SEEGER

The letter I got from General Ramey said something about "in the presence of the entire staff."

(*A beat.*)

BONNEY

Well, I suppose he meant the entire staff of *that particular project*, which, aside from Bill, was—just Parisi and me. And the two enlisted men, of course.

(*A beat.*)

SEEGER

Go ahead.

BONNEY

Bill and Parisi and I were in the control room. The enlisted men were in the testing room, setting up for the test. We were watching them on the monitors. Parisi had just brought in some coffee. One of the enlisted men, the Corporal, was opening the clamp on the arm. The other man, the PFC, was standing by, holding the grenade to be tested. A piece of tissue paper, part of the grenade's wrapping, was still around it. The Corporal couldn't open the clamp. It had been repaired improperly after the test of the day before and it was a little tight. The PFC put the grenade on the table and tried to help him. In the number two monitor, the close-up one, we saw the tissue paper around the grenade stretch tight and begin to tear; the firing lever had sprung away from the grenade's body. Either the pin had broken or there had never been a pin in it. Packing had kept the lever in place during shipment, and the man's hand had held it until he put the grenade down. Then the lever released. Bill said "Oh God" and ran out of the room. I pressed a button that rang a danger bell in the testing room, but the two men just looked around, not understanding how there could be any danger. Then one of them touched the grenade, rolled it back a bit, and there was the lever sticking up out of the tissue paper. They froze, and before they could come out of it, the door of the room opened and Bill burst in. He knocked them both away from the table and picked up the grenade. I suppose he was going to throw it into the corner of the room, where there was a shallow pit that would have lessened the explosion somewhat. It went off in his hand. We checked later and found a loose pin in the case of grenades.

(*A pause.*)

SEEGER

Colonel . . . did Bill seem in any way—depressed that morning?

BONNEY

No, he seemed no different than he was any other morning. Cheerful . . .

HELENA

He had been deeply despondent all that past month.

BONNEY

I saw no signs of—despondency.

HELENA

Just two weeks earlier you had called him into your office, and had asked him if anything was troubling him, and had suggested that he take a few weeks' leave.

(*A beat.*)

SEEGER

Is that—true?

BONNEY

I—don't remember anything like that. He was in—very good spirits. He did have some leave time coming to him, and I suggested that he take it then rather than in the summer, when we were expecting a heavy work-load. The suggestion had nothing to do with any despondency, though. The work-load is heavy in summer.

(*A beat.* SEEGER *is silent, looking at* BONNEY.)

HELENA

You're a poor liar, Colonel; you ought to take lessons from the General's aide.

BONNEY
        (*Rising.*)
May I go, sir?

HELENA
        (*Rising.*)
I thought Bill's death had only been misinterpreted. Now I think it is being deliberately lied about.

BONNEY

Sir.

HELENA

I don't believe a word he's spoken!

(*A beat.*)

SEEGER

Sit for a moment, Colonel.

BONNEY

I would like to get back to the—

SEEGER

(*On "get."*)
Sit, Colonel.

(*A beat.* BONNEY *sits.*)

RENA

Why do you go on?

(*A pause.* HELENA *sits.*)

SEEGER

There was no speaker system, no intercom, between that control room and the testing room?

BONNEY

There was, but . . . it wasn't working. It was being rewired; it hadn't been working for several days.

SEEGER

And you went on with the testing?

BONNEY

There was no real need for an intercom. The bell was the evacuation signal in case of danger.

HELENA

Why didn't the men obey it?

(BONNEY *looks at* HELENA. *No answer.*)

SEEGER

Why didn't the men obey the bell?

BONNEY

(*Looks at* SEEGER.)
Well, they were new men. They'd only been with us for a week or two.

SEEGER

Both of them?

BONNEY

Yes, both. Yes. I suppose they thought the bell had been sounded accidentally.

SEEGER

Didn't you question them?

BONNEY

Yes. Later, at the hospital. They said they couldn't see any danger so they thought the bell had been sounded accidentally.

SEEGER

You said you "supposed" they thought that.

BONNEY

No, that *is* what they thought. They said so. I did not come in
here prepared to *testify* this way! You—you mustn't pick at my
words; I'm telling the truth . . . The men thought the bell was
accidental, and then, when they saw the lever had sprung, they
froze. They were inexperienced. Twenty-year-olds.

SEEGER

They'd been trained. They must have been to Munitions School.

BONNEY

They hadn't been trained enough.

(*A beat.*)

SEEGER

That hand grenade, Colonel, was it different in any way from
other grenades, aside from its alloy casing?

BONNEY

No, except for that, a perfectly ordinary grenade; the lever on
a spring; deadly without a pin.

SEEGER

A five-second fuse?

BONNEY

Yes, a perfectly ordinary—grenade.

(*A beat.*)

RENA

Why do you go on this way?

(*A beat.*)

SEEGER

I go on because . . . Because it strikes me now . . . could Bill have seen the lever release, could he have run from one room, down a long corridor, and into another room, could he have picked up the grenade—all in the space of five small seconds?

(*A beat.*)

BONNEY

It wasn't a—long corridor.

HELENA

Thirty or forty feet, you said!

SEEGER

Thirty feet?

BONNEY

Less . . .

(*A contemptuous sound from* HELENA.)

SEEGER

Much less? Twenty? That's less than the width of this office . . .

HELENA

Say ten feet, or five! Erase the corridor completely! Erase Bill!

(*A beat.*)

SEEGER

How long was the corridor, Colonel?

BONNEY

I'm not—not sure. I told you, it's hard to be exact. Sixteen months . . .

SEEGER

You're still at Colleran, still at the Weapons Testing Center. How far is it from that control room to that testing room? Today, not sixteen months ago.

BONNEY

Let me think . . .

(*A pause.*)

SEEGER

Colonel . . .

BONNEY

I would say . . . twenty-five feet.

HELENA

You would say.

SEEGER

It's—not impossible . . . Bill was quick . . .

<table>
<tr><td align="center">RENA</td><td align="center">BONNEY</td></tr>
<tr><td>Five seconds is a long time!</td><td>Five seconds is longer than it sounds.</td></tr>
</table>

(*A beat.* SEEGER *looks at the two of them.*)

HELENA

Five seconds is five seconds.

(*A beat.*)

SEEGER

You say . . . a loose pin was found in the case of grenades.

BONNEY

That's right . . .

SEEGER

Pins don't fall out of grenades . . . I know grenades; it takes force to pull the pin.

BONNEY

I did not say that the pin had fallen out. Maybe the grenade was packed without a pin, and the loose one was only a coincidence. Maybe the grenade had a pin in it, a broken pin. There's no way of knowing.

SEEGER

That PFC, he never noticed that the grenade he was carrying had a broken pin? Or no pin at all?

BONNEY

There was the tissue paper around the grenade.

SEEGER

And when he put the grenade on the table, he didn't feel the lever moving as his fingers left it? Even through the tissue paper?

(*A beat.*)

BONNEY

Apparently not.

SEEGER

I think he would have felt it . . .

BONNEY

He was inexperienced.

SEEGER

(*Rising.*)
The spring has pressure; he would have felt it pushing . . .

BONNEY

He was a boy, a new boy.

SEEGER

He had nerves in his fingers.

BONNEY

It was the first test he worked on! That's why we were watching so carefully!

SEEGER

You said he'd been there a week or two! Both the enlisted men!

BONNEY

No tests before that! Paper work! All week. We were doing paper work. Charts . . .

(*A pause.*)

SEEGER

That clamp on the arm. It was tight because it had been repaired wrong after the test of the day before.

(*A beat.*)

BONNEY

Yes, I—I did say that. Yes. There *was* a test the day before. I had forgotten. But the PFC had only watched. He hadn't actually worked with the Corporal . . .

(*A beat.*)

SEEGER

Now you listen, Colonel . . .
          (*Coming around desk,* RIGHT.)
In a little over two hours I am to dedicate a building to my son's memory, because he gave his life to save that PFC and that corporal. I need the truth from you!

BONNEY

I've told you the truth!

SEEGER

An intercom that wasn't working; is that the truth? A grenade with no pin, covered up in tissue paper; is that true? Men without experience assigned to Weapons Testing? A ten-second run made in five seconds?

BONNEY

I've told you the truth.

SEEGER

(*Before* BONNEY *now.*)
What have you cooked up, you and that Parisi fellow?

BONNEY

(*Rising.*)
Sir—I'm sorry; I respect your rank, but General Ramey is my
commander, and I've already violated his orders by—talking as
much as I have.

SEEGER

What orders?

BONNEY

Policy. Policy at Fort Colleran—and here and at every post—to
avoid discussing on-post incidents with outsiders.

SEEGER

I'm no *outsider!*

BONNEY

I must—go to that luncheon . . .

(BONNEY *turns and goes* LEFT *towards door. A beat, then* SEEGER
*rushes after him, grabs him by the shoulder, swings him around
and pushes him roughly back towards* CENTER STAGE.)

SEEGER

You stay in that chair until I tell you to leave, God damn you!

RENA

Will!

(RENA *and* HELENA *have risen.*)

SEEGER

You sit down and remember who's the general in this room!

(BONNEY, *white-faced, has backed clumsily into the chair under* SEEGER*'s angry advance.* RENA *and* HELENA *have moved in.* HELENA *steadies chair with one hand.*)

RENA

Will, please! You mustn't! You have no right to push this man and shout at him!

SEEGER
(*Overlapping, starting on "push."*)
Get back there, Rena, and stay out of this!

(BONNEY *casts a desperate glance at* HELENA, *as though help might come from her direction.*)

RENA

You mustn't do this!

SEEGER

Get back, do you hear me? And stay back! I want you quiet!
(*Unwillingly* RENA *retreats a few steps.* SEEGER *turns on* BONNEY.)
Now you give me the truth of what happened that morning. Is she right; did Bill commit suicide?

BONNEY

General Ramey is my commander. I obey his orders. I always obey orders . . .

(*A beat.*)

SEEGER

Then you obey mine, you damned— What happened in that testing room?

> (*A pause.* BONNEY *is silent, ashen, his eyes staring robot-like straight ahead.*)

How did you get into that uniform? It's dirty with you inside it . . .

> (SEEGER *grabs* BONNEY *by his lapels and uproots him from the chair.*)

Open your mouth, you God-damned robot!

(HELENA *tries to wrest* BONNEY *from* SEEGER'*s grip.* RENA *rushes forward and pulls at* SEEGER'*s arm.*)

SEEGER	HELENA	BONNEY	RENA
There's a building I'm going to dedicate! I put his name on the list! You talk or I'll beat the truth out of you! Did he kill himself? Did he? Talk, God damn you! Did he? Did he?	Let go! God Almighty, you're going to— Let go of him!	Let go of me! Let go! Please, you're hurting me!	No! Stop! Stop it! Stop! *It's true! It's true! He committed suicide!* It's true! Stop it! He committed suicide. It's true . . .

(RENA'*s last few lines are in the clear,* SEEGER *having cut short his tirade when her words finally reached him. A beat.*)

RENA

He wrote me a letter . . . the night before . . . He wrote me . . .

(*A beat.* SEEGER *releases* BONNEY, *who sits weakly. All eyes on* RENA.)

SEEGER

A letter . . . ?

RENA

It was waiting for me, when we came off the ship . . .

HELENA

You've known, too, all along . . .

SEEGER

Where? Let me see it. Where is it?

RENA

Burned. I burned it, in the cellar.

(*A beat.*)

SEEGER

What did he say?

RENA

I—don't remember. Good-bye, forgive me . . . He didn't blame anyone . . .

SEEGER

What were his words?

RENA

I forget!

(*A beat.*)

SEEGER

You're lying. You wouldn't forget a letter like that. No one would. There *was* no letter. It's a lie. Another one of her afternoon stories. Burned in the cellar! What afternoon did you see that? It's a lie, to get my hands off this God-damned—
    (*To* BONNEY.)
—liar!
    (*To* HELENA.)
Liar!
    (*To* RENA.)
Liar! Liars, every one of you . . .
    (*To the heavens, thunderously.*)
LIARS!

(*A beat.*)

RENA

    (*Her eyes on* SEEGER.)
"Dear Mother . . . At last I have made one decision in this life of mine. By the time you read this you will know what the decision was. I don't want you to mourn me too long, Mother, and I don't want you to blame yourself for anything that's happened. I don't want Papa and Helena to blame themselves, either, but even on paper I haven't got guts enough to face them. I've disappointed them so much."

(*A beat.*)

BONNEY

He intercepted the enlisted men on the way to the testing room. "Give me the grenade," he said. "I'll set it up. You boys go have yourselves a smoke." They smelled—liquor on him, but they gave him the grenade, because he was an officer.

(NOTE: *throughout this passage no attempt is made to blueprint* SEEGER's *reactions. The throat-sounds of disbelief and of pain, the helpless turnings from one attacked flank to the other, these are for the actor and director to create between them. The overall effect, from the thunderous "Liars!" to the anguished "Oh God . . . !" should be of a towering bull being brought to its knees by picadors on either side.*)

RENA

"I can't go on, Mother. You and Papa are coming back from Europe and he is going to have me assigned to his new post. He wonders when I am going to make Captain in every one of those two-a-week letters of his, and now he is going to *help me* make Captain, and Major, and whatever else there is in this pointless, endless parade we're in. I'm so goddam *tired*, Mother . . ."

(*A beat.*)

BONNEY

He came into the testing room. We saw him on the monitor. Parisi turned on the intercom. "Where are the boys, Bill?" He didn't answer. He just went over to the table and stood there with the grenade in his hand. "Bill, what's the matter?"

RENA

"And then there's Helena. Now that she's expecting, I know she'll stay with me for the baby's sake. That's wrong; she should have left me long ago. She should have admitted she picked the wrong man instead of trying to make me into the right one. She's a tough giver-upper, though. She deserves someone a hundred times better than I am. I never realized it until this minute, but she and Papa are very much alike. They're strong, and they expect so much of themselves and of everybody else. I love them, Mother. If I didn't, I suppose I wouldn't hate myself so."

(*A beat.*)

BONNEY

He pulled the pin out of the grenade and laid the grenade on the table and leaned over the table with his eyes closed and his hands gripping the far edge of it. We shouted into the intercom and rang the danger bell. The enlisted men had been watching through the port in the door. They ran in and tried to pull him away from the table. He hung on.

RENA

"Good-bye, Mother, and forgive me. I know you will. I love you most of all, because you never expected me to be anything I wasn't. William."

BONNEY

They kept pulling at him. He turned and knocked them away—madman strength!—then turned again and flung himself across the table. At the very last second.

(*A beat.*)

RENA

His handwriting was so neat and small and fine . . . It never changed . . .

(*A pause. There are tears on* RENA's *face.* HELENA, *also crying, turns away.* SEEGER *stands shakenly between* BONNEY *and* RENA.)

SEEGER

Oh, God . . . ! Why did you keep it from me? Why did you burn it?

RENA

He was dead; you were alive.

SEEGER

(*Turning to* BONNEY.)
Flung himself, you said, on top of the—table . . .
(BONNEY *nods.* HELENA *sits on couch* DOWNSTAGE RIGHT. SEEGER *turns again to* RENA.)
You let me put his name on the list . . .

RENA

Could I have stopped you, without telling you?

SEEGER

Oh, God . . .
(*Turning away.*)
I thought I knew him . . . I thought he was . . . me . . . Eighteenth out of four hundred and nine . . . I thought he was me . . .
(*He strikes himself. A pause. He catches the edge of the desk, holds it to force himself forward.*)
Why did you lie? Liar! *Why did you lie?*

BONNEY

I was given orders; I obeyed them. My life is—obeying orders.

SEEGER

Ramey's orders?

(*A beat.*)

BONNEY

I called him. "Speak to no one," he said. "Get over here, quickly."
In his office, later, we . . . made our story. Facts and photographs had already been gathered and were beginning to leak.
We fit the story to them. Parisi and the enlisted men were . . .
ordered to agree.

SEEGER

Why? To keep clean his precious Fort Colleran?
          (BONNEY *is silent.*)
He'll pay for this, I swear he will! And stuck to his lie when the
dedication was announced; hid himself away, knowing what he
knew! He'll pay before a court-martial! You tell him I swear to
that! I wanted . . . such good things for him . . . Get out! Go
straight to General Ramey and tell him what's coming. There's
no dedication you have to stay for.

BONNEY

          (*Rising.*)
You're stopping it?

(*A beat.* HELENA *looks up.*)

SEEGER

Yes . . . Yes. I'm stopping it. Dedications—aren't for men who've been—pushed into dying . . .

(*A beat.* RENA *turns* UPSTAGE, *wiping her eyes.* BONNEY *goes* LEFT *to the door. He stops with his hand on the knob.*)

BONNEY

Are you sure you'll be able to stop it?

SEEGER

Of course. What do you mean?

(*A beat.*)

BONNEY

Perhaps you and I belong to different armies . . .

(BONNEY *exits, closing the door after him.* CORPORAL *rises as* BONNEY *passes through anteroom, then resumes seat.*)

SEEGER

Different armies? . . . He's—*crazy,* talking like that. . . . I'll get them here and tell them. Mr. McKay and General Vohs. They'll *order* me to stop the dedication!

RENA

(*Turning.*)

Will they?

SEEGER

Of course they will! I *know* their kind of men!

RENA

No, you don't, Will. You never have. You're blind with love.
That's why you've gone as high as you have, but no higher.
Love-blind people are useful for running the training camps, but
they get in the way where decisions are being made. You've only
been in the Army thirty-nine years; I've been in it all my life.

SEEGER

This—isn't *you*, Rena.

RENA
(*Without rancor, almost tenderly:*)
Oh, Will, how would you know what's me and what isn't me?
(*She goes* UPSTAGE *for her handbag.* SEEGER *watches her
dumbly.*)
I'm going home. I don't care whether the building is dedicated
to Bill or not.
(SEEGER *stares at her. With her handbag tucked under her
arm, she begins putting on, with difficulty, a pair of small
white gloves. The tears are in her eyes again.*)
He loved me most of all. Did you see that? Hear me read that?
And I was the one who hurt him most of all.

SEEGER

You—

RENA

By letting you do what you did to him. I had eyes, but I closed
them. I chose your happiness over his.

SEEGER

You *wanted* him in the Army . . .

RENA

I wanted what you wanted; that's all I've *ever* wanted. You
handed him to your Army—yes, yours, not mine—but I handed
him to you.
>   (*Trying to smile.*)

You're my Army. You're selfish, and overbearing, and thought-
less and stubborn. All you care about is following your own
map, regardless of how the people with you are tripping and
getting hurt. And I love you. That is the mystery of my life. I'm
fifty-four; sometimes I think I must be mad to love you the—
honeymoon way I do. I'm going home now. I'm going to pull
the blinds in the living room, and put on my green bathrobe,
and turn on the television set, and sit and watch. Don't make
fun of me anymore, Will. Please. It hurts me very much.

(RENA *exits* LEFT, *leaving the door open.* CORPORAL *rises as* RENA
passes through anteroom, then remains standing, facing office.
HELENA *rises.* SEEGER *makes a move to follow* RENA, *then stops.*)

SEEGER

Oh my God . . .
>   (*Turning.*)

Where do I begin to—comfort her?

HELENA

I don't know . . .

SEEGER

>   (*Looking off again.*)

I've buried her alive . . .
>   (*Turning.*)

And buried Bill dead . . .

HELENA

I helped you there. It took the two of us, pulling two ways, to break him.

> (SEEGER *and* HELENA *look at each other, their first un-armed moment.*)

He knew us well. Alike, he said . . . I'm more your child than he was.

(*A beat.*)

SEEGER

He was wrong, though, about—other things. And so is Rena, and Bonney. I'll show you.

> (HELENA *moves up, stands near* SEEGER. *His hand is on the telephone.*)

Sure, in the Army's lower levels you can find some—weakness, and deceit, and—selfishness. That's human! You'll find that in anybody, in any organization. My God, I don't say it's lily-white! But at the top, when the chips are down, it's—different. There's a system, and there's right, and there's—honor. I *know* that.

HELENA

I—hope so. I do . . .

> (*Recognizing the truth of what she is saying.*)

I do hope . . . !

(*A beat.* SEEGER *raises the receiver.*)

SEEGER

Officers Club. Please.

> (*He wipes his hand over his mouth, stays it on his cheek.*)

This morning, shaving, I smiled in the mirror . . .

(*The lights fade to total blackness, simultaneously coming up on* CORPORAL. *He is standing. He turns to the audience.*)

CORPORAL

The day is finding its final shape now. Boyd McKay, the Assistant Secretary of the Army, and General Vohs, the Deputy Commanding General of the First Army, make an unobtrusive exit from the Officers Club. In an olive-drab sedan, with an enlisted man at the wheel and a chromium star on the front bumper, they drive this way. Passing soldiers salute them. Now I claim the playwright's ancient privilege of basing one broad statement on the particulars of the play's action. Bear with me, please. An Army is, like all societies, made of men, and men are made of—scientists know what; phosphates and sulfates; you've heard it before; we function as we can, bend with the breeze, turn with the tide, build our puny campfires and elbow and gouge for the nearest, safest place. And so on. And then comes a man like Seeger, who sees heaven on this earth, and tramples us in his pursuit of it. We don't like him much; it's *good* to see his eyes forced open; he, with his complacency of system and honor and goodness and right, crashing along, while we, with our toes trodden, are slapped with extra drill on Saturday afternoon because the Captain is trying every which way to make Major! There's your system and honor and goodness and right. But here is the statement; agree or disagree; heaven begins in the eye of a human. No dome was ever raised without walls to support it, no walls ever erected without foundations to hold them, no foundations ever laid without the ground being cleared to receive them. And who begins the clearing of the ground? One man, maybe mad, who has seen in the air the outline of a shimmering dome. We'll go on with the play now. Seeger, with Vohs and McKay . . .

(*Lights come up full in office and fade to half on* CORPORAL. *Cyclorama is a deep empurpled blue.* SEEGER, *with his jacket on and carefully buttoned, stands behind the desk.* VOHS *sits* DOWN- STAGE RIGHT *of desk,* MCKAY *sits* DOWNSTAGE LEFT *of desk.* HELENA *sits near* SEEGER, UPSTAGE RIGHT. *The door is closed.* CORPORAL *eases into swivel chair.* SEEGER *wipes his palms inconspicuously on his trouser sides.*)

SEEGER

Gentlemen . . . I've learned a—terrible truth, here in this office, since the parade. My son's death was—not the heroism described in the official report. It was—an act of suicide. The enlisted men were injured trying to save *him.*

(*A pause.* VOHS *and* MCKAY *look at one another.*)

VOHS

Are you certain of this?

SEEGER

Would I say it if I weren't certain? My wife received a letter; he made his intention plain. She burned the letter, out of—con- cern for me. It was I who—pushed him . . . Lieutenant Colonel Bonney has admitted the entire truth. General Ramey *concealed* the truth to keep a black mark off Fort Colleran. Mr. McKay, I urge you as strongly as I can to bring him to account for his— disgraceful act. He shames his uniform. Bonney was his partner in the lie, but Bonney's only fault was obedience. Which I never knew till now could *be* a fault . . . In light of all this . . . I am going to call Troop Command and give orders for the dismissal of the troops and the cancellation of the dedication ceremony.

(VOHS's *and* MCKAY's *eyes meet again.*)

The Recreation Center will stay undedicated until you and your superiors have had a chance to choose a—more fitting recipient for the honor, although I *would* like to let the men go ahead with the—dance they've planned there for this evening. I thought it proper to inform you of this before calling Colonel Parmalee, the Troop Commander.

(*A pause.* VOHS *and* MCKAY *are still in mute conference.* SEEGER *watches them, and reaches slowly for the telephone.*)

MCKAY

One moment, please, General . . .

(*A beat.* SEEGER's *fingertips are on the receiver.*)

SEEGER

Mr. McKay . . .

MCKAY

The ceremony should, of course, be stopped, and another recipient chosen for the dedication. Your willingness to call Colonel Parmalee, considering the—public embarrassment that might result for you and your wife . . . and your daughter-in-law . . . reflects well on your integrity and your respect for the significance of the honor. The ceremony should be stopped. There would be no question at all about it, if the significance of the honor were the only factor involved.

(*A pause.*)

SEEGER

There's . . . another factor . . . ?

MCKAY

There is. Yes, there is . . .

(*A beat.* HELENA *shifts forward.*)

A building such as this recreation center serves a dual function; you must be aware of that. Its first function is the objective one of giving the enlisted men recreational facilities. Its second function, less objective but no less important, lies in the area of—public relations. This is not a pleasant area for men like us to work in, but it's one in which we *must* work so long as this country is a democracy and not a dictatorship. We must create a favorable image of the Army in the mind of the public; we must gain the approval which is given us in war and denied us the day after the victory; we must win, finally, the *appropriations* that are essential to the defense of the very people who would withhold those appropriations. To achieve all this we must rely on a program of public persuasion, public relations. Impressive recreation centers for the enlisted men are a part of that program. The ceremony dedicating such a building, therefore, also serves two purposes. One, it honors a man and puts a name on the building, and two, it *points attention* to the building, so that the building can perform to the fullest its public relations function.

SEEGER

And you feel that this—second purpose of a dedication is—as important as its first purpose . . .

MCKAY

Ultimately, I feel that it is more important.

(*A beat.*)

SEEGER

You want the ceremony to go on.

MCKAY

I do, and I believe General Vohs will agree with me.
(*A beat.* VOHS *nods.*)
Your Public Information Office and First Army's P.I.O. have created a considerable amount of interest in the event. Changing the recipient of the dedication could not be explained in any way that wouldn't bring bad publicity rather than good. We regret as much as you do the necessity to take a less than honest course, particularly when it's your own son who's involved, but you must bear in mind that the Army's final mission is not to dispense honors with justice; it is to defend this country; that is our single purpose.

SEEGER

The final mission . . . the end; that's what counts . . .

MCKAY

Yes.

SEEGER

(*Turning part way towards* HELENA.)
And the end is I made him a soldier . . .

(*A beat.*)

MCKAY

I beg your pardon?

SEEGER

Don't you think the—*way* the mission is accomplished counts, too? An honor for heroes shouldn't be made into a—tool for public relations.

MCKAY

It's past one-thirty, General; a bit late for arguing the-ends-and-the-means. In the circumstances, you will not be expected to perform the dedication yourself. The Brigadier who commands your Ordnance Schools . . .

VOHS

Timmerman.

MCKAY

General Timmerman will stand in for you at the ceremony. We'll tell the reporters that you've been taken ill. One of them remarked on your paleness on the platform, so the story should hold water. Would you call General Timmerman, please?

(SEEGER *stares at* MCKAY *disbelievingly*.)

Would you get General Timmerman here, please? He'll have to prepare a speech.

SEEGER

You aren't the Secretary, you're his assistant. And you're not General Del Ruth; you're his deputy. I don't believe that either the Secretary or General Del Ruth would feel about this the way you men feel.

MCKAY

I assure you they would.

(*A beat.*)

SEEGER

We'll see. We'll just see . . .
            (*Takes up telephone.*)

MCKAY

What are you—

SEEGER

Put me on the Governors Island trunk line.

MCKAY

            (*Rising.*)
You won't reach General Del Ruth!

SEEGER

We'll see about that . . .

VOHS

He's not on the Island.

MCKAY

You're wasting your time! And *our* time as well!

VOHS

            (*Rising.*)
He won't speak to you, Seeger. Hang up . . .

SEEGER

Headquarters, please.

VOHS

Hang up, Seeger!

MCKAY

He knows your son killed himself! He knows . . . And the Secretary knows, too.

SEEGER

(*Lowering the receiver.*)
What—?

VOHS

We've *all* known, since the day it happened . . .

(*A beat.*)

HELENA

Oh, no . . . !
      (*The receiver clicks in* SEEGER's *hand. He hangs it up, missing the cradle once.*)

SEEGER

You've—known—?

MCKAY

Did you truly believe that Ramey took it on his own authority to issue a false report?
      (SEEGER *lowers himself into his chair, staring at* MCKAY.
      VOHS *sits.* MCKAY *remains standing.*)
Another officer had committed suicide five days earlier, at Fort Bliss. Word of a second suicide, within so short a period, would have been disastrous, not only in terms of outside reaction, but disastrous to morale within the Officer Corps itself. Ramey was given orders. He obeyed them.

SEEGER

(*A hand over his eyes.*)

Oh, my God . . . my . . .

(*Lowering hand.*)

This is why Del Ruth couldn't—couldn't face coming . . . ! Why the—Secretary isn't here, either . . . ! Wait, wait, I'm lost now. You *knew* Bill committed suicide, and—still you—chose him for the dedication?

(*A beat.*)

MCKAY

His name was submitted. We went by the record.

SEEGER

The record was a lie . . .

(*A beat.*)

MCKAY

We were obligated to study the records of all men submitted . . .

SEEGER

You knew his record was a lie! Your lie!

MCKAY

Yes, God damn it, we knew! I told you, didn't I? This is a public relations project! Don't you know why those reporters are here today? Don't you know why your P.I.O. had such an easy time stirring interest in this dedication?

SEEGER

A high honor's being given . . . A fine building . . .

MCKAY

(*Turning away.*)

Oh, God!

SEEGER

They're here because they think Bill was a hero . . .

MCKAY

(*Turning to him.*)

The interest in this dedication is *human* interest! You're his father! A father is dedicating a building to his son! That's why they're here! Do you think those reporters or their readers give a *damn* about Army honors? *Sentiment* is what attracts them!

SEEGER

That's why—you chose Bill, knowing the truth about him? Because he was my son? For human interest?

MCKAY

Because he was your son. Because when something useful is handed to us we have to use it. Because we don't get handed much that's useful. We haven't yet learned the secret of spinning gold out of thin air.

(*A pause.*)

SEEGER

Where did I—put my life? What uniform is this? What army am I in?

MCKAY

The Human Army! What did you *think* you were in? The Ce-
lestial Army of Sweet Jesus? Angels on parade?

SEEGER

You're *less* than human!

MCKAY

We're no better and no worse than you are! Maybe *we've* used
you, didn't *you* use your *son?* Any wrongs we've done, you've
done, too! We're you, no better and no worse!

SEEGER

I've never done wrong knowing I was doing it!

MCKAY

Life has been easy on you! I've never done wrong *without* knowing I was doing it! Don't think your ignorance constitutes virtue,
though; it only constitutes ignorance!

VOHS

Boyd—

MCKAY

I'm sorry, but I am up to here with innocent baby-eyes looking at
me as if I were— I had a law practice, General, a profitable one, and
I gave it up because I thought there was a useful, clean job I could
do, because *I* had innocent baby-eyes, too, once upon a time. Well,
I spent three damned years on my knees in front of appropriations
committees and got nothing each day except a bad temper to take
home and lash my wife with, and then I grew some scales over my
big baby-eyes and faced up to the truth of this world; it's hostile to

us, this ball we're on, and you can't grow anything green without shoving your hands wrist-deep into dirt and mud and manure. I've acknowledged my membership in the Grand Human Army of The Filthy Hand; I buy drinks for the committeemen and kiss their behinds when I can, I order bronze plaques with convenient lies inscribed on them, and I sub for the Secretary when he's too sick of the smell of *his* filthy hands, and we hope, both of us, all of us, that someday something green will grow. And we are up to here with people like you, the *ignorant* ones with their imaginary gloves on, staring at us as if we were Judas Iscariot. How clean are your own hands, General? Now call Timmerman and get him here to learn a speech. The reporters will be disappointed but they'll file their stories anyway, now that they've come.

(*A pause.*)

SEEGER

I can't allow this to happen . . .
        (*Rising.*)
I'm the Commander of this post.

(*A beat.*)

MCKAY

In this desk somewhere, there is a paper addressed to you and signed by General Del Ruth. It does not say the building *may* be dedicated to Lieutenant William J. Seeger, Junior; it says the building *will* be dedicated to Lieutenant William J. Seeger, Junior. It is an order, not a grant of permission.

(*A beat.* SEEGER *looks about as though at a new and foundation-less world.*)

SEEGER

It's an order . . . that I—won't obey . . .

(*A pause.*)

VOHS

Seeger, believe me, I'm your friend. It's impossible for you to stop this dedication. If you try, you will—hurt yourself, very much.

(*A beat.*)

HELENA

Suppose we tell the reporters the truth about Bill?

MCKAY

Have you any proof to give them? Bonney won't talk again, you can be sure of that. Nor will anyone else. And the penalty for unauthorized statements to the press can be truly grave, as the General knows. You will prove nothing. The record will stand. Your husband is dead, Mrs. Seeger; you seem intelligent; do you honestly believe it matters what words appear on a plaque, on a glorified gymnasium, on a class B military establishment? The plaque is only bronze; it will last much less than eternity.

SEEGER

It *does* matter. If it doesn't, I might as well have died when I joined up! Thirty-nine years of service I've given you! Butchered my son! And buried my wife alive! It *has* to matter!

MCKAY

All right, General. Cards on the table, and the Secretary stands behind me. The soldier who disobeys an order is relieved of his duty and the order is carried out by the man who succeeds him. That is the meaning of the word "army." If you deliberately disobey Del Ruth's order, you will be relieved of this command and the order will be carried out by someone else tomorrow or Monday. In that event, your elevation to permanent Major General will become extremely unlikely. Stars are given for service, not opposition. Now you know the price of what you're buying.

(*A pause.* SEEGER *stands as if at the rim of a cliff.* HELENA *rises, moves to* SEEGER's *side. He turns toward her.*)

HELENA

I don't know what to call you when I'm not saying "General" mockingly . . . Father . . . he's right; Bill is dead, and the plaque is only bronze. I came here with a neurotic shield; there was even some truth in that aide of yours. I had neurotic arrows, too, and now that I've drawn blood, I've lost heart. Or *found* heart, maybe. Let them do it their way. Don't hurt yourself on Bill's account, or mine. Bill's beyond knowing, and even if he weren't, he would say, too, "Let them do it." You don't owe him this. Neither of us owes him anything, except sorrow.

(*A pause.* SEEGER *touches* HELENA's *cheek, considers for a moment, and moves to the telephone. He picks it up.*)

SEEGER

Troop Command, please.

MCKAY

Put down that phone.

SEEGER

I'm the commander of this post. There will be no dedication.

VOHS

(*Rising.*)

Boyd, you have no authority to stop him.

SEEGER

Colonel Parmalee, please. General Seeger.

MCKAY

Please don't do this . . .

SEEGER

Colonel? This is Seeger. I am calling off the dedication ceremony. I want the troops dismissed. Immediately. Yes, I did.
And I also want the stands in front of the Recreation Center
to be taken away. Station a man there to tell people the ceremony is cancelled. The dance can go on as scheduled, but
the plaque outside the building is not to be uncovered.
No, there is no explanation; just these orders. Obey them,
please.

(*He hangs up.*)

MCKAY

(*To* VOHS:)

Get to a phone, an outside phone, and call Del Ruth. I'll catch
the reporters before they leave the Club.

(*To* SEEGER:)

You haven't cancelled the dedication, General; you've postponed
it for a day or two.

SEEGER

If anyone, *anyone*, dedicates that building in my son's name, I will *make* an unauthorized statement to the press, regardless of the penalty. There will be publicity even if there is no proof.
(*A beat.*)

MCKAY

You've committed suicide, as surely as your son did.

(MCKAY *exits. As he passes through anteroom* CORPORAL *rises and remains standing.*)

VOHS

I'll try to soften Del Ruth. Expect no miracles, though; McKay and the Secretary hold the power.

(VOHS *exits. When he has passed through the anteroom,* CORPORAL *resumes his seat.* HELENA *has moved* DOWNSTAGE RIGHT *after* MCKAY*'s exit.* SEEGER *still stands behind the desk. They look at one another. A pause.*)

SEEGER

It's true; there'll be no miracles. I disobeyed. They'll snap me in two.

HELENA

They ought to—shine your shoes.

SEEGER

No, no, no . . . They're the ones who put me here . . . Will you stay a while?

HELENA

I can't . . . There's Billy . . . If I make it to the airport by three,
I can feed him his breakfast. He's cranky in the morning.

SEEGER

I'll drive you to the plane . . .

HELENA

Rena's at home, alone . . .

SEEGER

Yes . . .
> (*A beat.* HELENA *turns and goes to the couch for her
> belongings.*)
Helena . . . I—loved Bill . . .

HELENA

> (*A pause, and a letting-go.*)
I know you did . . .

SEEGER

You did, too.
> (*A beat.*)

HELENA

Will you visit us?

SEEGER

Can we?

HELENA
(*Turning to him, smiling.*)
Yes. *Please* . . .

(*Lights fade to half and come up full on* CORPORAL *seated in swivel chair. During the following,* HELENA *slowly picks up her purse and satchel, and exits,* LEFT, *looking back at* SEEGER. *He watches her go, then pockets a few things from his desk drawer, picks up his cap, and moves* DOWNSTAGE *of desk.*)

CORPORAL
(*Turning to audience.*)
On the following Monday morning, General Seeger was ordered to Walter Reed Hospital in Washington, for a routine physical check-up. This had the effect of placing him on sick-leave, and in his absence command of the post was assumed by Brigadier General Paul Timmerman, the Commander of the Ordnance School.
(*Rising and moving* DOWNSTAGE CENTER.)
A week later Seeger returned, but he was still carried on sick-leave and did not appear in Headquarters Building. Timmerman retained command. At the end of the month, General Seeger was retired from active military duty in the permanent rank of Brigadier General; one star. Retired, he went with his wife to San Francisco, and there, fourteen months later, he died of a coronary thrombosis. I saw his obituary over my good civilian coffee one morning. He was fifty-eight. He was survived by his wife, his daughter-in-law, and his grandson. The Recreation Center was never dedicated to anyone. It slipped gradually into use, and one day the curtain and plaque were gone from beside its entrance. Where the plaque had been there were only four

small pock-marks, as though four bullets had been fired from a distance against the stone. I revisited the post two months ago. The pock-marks are still there.

SEEGER

Corporal.

(*Lights come up in office.*)

CORPORAL

(*Turning* UPSTAGE.)

Sir?

SEEGER

I'd like you to stay here for a few minutes . . .
(*Coming* DOWNSTAGE.)
I'll send someone to relieve you. Calls will be coming in; from Governors Island, maybe from Washington. Tell whoever calls that I've gone home and can be reached there.

CORPORAL

Yes, sir.

(*A beat.*)

SEEGER

(*The cap turning in his hands.*)
I guess there's . . . nothing else . . .

(*A beat. He turns and starts* LEFT *toward door.* CORPORAL *comes to attention and salutes.*)

CORPORAL

Sir.

(SEEGER *turns.* CORPORAL *holds the salute.*)

SEEGER

Oh.

(*Distractedly he returns the salute.* CORPORAL *drops his arm.* SEEGER *exits.* THE CURTAIN FALLS.)

THE END

NOTEBOOK
WARRIOR

INTRODUCTION

(NOTEBOOK WARRIOR)

At age 22, having contributed several half-hour episodes of suspense and fantasy fare to 1950s television shows such as "Lights Out" and "The Clock" (rough precursors to anthology series such as *The Twilight Zone*), Ira Levin wrote his first novel—*A Kiss Before Dying*. He'd sold his soon-to-be *Edgar Award*–winning suspense classic in 1953 to publishers *Simon & Schuster*—but before it could hit bookstores, he was drafted into the United States Army at the tail end of the Korean War; the war ended while he was completing basic training.

That conflict which Levin experienced—of a young man with a burgeoning career being forced by the draft to abandon his personal interests in support of his country's—forms the crux of *Notebook Warrior*. When the teleplay first aired, *The Atlanta Journal* said it "takes a realistic view of some of the problems encountered by young men whose advancing careers are interrupted by the draft." Levin described his own circumstance at the time as ". . . an oddly-divided life. You know, it was getting up at the crack of dawn and saluting the officers—and at the same time the book had done well, and I was kind of frustrated about not being able to get on to something else."

"A plain dog-soldier guarding the ramparts of democracy" (as he'd later write in a humorous personal essay) with almost two years of peacetime service remaining, the creatively-inclined

Levin found himself assigned to the highly technical radar school at Fort Monmouth, New Jersey. It couldn't have been a worse fit. After months of genuinely *trying* to master the intricacies of *Ohm's Law for Alternating Current*, he marched himself over to the base's *Public Information Office*, and made a proposition: if granted the necessary time and resources, he—a credentialed TV writer—could fashion a television play about the base's activities, which would stand a real chance of making it onto commercial television.

Offer accepted. Levin was transferred to the *P.I.O.*, and with the assistance of the base's personnel, he created *Notebook Warrior*—a highly autobiographical tale concerning (by way of artistic license) a young violinist plucked from his burgeoning music career by the draft, only to struggle with the highly technical demands of the radar school at Fort Monmouth. (Write what you know.)

As the play's opening lines relate, the term *Notebook Warrior* refers to those noncombat GIs attending the Army's technical schools. There were some five thousand such GIs within the larger *Signal Corps* to which Levin had originally been assigned at the sizable Fort Monmouth, all studying various aspects of 1950s telecommunications technology.

Notebook Warrior was broadcast live on September 14, 1954 as the first episode of the second season of *The United States Steel Hour*, which had just won the Emmy Award for *Best Dramatic Program*.

It starred a young Ben Gazzara as the fictional violinist *Richard Elgin, Jr.* As *Life* magazine reported, "one of the neatest camera tricks ever devised" was utilized to create the illusion of (non-violinist) Gazzara "playing" his instrument. This technique employed no less than three professional violinists: two to hold and articulate Gazzara's violin (one its strings, the other its bow) while the camera remained fixed on his face and torso—and a third to actually play the required passages on their own separate instrument. The illusion was apparently seamless, and utterly convincing.

Most notably however with respect to casting, Elgin's *father* (Richard Elgin, Sr.) was played by Sidney Blackmer—who would later originate the role of *Roman Castevet* in the iconic 1968 film adaptation of Levin's occult classic *Rosemary's Baby*.

Notebook Warrior proved a success for all concerned, and after its airing, Levin was transferred to the *Army Signal Corps Pictorial Center* in Queens, New York (which housed an on-site barracks, in addition to its production facilities). There, he was tasked with scripting training films such as *The Quartermaster Semi-Mobile Field Bath*, and its inevitable sequel *The Quartermaster Semi-Mobile Field Laundry*. To his almost unimaginable good fortune, his Queens billeting allowed Levin to take the subway home most weekends to his family's Upper West Side apartment. Not bad for an enlisted man.

In 1956, two years after its *Steel Hour* premiere, *Notebook Warrior* was staged anew on NBC's *Matinee Theatre*—in color, no less (a new technology at the time). As no recordings of either broadcast are known to us to have survived, and as *Matinee Theatre* appears to have made cuts in cast size, running time, and *content* (it was a daytime broadcast, unlike the nighttime *Steel Hour*), we've attempted to remain faithful to the original 1954 presentation.

In 2022, streaming giant *Netflix* purchased a three-hundred-acre parcel of the now decommissioned Fort Monmouth to construct a massive film and television production complex on the former base. While the creation of such content might seem like a radical repurposing of the facility, it's in part actually taking a page from *Notebook Warrior*'s, um . . . notebook.

Nicholas Levin

New York

March 2025

Ben Gazzara and Sidney Blackmer in *Notebook Warrior* (1954)

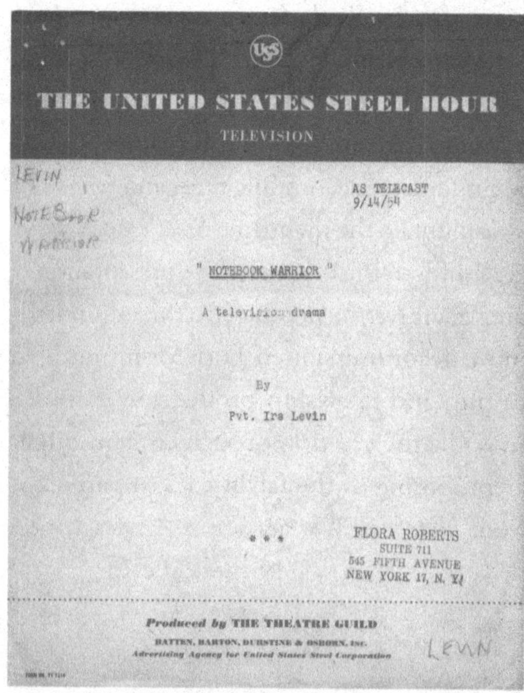

Production script
title page

NOTEBOOK WARRIOR

Notebook Warrior was originally presented on *The United States Steel Hour* on September 14th, 1954 with the following cast:

PRIVATE RICHARD ELGIN, JR. . . . . Ben Gazzara
CAPTAIN DUGGAN. Richard Kiley
RICHARD ELGIN, SR. . . . . .Sidney Blackmer
PRIVATE GREENLEAF . . . . Bob Scheerer
PRIVATE BEIDERMAN . . . . .Jack Naughton
PRIVATE LASKO . . . . .Ray Boyle
SERGEANT CRESCA . . . . .Rudy Bond
COROPORAL DANE . . . . Mitchell Agruss
FIRST INSTRUCTOR SANSOME. . . . . Perry Fiske
SECOND INSTRUCTOR WILSON . . . . .P. Jay Sidney
PRIVATE NORDLINGER. . . . . David Leland
THIRD INSTRUCTOR (UNNAMED) . . . . .Dick Grayson
PRIVATE RUSSELL . . . . Bob Hastings
PRIVATE CALDER. . . . . Lawrence Blauvelt

The production was directed by Alex Segal, and produced by *The Theatre Guild*.

ACT ONE

FILM OF SOLDIERS MARCHING

Oh, you knucklehead!

Oh, you knucklehead!

Oh, you knucklehead!

Oh, you knucklehead!

You had a good home and you left!

You're right!

You had a good home and you left!

You're right!

You wouldn't go back if you could!

You're wrong!

You wouldn't go back if you could!

You're wrong!

Sound off!

One, two!

Sound off!

Three, four!

Break it on down!

One, two, three, four,
One, two—three-four!

GI fork and GI Knife!

GI fork and GI knife!

Gee I hate this Army life!

                Gee I hate this Army life!

GI brush and GI comb!

                GI brush and GI comb!

Gee I wish I was back home!

                Gee I wish I was back home!

Sound off!

                One, two!

Sound off!

                Three, four!

Break it on down!

                One, two, three, four,
                One, two—three-four!

DISSOLVE TO FILMED RADAR IMAGERY,
ACCOMPANIED BY ELELCTRONIC SQUEAKING.

DISSOLVE TO A MILITARY CLASSROOM, IN
WHICH A CENTRAL TABLE AND ONE OR
TWO WORKBENCHES SIT. PRIVATES ELGIN,
GREENLEAF, LASKO, BEIDERMAN AND RUSSELL
(PLUS EXTRAS) ARE SEATED, BEING ADDRESSED
INFORMALLY BY CAPTAIN DUGGAN.

CAPTAIN DUGGAN'S PRE-RECORDED
NARRATION BEGINS. ONCE ESTABLISHED, WE
CAN MAKE OUT HIS LIVE COMMENTS TO THE
MEN SOFTLY UNDERNEATH IT.

CAPTAIN DUGGAN (RECORDED)
Notebook Warrior. In civilian English, that's a GI attending one
of the Army's technical schools. We have around five thousand

"Notebook Warriors" here at Fort Monmouth, New Jersey, studying radio and photography, telephone and teletype. I'm in command of a company of these student-soldiers. Duggan is my name. James Duggan, Captain, Signal Corps, U.S. Army. Most of the men in my outfit are studying radar. I would like, if I may, to tell you about one of the men in my company. Pvt. Richard Elgin, Junior, of New York City. Perhaps you've heard of him.

DUGGAN (LIVE) TO MEN

The way I understand it, you're in this area for the first 18 weeks, and then you go over to the 900 area for the rest of the course. You've got a lot good equipment to work on and a lot of good instructors to learn from; it's up to you guys to make the most of it. Don't kid yourselves, the training you get here would cost you plenty on the outside.

DUGGAN (RECORDED)

I've reconstructed Private Elgin's story from scenes I've witnessed, scenes that have been described to me, and scenes that I have filled in with my imagination. If in the telling of it, I appear at times too much the hero, I hope you will forgive me. Also, if at times I appear too much the villain. It began on Elgin's first day at the Signal School.

DUGGAN (LIVE) TO MEN

If you could get it. You couldn't get a lot of it because you're going to be working with equipment that isn't available outside the Army. So it's a good opportunity that you've got here. The instructors run things pretty informally, I understand, so don't be afraid to ask them to go over something that you might have missed the first time.

(FIRST INSTRUCTOR SANSOME ENTERS FRAME)

This is Mr. Sansome, your instructor for the first week of the course. At this point, you become the school's babies, and my job becomes just seeing that you aren't gypped out of your chance to pull KP and guard duty. Have fun and work hard.

(DUGGAN EXITS FRAME)

(SOUND: DOOR CLOSING)

FIRST INSTRUCTOR SANSOME
Capt. Duggan mispronounced the name. It's Sansome.

PRIVATE BEIDERMAN
Rhymes with handsome?

SANSOME
That's right. When I call off your names—and stop me if I do any mispronouncing—sound off and let me know what experience you've had in electronics, engineering, TV and so on . . . Greenleaf, John A.

PRIVATE GREENLEAF
(Southern accent)

Here. I don't have any real experience in electronics or anything, but I used to fool around with radio some. My brother-in-law's a ham operator. I worked on some of his equipment with him.

SANSOME
Russell, Robert A.

PRIVATE RUSSELL

Yo. Two years TV course. Trade school, then I did repair work for, oh eight months or so, AM, FM, TV.

SANSOME

(*Consults roster*)

Elgin, Richard, Jr.

PRIVATE ELGIN

(*Lifts hand*)

Here.

(*Pause.* SANSOME *looks at him, waiting.*)

No experience. I can turn a radio on and off.

(*Everyone smiles*)

SANSOME

What did you do in civilian life?

ELGIN

(*Pause*)

I was a musician.

BEIDERMAN

Played an electric guitar.

ELGIN

(*Wryly*)

A violin. No electricity.

SANSOME

Did you study any science?

ELGIN

I studied music.
(*The coldness in his voice produces an uncomfortable
pause*)

PRIVATE LASKO

How'd you get into radar?

ELGIN

<u>You</u> tell <u>me</u>. I'm dying to know.

(*Another pause*)

SANSOME

(*Smiling*)
Well, Uncle Sam knows best.

ELGIN

I'm glad <u>you</u> think so.

SANSOME

I think so. Beiderman, William G.

BEIDERMAN

I was a junior draftsman with a company that made auto parts.
I worked in the . . .

DISSOLVE TO FILMED CLASSROOM MONTAGE
(CLOSE SHOTS OF HANDS DRAWING CIRCUIT
DIAGRAMS, TAKING NOTES, SOLDERING
WIRES, ETC. OVER THIS WE HEAR:)

DUGGAN (RECORDED)

To understand radar it is necessary to understand television, and to understand television it is necessary to understand radio. The course that Elgin was taking, a thirty-three week course, began that way; with radio and television. The instructor, early in the course, was unaware of the difference between Elgin and the other students. But the other men in the class caught on and, at the end of the fourth week, brought it out into the open.

(SHOT OF ELGIN STANDING BEFORE WORKBENCH ON WHICH AN OVERTURNED RECEIVER LAYS. AT OTHER BENCHES OTHER SOLDIERS WORK ON RECEIVERS.)

(ELGIN, *a pair of pliers in his hand, looks around surreptitiously. He returns his attention to the exposed wiring of the receiver, wavering on the point of a decision. Finally he reaches in with the pliers, grips a wire and pulls. It is stronger than he expected but he manages to break the connection. He looks at the pliers for a moment, then drops them on the bench. He looks at the receiver and at his hand: It is trembling slightly.*)

SECOND INSTRUCTOR WILSON

Anything wrong, Elgin?
(*He has come up behind* ELGIN)

ELGIN

(*An instant to recover*)
It – it doesn't work, Mr. Wilson.
(*Indicating set*)
I'm not getting a signal through.

WILSON
(*Looking in back*)
Everything plugged in?

ELGIN
Yes.

WILSON
(*Leaning over receiver*)
Did you try to troubleshoot it?

ELGIN
Yes, but I couldn't find anything.

(*A moment of suspense while* WILSON *glances over the wiring*)

WILSON
Look, here it is. This wire here.

ELGIN
(*Uncomfortably*)
Oh . . .

WILSON
You mean you didn't notice that? It could have bitten you.

ELGIN
No. I checked, but . . .

WILSON
(*Looks at receiver again. Casually*)
How did it happen?

ELGIN

I don't know. I must have caught it on something.
(*Shakes head, gently*)

WILSON

You failed this morning's test, didn't you.
(ELGIN *nods*)
I don't know how I'm going to give you a high enough lab grade
to pass for the week.
(*Straightens up*)
Well, get out your soldering iron and fix it up. You better check
the readings on that 5O-L-6 again. If what you have is right,
your whole bench would be melted by now.

(ELGIN *stands for a moment, looking at the receiver. Then turns to
his tool chest, opens it and takes out his soldering iron*)

(SOUND: KNOCK ON DOOR)

DUGGAN

(*At door*)
Mr. Wilson?

WILSON

Yes?

DUGGAN

I'm Captain Duggan. These men are in my company.

WILSON

Oh. Come in.

DUGGAN

(*Entering*)

Good morning. I know we're supposed to keep our noses out of the classroom work, but I thought I'd see what the men do when we chase them out in the morning. How're they doing?

WILSON

Okay. A couple of fireballs, one eight-ball. The usual.

DUGGAN

Quite a setup.

WILSON

You ought to see the stuff they work with later on.

DUGGAN

. . . Who's the eight-ball?

WILSON

That one there. Elgin. All thumbs.

DUGGAN

He's probably got one of the most . . . dexterous sets of hands in the whole country. He's a violinist; a good one.

WILSON

Well, he's all thumbs in a radio receiver. And deadwood in the discussions.

DUGGAN

Give him time. He's a bright boy. I checked his papers when he came into the company.

WILSON

Bright boy or no bright boy, he'll never be a radar repairman.

DUGGAN

He isn't failing is he?

WILSON

I think he is. I haven't made up the lab grades yet.

DUGGAN

Well, thanks for the look-see . . .
>   (DUGGAN *goes to* ELGIN)
Having trouble finding your way around in there?

ELGIN

Yes, sir.

DUGGAN

Stick with it.

ELGIN

Yes, sir.

(DUGGAN *leaves the classroom, as two soldiers —* LASKO *and* BEI-
DERMAN *— saunter over to* ELGIN. BEIDERMAN *stands behind*
ELGIN, *scraping the tip of a soldering iron.* LASKO *lounges against*
ELGIN's *workbench. He picks up* ELGIN's *pliers.* BEIDERMAN *and*
LASKO *speak in mock-German accents.*)

LASKO

>   (*To* BEIDERMAN)
Ach du lieber, Fritz. I tink dis feller's in der wrong army!

BEIDERMAN

Ja wohl, ja wohl.

LASKO
(*Pantomiming with pliers*)
In der set mitt der pliers, out-gepullen der vire.

(ELGIN *stiffens guiltily*)

BEIDERMAN

Ja wohl!
    (*Pause*)

LASKO

I tink dis feller's an American shpy. Dey send him to louse up
De Fuhrer's radar school.

BEIDERMAN

(*Correcting*)
Mistook der school up-gelousen.

(ELGIN *smiles nervously at* LASKO)

LASKO

(*Slowly, not smiling*)
Crazy, mixed up radar repairman.
    (*Pause.* ELGIN, *angry, turns to bench, plugs in soldering iron.*)
    (LASKO *twists his head to read label on the receiver*)
"Dis piece uf eqvipment cost you undt your family two hundred dollars. Treat idt carefully." Yah, I tink he's an American
shpy. He—

(ELGIN *turns, takes pliers from* LASKO's *hand, puts them on bench*)

ELGIN

Okay. Very funny. Martin and Lewis.
(*Turns to bench*)

LASKO

Not very funny. Very serious. Das firing squad for this fellow.

ELGIN

(*Turning*)
Look, do me a favor. Knock it off, will you? Mind your own business.

LASKO

(*Dropping accent*)
It <u>is</u> my business.
(*Pause. Earnestly*)
I'm the class leader, aren't I? What am I supposed to do, stand around and watch you bust up equipment?

ELGIN

(*Busy at receiver*)
I didn't bust anything.

(GREENLEAF *has joined the group during the above. He puts his hand on* ELGIN's *shoulder.*)

GREENLEAF

I wish you boys would quit harassing my father.

LASKO

This crazy character's going around busting up equipment.

ELGIN

I didn't bust anything.

LASKO

We saw you put —

GREENLEAF

Look, Mr. Wilson's giving us the evil eye. Back to the benches.
(*He makes fly-shooing motions*)

LASKO

I don't get you, Elgin. Honest, I . . . I'll admit this is still the
Army, but it isn't such a bad deal, is it?

GREENLEAF

(*More motions*)
Shoo! Shoo!

LASKO

(*Disgustedly*)
Ahhhhh . . .

(*He turns and exits,* BEIDERMAN *following*)

GREENLEAF

That boy has delusions of corporal.
(ELGIN *smiles.* GREENLEAF *leans on the bench and looks*
at ELGIN'*s work.*)
Oh, man, you solder like a Wac.

ELGIN

Thanks for taking them off my back.

GREENLEAF

Give me that iron. You have to kind of heat the connection
before you apply the solder . . . like this . . .

WILSON (OUT OF FRAME)

Say men, I've got your marks now.

> (ELGIN *and* GREENLEAF *turn. All the men turn to face*
> WILSON, *who's seated in the center of the room.*)

The first mark is this morning's test, the second is your lab grade
and the third is the average for the week.

(CAMERA BEGINS MOVING IN ON ELGIN,
WHO IS LOOKING AT THE PLIERS IN HIS
HAND. WILSON READS:)

Beiderman: ninety, eighty, eighty-five. Calder: seventy-five,
eighty-five, eighty.

> (ELGIN *freezes in expectation*)

Elgin: fifty-five, sixty-five, sixty.

> (ELGIN *turns to bench. He toys sullenly with the pliers.*)

Lasko: ninety, ninety, ninety. Greenleaf: eighty, eighty-five,
eighty-three. Russell: eighty-five, ninety, eighty-eight . . .

FADE OUT

FADE IN (ORDERLY ROOM)

(*The company clerk,* CORPORAL DANE, *and the first sergeant,*
CRESCA, *are at their desks.* CRESCA *is an elderly man with a sleeve
full of hash marks.* DANE *is typing.*)

(SOUND: KNOCK ON DOOR)

ELGIN

Sergeant Cresca?

CRESCA

Come in.

(SOUND: DOOR OPENING; CLOSING)

No passes until five o'clock.

(ELGIN ENTERS FRAME,
TUCKS HIS FATIGUE CAP UNDER
HIS ARM)

ELGIN

(*Sullenly*)

My platoon sergeant told me you wanted to see me, Elgin.

CRESCA

Elgin . . . Elgin . . . The C.O. wants to see you. Wait here.

(CRESCA EXITS FRAME)

(SOUND: KNOCK ON DOOR)

DANE

(*Looks at* ELGIN *curiously*)

You're the violinist, aren't you?

(ELGIN *nods*)

I read the piece in the Monmouth Message. Did you really play in Carnegie Hall?

ELGIN

(*Flatly*)

Anybody can play in Carnegie Hall. You just rent the place for a night and sell tickets.

DANE

The message said you'd made records, too.

CRESCA

(OFFSTAGE)

Yessir, will do, sir.

(CRESCA COMES INTO FRAME)

(*To* ELGIN)

Report to the C.O.

ELGIN

What's it about?

(CRESCA *shrugs his ignorance*)

(ELGIN EXITS FRAME. CRESCA SITS AT DESK. DANE STARTS TO SAY SOMETHING.)

CRESCA

(*Pointing at* DANE's *work*)

Type!

(SHOT OF DUGGAN SITTING AT HIS DESK)

(SOUND: KNOCK ON DOOR)

DISSOLVE TO OFFICE

DUGGAN

Come in.

(SOUND: DOOR OPEN AND CLOSE)

(ELGIN ENTERS FRAME AND ADVANCES TO
DUGGAN'S DESK. HE COMES TO ATTENTION
AND RENDERS A NONE-TOO-PERFECT SALUTE)

ELGIN

Private Elgin reporting to Captain Duggan as ordered, sir.

DUGGAN

(*Returns salute*)
At ease, Elgin.
(ELGIN *stands at ease*)
You can sit down if you'd like to.

ELGIN

Thank you, sir.
(*Lowers himself onto front of chair, his cap in his hands.
Pause.*)

DUGGAN

Is everything all right, Elgin?

ELGIN

(*Slightly bewildered*)
Yes, sir.
(*Pause*)

DUGGAN

(*Lifts sheet of paper*)

This is a list from the schools. The men who have to attend make-up classes next week.

(*Pause.* ELGIN *looks down with a here-comes-the-lecture frown.*)

I hardly expected to find <u>your</u> name on it.

(*Pause*)

Did you fail for the entire week or only in the lab work?

ELGIN

The entire week. Sir.

(*Looks up again, coldly*)

I'm being washed back two weeks.

DUGGAN

(*Playing with pencil*)

Is there any personal problem that might be interfering with your work? Any trouble at home?

ELGIN

No, sir, there isn't.

DUGGAN

Then . . . ?

ELGIN

(*A hint of resentment and defiance*)

Sir, I find the course very . . . very difficult and . . . uninteresting. I'm the only one in the class with no background or experience in the field. It makes it very difficult.

DUGGAN

I've looked at your records, Elgin. You scored exceptionally highly in the aptitude tests that have a . . .
>   (*Observing* ELGIN's *expression*)

I see you don't think too highly of the aptitude tests.

ELGIN

I'm a concert violinist and I'm in radar.

DUGGAN

I know you're a violinist. Unfortunately there's no string section in a military band. But there <u>is</u> a crying need for men capable of learning electronics.
>   (*Pause.* DUGGAN *picks up list of make-up students, drops it again.*)

Have you been studying?

ELGIN

>   (*Pause*)

Sir, down at school they told us that our Company Commanders are only responsible for our <u>military</u> training.
>   (*Pause*)

DUGGAN

Have you been studying?

ELGIN

>   (*Defiant*)

No, sir, I haven't.

DUGGAN

Why not?

ELGIN
(*Sitting back in chair*)
We aren't assigned any homework.

DUGGAN
But apparently you need it.
(*Pause*)
What did you do when you were studying music and you found a piece that gave you trouble? You went home and you practiced . . .

ELGIN
(*Interrupting, leaning forward*)
This isn't music! This is vacuum tubes and oscillators and circuits and —

DUGGAN
It's something that has to be learned!
(*Pause*)

ELGIN
(*Tense*)
Can I speak frankly, sir?

DUGGAN
Go on.

ELGIN
I didn't <u>ask</u> to join this army. I didn't ask to go to radar school. I spent fourteen years preparing for a career, a career that was just starting when I got that letter from my "friends and neighbors". Well, I'm stuck. I'm stuck for two years. But I'm going to keep as much of those two years for myself as I possibly can.

I'm not going to sit in the barracks studying diagrams when I can be in the library listening to music. I'm not going to squirm through lectures when I can keep a pocketbook inside my notebook and read a decent novel.

> (*Pause*)

I'm not going to be a radar repairman when I can just be a dumb joe who files paper or walks his post and gets out as quick as he can.

DUGGAN

> (*A long pause*)

You seem to have thought it out very carefully.

ELGIN

You can GI all you want, but you can't paint a brain olive drab.

DUGGAN

Very clever.

ELGIN

Not original. Something my father said.

DUGGAN

> (*Pause*)

He sounds like a witty man.

ELGIN

He is.

DUGGAN

All right. You spoke frankly. Now it's my turn.

> (*Pause*)

You're being foolish.

ELGIN

(*Stands*)

Am I dismissed, sir?

DUGGAN

No, you are not.

(*Pause*)

You're being foolish because you're deliberately refusing to adapt to your environment. I don't mean the immediate environment of radar school; I mean the overall environment of this country and this age, an environment which happens to include two years in the army. Very unfortunate. But it's the environment into which you were born. You can either adapt or refuse to adapt. I think you've studied enough biology to know what happens to species that don't adapt to their environment; they don't survive.

ELGIN

There are some things that it's wrong to adapt to! It would be . . .

(*Gropes for word*)

DUGGAN

Self-betrayal?

ELGIN

Yes!

DUGGAN

You would rather keep yourself as you were the day before you got the letter from the friends and neighbors.

ELGIN

Yes.

DUGGAN

Deliberately refusing to grow.

(*Pause . . .* ELGIN *reacts*)

So that at the end of two years, those two years might as well never have been lived at all.

ELGIN

Yes.

DUGGAN

Isn't <u>that</u> self-betrayal? Isn't that <u>really</u> putting a two-year hole in your life?

(*Pause*)

Isn't growth in <u>any</u> direction better than no growth at all?

(*Pause . . .* ELGIN *is confused, angry at his confusion*)

Think it over.

(*Pause*)

Now you're dismissed.

(ELGIN *turns from desk*)

Elgin!

(ELGIN *stops, turns*)

A salute!

(ELGIN *salutes awkwardly.* DUGGAN *returns salute and* ELGIN *exits frame.*)

(SOUND: DOOR OPEN AND CLOSE)

(DUGGAN *looks at make-up list again, looks at door, shakes his head*)

DISSOLVE TO BARRACKS

(*A radio is blaring out "Dear John".* LASKO *and* RUSSELL, *in civilian slacks and zipper jackets, are consulting the movie program tacked on the bulletin board.*)

LASKO

Old man break your back?

RUSSELL

I used to <u>love</u> Friday nights. You had the whole weekend ahead of you. <u>Now</u> what'ya got? Saturday morning inspection. My mother says this is good for me. My mother says I'm a slob and the Army is gonna make me neat and tidy.

LASKO

She's right. I'm gonna write her a letter and tell her how beautifully you're developing. When you go home Christmas she ought to make you stand at inspection every day.

RUSELL

I bet she'd do it! She's absolutely batty on the subject of me being a slob. I think it's something psychological.

LASKO

It's just that you're such a slob, that's all.

RUSSELL

Oh great. I've got a <u>new</u> mother.

(RUSSELL EXITS FRAME,
AS NORDLINGER ENTERS)

NORDLINGER

Hey, Lasko.

LASKO

Yeah?

NORDLINGER

You're from Texas, aren't you?

LASKO

Yeah . . .

NORDLINGER

Do you know what a Texan is?

LASKO

I give up. What's a Texan . . .

NORDLINGER

Well, this is just a little joke that Nagle told me.

LASKO

Go ahead. What's a Texan?

NORDLINGER

A Texan is a Mexican who didn't have enough gas to get to
Arizona.

LASKO

That's a very stupid thing to say. It's not only stupid, it's also
bigoted and prejudiced. It's anti-Texas, it's anti-Mexican, and
I think it's even anti-Arizona. Don't you think there's enough

bigotry and prejudice in this horrible world without you adding to the amount? How would you like it if I said, "What's a guy from Massachusetts" and you said, "I give up, what'" and I said "A guy from Massachusetts is a drooling idiot with B.O. and a bunch of drunken children." How would you like that? Would that strike you as a friendly, American-type thing to say? Or would you think that I was being bigoted and prejudiced, unfair and inaccurate . . .

(DURING THE ABOVE, NORDLINGER AND LASKO EXIT FRAME, STILL ARGUING, AS GREENLEAF AND BEIDERMAN ENTER, WEARING CIVILIAN SLACKS AND ZIPPER JACKETS)

GREENLEAF

Nordlinger must have mentioned Texas without kneeling towards Dallas.

BEIDERMAN

Poor Nordlinger . . .

(*They examine the movie program tacked on the bulletin board*)

BEIDERMAN

There's a dance at the service club.

GREENLEAF

You go dance with those dogs. I'm going to admire Susan Hayward.

BEIDERMAN

Susan Hayward? Where?

GREENLEAF
(*Pointing to program*)
Right there. Theater number two.

BEIDERMAN
Ee-good-gad! I thought it said <u>Louis</u> Hayward!

GREENLEAF
You're cracking, Dad. You've been in this army far too long.
Let's get Elgin.

BEIDERMAN
Elgin?

GREENLEAF
Oh, he's all right. Come on.

(*They go down the aisle towards* ELGIN*'s bunk*)

BEIDERMAN
I thought it was one of those Monte Cristo things. Monte Cristo's Second Cousin Returns.

GREENLEAF
In glorious black and white.

(ELGIN, *in T-shirt and slacks, is lying on his bunk, his hands beneath his head, staring at the mattress of the bunk above him. The
radar training manual is on his chest.*)

GREENLEAF
Why don't you get up off your back and we'll go to the six
thirty-show. They got Susan Hayward.

ELGIN

(*Distantly*)

I have to call New York.

GREENLEAF

You can make your call after the show, can't you, Dad?

ELGIN

(*Sitting up, looking at the manual*)

No. I have to call now.

BEIDERMAN

(*Puts foot on footlocker, tying shoelace*)

Yeah, I notice how you're running to the telephone center. You want to watch out you don't fall and break a leg.

ELGIN

(*Putting down manual, standing*)

Yuk, yuk, yuk.

(*Takes jacket from wall locker*)

See you later.

(*Pulling on jacket, he exits*)

GREENLEAF

He was lying there like that for an hour. I don't think he ate chow.

BEIDERMAN

(*Finishing shoelace*)

Smart move.

GREENLEAF

(*Looking at watch*)

It's early. We can stop by the telephone center and wait for him.

BEIDERMAN

What for?

GREENLEAF

I worry about the boy. I think all this hillbilly music is driving
him slowly insane.

BEIDERMAN

That I can believe.

DISSOLVE TO PHONE BOOTH

(CLOSE-UP ELGIN IN TELEPHONE BOOTH, THE RE-
CEIVER TO HIS EAR. HE LOOKS THOUGHTFUL AND
DISTURBED.)

ELGIN

Operator—New York City—Murray Hill 4-3598.

(SOUND: PHONE RINGING AT OTHER END,
RECEIVER BEING LIFTED)

RICHARD ELGIN, SR. (FATHER)
                   (SOUND EFFECT: TELEPHONE FILTER)

Hello? . . . Hello?

ELGIN

Hello, Dad? Richard . . .

FATHER

Richie! How _are_ you?

ELGIN

Fine. How are you?

(SPLIT SCREEN — ELGIN AND FATHER)

FATHER

(NO FILTER)

Fine. Why are you calling? Is anything wrong?

ELGIN

No, nothing's wrong.

(*He pauses and his* FATHER *breaks in*)

FATHER

Richie, I got the score of that Kabalevsky concerto we were talking about. I'm going over it right now and—

ELGIN

(*On word "right"*)
I had a talk with my company commander this afternoon.

FATHER

What? What did you say?

ELGIN

I said I had a talk with my company commander this afternoon.
(*Pause*)
He's . . . he's not bad. Very intelligent.

FATHER

(*Pause. A certain wariness*)
What did you talk about?

(SPLITSCREEN ENDS)

ELGIN

(GREENLEAF *and* BEIDERMAN *are now outside the booth waving in at* ELGIN. *He turns away.*)
I failed the weeks' work. I'm being washed back two weeks.

FATHER
(SOUND EFFECT: TELEPHONE FILTER)

Oh.
(*Pause*)
Listen, Richie, don't feel bad. Everything is working out beautifully.

ELGIN

Beauti . . . ?

(CUT TO FATHER)

FATHER

I spoke to Ozzie today. That friend of his got in touch with a man in Washington. A million phone calls, Richie, and the end of it is that there's an opening in Special Services. It's at Governor's Island, and they're anxious, very anxious, to have you!

(CUT TO ELGIN)

ELGIN

(*Mixed enthusiasm, looking out at* GREENLEAF *and*
BEIDERMAN *who are caricaturing impatience*)

Fine.

FATHER

Governor's Island! Think of it, Richie. You'll be able to come
home every day and practice. And the only hitch was that the
radar school had top priority! I told you that once they saw they
had you in the wrong place . . .

ELGIN

(*Pause*)

I didn't flunk <u>out</u>, Dad. I was just washed back two weeks.

(*Pause*)

They don't flunk you out unless you fail the same week twice.
Or fail the nine week comprehensive.

FATHER

Oh . . .

(*Meaningfully*)

They can't expect you to become a radar expert overnight . . .

ELGIN

(*Quickly*)

Dad, listen . . . Captain Duggan said something today . . . well,
he mentioned that there's a terrific need for men who can learn
electronics . . .

FATHER

(*Pause*)

Just a minute, Richie. What's the matter?

ELGIN

Nothing's the matter. He just said that there's this need for men who can learn electronics.

FATHER

You know how hard I've worked on this, don't you, Richie? How important it is that you keep on practicing?

ELGIN

(GREENLEAF *is tapping on glass and pointing to wrist watch*)

I know, but . . .

FATHER

There are hundreds of boys in the army who are <u>anxious</u> to study radar, but how many are there with your talents . . . your gifts?

ELGIN

(*Uncomfortably*)

I know . . .

FATHER

It isn't as if the country were at war, Richie. We're entitled to think of ourselves a little bit. What was all the practicing for? Why did we work so hard all these —

(GREENLEAF *has been tapping on the glass during the above lines. Now* ELGIN, *his face reflecting his inner tension, covers the phone's mouthpiece with his left hand and flings open the door.*)

ELGIN

Cut that out! What's the matter with you? I'm trying to talk
and you're —
(*Unable to find words*)

GREENLEAF

(*Stepping back*)
Ex<u>cuse</u> me!

ELGIN

What do you want? Nobody asked you to wait!
(*He slams the door shut*)

BEIDERMAN

Holy . . . ! That little . . . Come on, Greenie, let's blow!

(*They exit:* BEIDERMAN *angry,* GREENLEAF *hurt*)

(CUT TO ELGIN IN PHONE BOOTH —
BREATHING HARD)

FATHER

Richie? What's going on there?

ELGIN

(*Dully*)
Nothing.

FATHER

(*Pause*)
Remember who you are, Richie.

(*Pause*)

Now . . . tomorrow's Saturday; will you be getting a pass?

ELGIN

I think so.

FATHER

Good. I want to go over this Kabalevsky with you. I'm marking out the hardest passages but it isn't as difficult as it sounds. There's a little tricky finger work in . . .

FADE OUT

END OF ACT ONE

ACT TWO

(*Shots of soldiers taking practical examination*)

DUGGAN (RECORDED)

At the end of the ninth week of the radar course, the men are given a two-day comprehensive examination. The ones who pass it go on to the advanced work. The ones who fail are dropped from the school. The first half of the exam is a written test. The second half is practical work.

(*Pause*)

There is something wrong with each radio set. The men are given twenty minutes to find out what. They call it "trouble-shooting."

(CUT TO SHOT OF CLOCK, THEN TO SHOT OF ELGIN AT BENCH. AT FIRST GLANCE HE APPEARS BUSY, BUT IN CLOSE SHOT WE SEE THAT HIS HANDS ARE IDLE. HIS FACE IS STRAINED, DETERMINED: WE CAN SEE THAT THIS MALINGERING IS NOT EASY FOR HIM)

(THIRD INSTRUCTOR ENTERS FRAME)

NORDLINGER

Psst! The amplifier! Psst!

THIRD INSTRUCTOR

Find it yet?

ELGIN

No, Sir.

THIRD INSTRUCTOR

(*Pause. Significantly*)

Did you check the amplifier stage?

ELGIN

Yes, Sir.

THIRD INSTRUCTOR

With the schematic?

ELGIN

Yes, Sir.

THIRD INSTRUCTOR

(*Pause*)

Time's almost up.

(THIRD INSTRUCTOR MOVES OUT OF
FRAME. ELGIN WATCHES HIM GO, THEN
STANDS LOOKING EXPRESSIONLESSLY AT
EQUIPMENT, NOT TOUCHING IT.)

THIRD INSTRUCTOR

Time. All right everyone move over to the next position.

(ELGIN *sighs as though an irrevocable decision has been made. Pan down to his hands, wiping each other.*)

NORDLINGER

You got rocks in your head? I was giving you the straight G-2—!

ELGIN

Yeah, I know.

DISSOLVE TO BARRACKS

(SOUND: RECORDING OF HILLBILLY MUSIC)

(SHOT OF LASKO, STANDING NEAR BUNKS)

(ELGIN *is sitting on his bunk.* RUSSELL *and* PRIVATE CALDER *are changing into their civvies.*)

LASKO

(*Shouting*)
Who wants to sell their long weekend pass? Russell! You want to sell your long weekend pass?

RUSSELL

(*Gives a fiendish cackle and points to photograph on wall locker*)
If you had a girl like that, would you sell your long weekend?

LASKO

(*Strikes pose of intense scrutiny — deliberates*)
Yes. And if I couldn't sell it I would pay someone to take it.

RUSSELL
(*Wincing*)
Oh, you're <u>green</u> with envy! Green!

LASKO
Listen, I'm broadminded; you want to date a buffalo, that's your business.

RUSSELL
(*Calling to photograph*)
He's jealous, Diane! Don't listen to the poor green maniac!

LASKO
(*Moving on*)
Who wants to sell their long weekend pass?

PRIVATE CALDER
I thought it was against the rules to sell passes.

LASKO
Gee, you're right. I forgot.

CALDER
Remember? The Captain said no selling passes or KP or guard duty . . .

LASKO
You're right, Calder, you're right. How would it be if someone <u>gave</u> me his pass and I <u>gave</u> him a couple of bucks? 'Cause I liked him.

CALDER
I don't know . . .

LASKO

Maybe I'd better go ask the Captain, huh? Bless your little enlisted heart. Who wants to sell —
(*Sees* ELGIN. *Goes to him. Gruffly*)
You got a long weekend pass?
(ELGIN *nods*)
You want to sell it?
(ELGIN *shakes his head —* LASKO *exits, still on the hunt*)
Who wants to sell their long weekend pass?

(GREENLEAF ENTERS FRAME)

GREENLEAF

(*To* ELGIN)
You don't <u>look</u> like a man with a Friday night pass.
(ELGIN *smiles thinly*)
You're gonna have to run like a bunny if you're gonna catch the five-thirty train.

ELGIN

(*Looks at watch*)
I can always wear my uniform and pick up a ride.
(*Rises and moves to wall locker*)

GREENLEAF

How'd the big test go?

ELGIN

(*Unlocking locker*)
It went.

GREENLEAF

Failed?

ELGIN

Mn-hmm.

GREENLEAF

What happens now?

ELGIN

(*Takes out uniform, hangs it on locker door*)
Faculty board Monday or Tuesday. And then —
(*Shrugs*)
There's a chance I may get into Special Services.

GREENLEAF

Good deal!

ELGIN

It's not definite yet. Anyhow I'll be getting out of this lousy
student company.

CRESCA

(*On two-way loudspeaker, over din*)
Third platoon!
(*There is a chorus of shushing; "At ease!" "Knock off the
noise!" "Cut that radio!"*)

(CUT TO SHOT OF BEIDERMAN NEAR
BULLETIN BOARD)

Third platoon!

BEIDERMAN

(*To loudspeaker*)
You're coming in like a bell!

CRESCA

Is Elgin there?

BEIDERMAN

Elgin!

(Other men repeat the call)

ELGIN

(Coming forward)

Here I am.

BEIDERMAN

Here he is, Sarge.

CRESCA

Elgin?

ELGIN

Yes?

CRESCA

Get over here on the double. The C.O. wants to see you.

ELGIN

(Pause)

Okay.

(A moment of silence)

LASKO

(Softly)

Dum-da-dum-dum . . .

(ELGIN *turns and goes grimly to his bunk. Conversations resume,
the radio is turned up again*)

(SOUND: RECORDING OF DIFFERENT
HILLBILLY MUSIC)

GREENLEAF

What does he want?

ELGIN
(*Taking cap from bunk*)
He wants to give me lecture number three hundred and nine,
that's what he wants.
(*Puts cap on. Vehemently*)
I'll see you later.

(HE EXITS. CAMERA STAYS ON
GREENLEAF, WHO LOOKS BAFFLED.)

DISSOLVE TO OFFICE

(DUGGAN *at desk*)

(SOUND: KNOCK ON DOOR)

DUGGAN

Come in.

(SOUND: DOOR OPEN/CLOSE)

(ELGIN ENTERS FRAME, HIS CAP UNDER HIS ARM,
HIS LIPS COMPRESSED RESENTFULLY. HE SALUTES.)

ELGIN

Private Elgin reporting to Captain Duggan as ordered, sir.

DUGGAN

(*Returns salute*)

At ease, Elgin.

(*A slight lessening of* ELGIN's *rigidity*)

You can sit down if you want.

(ELGIN *remains standing.* DUGGAN *takes a deep breath.*)

It looks like congratulations are in order. For succeeding in not becoming a radar repairman.

(*Pause. Their eyes lock.*)

I don't think it was easy, was it? Till now you've probably done your best in everything . . . Was it easy to fail? Was it easy to fail?

(*Pause. Sternly*)

I asked you a question, Private Elgin. Was it easy to fail?

ELGIN

(*Grimly*)

I don't know, sir!

DUGGAN

(*Pause. Strikes desk in anger at impasse. Leans forward earnestly*)

Elgin, I'm gonna make you understand how important this is if it's the last thing I do. Not only for the Army, but for you! You were given a job to do and you failed it. Intentionally. These are the things that form a man! Or <u>de</u>form him!

(*Pause. Striving to get across to* ELGIN)

You'll be up before the Faculty Board Tuesday morning; if you ask them, they'll give you another chance! If necessary, I'll speak —

ELGIN

I failed! It would be wasting time giving me another chance!

DUGGAN

You failed because you wanted to fail!

ELGIN

I failed because the Army made a mistake! I'm an artist, not a mechanic! They think they can take a person and twist him into anything they want! Throw 'em in the hopper and stamp 'em out all alike! Well, they can't!

DUGGAN

(*Skipping a beat*)

Is that you or your father talking?

ELGIN

(*Pause. Low, intensely*)

My family affairs are <u>not</u> your concern, Sir.

DUGGAN

(*Heatedly*)

When they seem to be messing up your whole two years in the Army? Maybe your whole life?

(*Pause*)

What kind of man <u>is</u> your father? What other clever remarks does he have besides the one about painting brains olive drab? What kind of poison does he feed you every weekend?

ELGIN

(*Struggling for control*)

I would like to be dismissed, Sir!

DUGGAN

And I would like you to think! You still have a chance to do the —

ELGIN

(*Cutting in*)
I have half an hour to catch my train!

DUGGAN

(*Pause. Down to normal pitch*)
You're going on pass tonight?

ELGIN

(*Senses the danger — firmly*)
Yes, sir.

DUGGAN

Going home?

ELGIN

(*Pause*)
Yes, sir.

DUGGAN

(*Pause*)
I'm sorry, Elgin, but I'm going to tell Sergeant Cresca to pull your pass. For one weekend, this weekend, I want you to think for yourself. The Faculty Board will —

ELGIN

(*Interrupting furiously*)
Sir, this is my squad pass! I haven't had a Friday night since I've been here! You can't —

DUGGAN

(*Pause*)

I can't what?

ELGIN

(*A bit frightened of what he is saying, but going ahead
anyway*)

You can't pull my pass like that, without a reason.

(*Pause*)

I'll go to the Inspector General.

DUGGAN

I gave you my reason, Elgin. I want you to think for yourself.
You want a more orthodox reason?

(*Pause. Quickly*)

What's your fourth general order?

ELGIN

(*Caught off guard*)

My fourth general order is to repeat all . . . to report . . . to
report all . . . Sir, my fourth general order . . .

DUGGAN

You don't know your general orders. Your pass is pulled.

(*Calling*)

Sergeant Cresca!

(*Stands*)

ELGIN

I <u>know</u> them! You didn't give me a chance!

DUGGAN

Your fifth general order!

ELGIN

To quit my post only when properly relieved!

DUGGAN

The seventh!

ELGIN

To talk to no one except in the line of duty!

DUGGAN

(*Coming around desk*)
The tenth!

(SOUND: DOOR OPENING)

ELGIN

To salute all officers and all colors and standards not cased!

(CRESCA COMES INTO FRAME, AT REAR)

CRESCA

Yes, sir?
(*He looks on curiously*)

DUGGAN

The eighth!

ELGIN

Sir, my eighth order is to give an alarm in case of fire or disorder!

DUGGAN

(*Confronting* ELGIN *now*)
The ninth!

ELGIN

Sir, my ninth general order is to call the corporal of the guard
in any case not covered by instructions.

DUGGAN

The sixth!

ELGIN

Sir, my sixth general order is to receive, obey and pass on to
the sentinel relieving me all orders of the officer of the day, the
officer . . .
    (*A harried pause*)
Sir, my sixth general order is to receive, obey and pass on to
the sentinel relieving me all orders of the commanding officer,
the . . . the . . .
    (*Another pause*)
Sir, my sixth general order . . .

(*During the above exchange both* DUGGAN *and* ELGIN *have been
letting off all the steam they have had to hold in because of their
officer-enlisted man relationship. Now* ELGIN *has reached the boil-
ing point of tension and frustration; his right arm lifts and his
hand flexes spastically.* DUGGAN*'s left hand shoots out and grabs*
ELGIN*'s arm.*)

(CLOSE SHOT OF DUGGAN'S
HAND GRIPPING ELGIN'S ARM)

(CLOSE SHOT OF CRESCA, REGISTERING SURPRISE)

(IN MEDIUM SHOT, DUGGAN GIVES ELGIN A PUSH. ELGIN FALLS BACK A STEP OR TWO. HE STANDS DEFENSIVELY HOLDING HIS ARM WHERE DUGGAN GRIPPED IT. THERE IS A MOMENT OF FROZEN ACTION. CAMERA RECAPITULATES CRESCA'S SURPRISE, DUGGAN'S EXPRESSION OF PAINED RESOLUTION AND ELGIN'S ANGER AND CONFUSION. ELGIN LOOKS AROUND DESPER-ATELY FOR A MOMENT THEN FLEES.)

(DUGGAN *stands motionless, his hands fisted*)

CRESCA
(*Managing to find his tongue*)
Sir? Did you . . . want something?

(*No response from* DUGGAN. CRESCA *waits for a moment, then backs away.*)

(CAMERA HOLDS ON DUGGAN)

DISSOLVE TO ORDERLY ROOM

(DANE, *standing behind his desk.*)

(SOUND: DOOR CLOSING)

(CRESCA ENTERS FRAME)

DANE
(*Softly, excitedly*)
What happened? What is it?

CRESCA
(*A shocked whisper*)
The old man . . . He grabbed the kid, pushed him around . . .
Elgin tried to sock the old man. The old man grabbed him and
shoved him —

DANE
Are you kidding?

CRESCA
I never saw the old man so mad in all'a my life. Did you ever
see him do anything like that?

DANE
Holy mackerel . . .

DISSOLVE TO BARRACKS

(ELGIN *at his bunk, furiously unbuttoning his fatigue jacket.*
GREENLEAF *rises from adjacent bunk.*)

GREENLEAF
Where's the conflagration?

ELGIN
(*Takes jacket off*)
That . . . He pulled my pass!

GREENLEAF

(*Watches* ELGIN *take khaki shirt from hanger*)

Where you going if he pulled your pass?

(ELGIN *puts shirt on. No answer.*)

You going AWOL?

ELGIN

(*Buttoning shirt*)

He knows what he can do with his pass!

GREENLEAF

(*Pause*)

You don't want to bug out, Dad. There's gonna be bed-check
tonight.

ELGIN

Stuff my bunk and tear it down tomorrow morning.

GREENLEAF

(*Pause*)

You want me to blow up the orderly room? Through the loudspeaker?

(ELGIN *is silent, sitting on bunk. He starts to remove his boots.*
GREENLEAF *rises and goes up the aisle to the bulletin board. Reach-
ing up he attaches two imaginary wires to the loudspeaker. He
backs away, moving down the aisle, feeding out the wires as he goes.
Back at* ELGIN*'s bunk, he attaches the wires to the base of an imaginary detonator, waits a moment with his hands on the plunger,
and then pushes it down. He simulates the roar of an explosion.
Straightening, he squints at the horizon, brushes his hands, and
sits down on the footlocker.*)

GREENLEAF

I blew up the orderly room.
>   (*No comment from* ELGIN)
Now Captain Duggan is dust and ashes.
>   (*Pause*)
You don't want to go AWOL, do you, Dad . . .

ELGIN

I've got a long weekend coming and I'm gonna take it! My father's expecting me.

GREENLEAF

They're sure to miss you in the morning.

ELGIN

>   (*Pause. Low, intense*)
Listen! I don't care if they <u>do</u> miss me! For all I care you can go in to Duggan and <u>tell</u> him I'm gone. I'll be back Monday morning for reveille and he won't dare report me AWOL tomorrow!
>   (GREENLEAF *looks at him with surprise*)
All I have to do is make one little phone call — to the I.G. — and Duggan's had it! He grabbed my arm, hard, and pushed me. Cresca was looking, so I've got a witness. You know what they do to a C.O. who roughs up one of his men?
>   (*He resumes his hasty dressing*)
One little phone call to the I.G. . . .

GREENLEAF

>   (*Pause*)
What did he want to rough you up for?

(ELGIN *goes right on dressing*)

DISSOLVE TO OFFICE

(DUGGAN *is standing, smoking a cigarette. He turns, snuffs out cigarette in ashtray on desk.*)

DUGGAN

(*Calling*)
Sergeant Cresca.

(SOUND: DOOR OPENING)

CRESCA

(ENTERING FRAME)

Sir?

DUGGAN

Get Elgin back in here, please.

CRESCA

Yes, sir.
(CRESCA *withdraws*)

DISSOLVE TO BARRACKS

(SHOT OF BARRACKS LOUDSPEAKER)

CRESCA

(*On loudspeaker*)
Third Platoon!

CALDER

(*To speaker*)
Yes, sir — third platoon.

CRESCA

(*On speaker*)
Is Elgin there?

CALDER

Elgin!

GREENLEAF

He isn't here.

BEIDERMAN

He isn't here.

CALDER

(*To speaker*)
He isn't here.

DISSOLVE TO OFFICE

(DUGGAN *is seated at desk*)

(SOUND: KNOCK ON DOOR)

DUGGAN

Come in.

(SOUND: DOOR OPENING)

CRESCA

(*Entering*)

Sir, Elgin isn't in the barracks.

(*Pause*)

I tried the day room, too!

(CRESCA *waits a moment, then withdraws*)

(SOUND: DOOR CLOSING)

(DUGGAN RISES. AFTER A SECOND HE TAKES HIS CAP FROM DESK AND EXITS FRAME. CAMERA STAYS ON DESK.)

(SOUND: DOOR OPENING, SLAMMING)

DISSOLVE TO BARRACKS

(SHOT OF GREENLEAF LYING ON BUNK, READING A MAGAZINE)

CALDER

(OFFSTAGE)

Atten-shun!

(GREENLEAF *drops magazine and hops to attention.* DUGGAN *is standing near bulletin board, returning* CALDER's *salute.*)

DUGGAN

At ease.

(*The men stand at ease*)

Is Elgin here?

CALDER
(*Coming to attention*)
No, sir.
(*Indicating loudspeaker*)
They just were . . .

DUGGAN
Does anyone know where he is?
(*Silence*)
Where's his bunk?

NORDLINGER
That one there, sir.

(DUGGAN *goes to* ELGIN*'s bunk.* BEIDERMAN *and* GREENLEAF *are standing near it.* DUGGAN *looks at them. They come to attention.*)

DUGGAN
Do you know where Elgin is?

BEIDERMAN   GREENLEAF
No, sir.   I don't know, sir.

DUGGAN
Did he come back here after he was called to the orderly room?

BEIDERMAN
Yes, sir.

DUGGAN
What did he do?

GREENLEAF

(*Pause*)

He went out again, Sir.

DUGGAN

Still in his fatigues?

GREENLEAF

No, Sir. He changed into his class A's.

DUGGAN

And he didn't say where he was going?

GREENLEAF

I . . . I don't know, sir.

DUGGAN

You don't know? Did he or did he not say where he was going?
(*Pause*)
Listen soldier and listen good—the penalty for helping a man
go AWOL is as serious as the penalty for going AWOL—
you get that. Did Elgin say he was going to New York, to
his home?

GREENLEAF

(*Pause. Almost inaudibly*)

Yes, sir.

DUGGAN

(*Softly*)

Thank you.
(*He turns and goes up the aisle*)

CALDER

Atten-shun!

(*The men come to attention.* CALDER *salutes.* DUGGAN *returns the salute and goes out.*)

(SOUND: DOOR SLAMMING)

(*The men breathe deeply and relax, breaking out into a buzz of excited conversation.* GREENLEAF *sits on a footlocker. He looks at* BEIDERMAN; BEIDERMAN *looks at him.*)

END OF ACT TWO

ACT THREE

DISSOLVE TO HALLWAY

(ELGIN *standing in front of door. He presses doorbell button.*)

(SOUND: BUZZER AS HEARD FROM OUTSIDE)

FATHER'S VOICE

Coming.
(*Pause*)
Who is it?

ELGIN

Me, Dad.

(*Door opens*)

FATHER

(*Warmly*)
Richie!

(*He is gray-haired, around fifty. He wears an old smoking jacket and his shirt collar is unbuttoned.*)

ELGIN

Hi.

FATHER
(*Opening door wide*)
I didn't expect you so early!

ELGIN
(*Entering, taking off cap*)
I got a ride.

(CUT TO SAME SCENE FROM OTHER SIDE OF DOOR)

FATHER
(*Closing door*)
And in uniform.

ELGIN
(*Putting cap on table next to door, smiling*)
It makes it easier to hitch-hike.

FATHER
(*Clasps* ELGIN's *arm. Leads him into center of room.*)
Did you eat?

ELGIN

Hot dog on the turnpike.

FATHER
(*Shakes head ruefully*)
Hot dog . . .

(LIVING ROOM IS FURNISHED WITH DARK, HEAVY
PIECES, CLUTTERED WITH RECORD ALBUMS, A
FEW PILES OF SHEET MUSIC, BRIC-A-BRAC, ETC.
SOFA, PIANO, DESK, MUSIC STAND NEAR PIANO,
CABINET, ETC. PHOTO OF ELGIN ON PIANO.)

(*Leaving* ELGIN *in center of room,* FATHER *goes to desk*)

FATHER

Look, Richie. Here's this Kabalevsky I told you about —

ELGIN

Dad.
   (*Pause.* FATHER *turns.*)
You can call Ozzie.
   (*Pause*)
I'm through with radar school.

FATHER

What happened?

ELGIN

I failed the test today. The nine week test.

FATHER

   (*He looks at* ELGIN *expressionlessly for a moment, then goes
   to telephone and dials a number. Holding receiver to his ear,
   his eyes meet* ELGIN*'s again.* ELGIN *turns away. He goes to
   the piano and stands with his hands on it.* FATHER *looks concerned—as if he is about to speak—then wakens to telephone.*)
Hello, Ozzie? Richard.
   (*Pause—*ELGIN *sits dispiritedly at piano*)

Richie is out of that radar school. They realized that they had him in the wrong place, that's all.

> (ELGIN *picks out a melody softly, with one finger, his face expressionless*)

Good.

> (*Pause*)

How long will it take?

> (*Pause*)

(CLOSE-UP OF FATHER)

Ozzie, I . . . I don't know how to thank you for all this. You know how much it means to me, to Richie. If there's ever anything that I can do for you, anything at all . . .

> (*Pause*)

Thank you, Ozzie. Thank you a thousand times.

> (*Pause*)

Goodbye.

> (*He hangs up. Pause*)

He can't get in touch with his friend tomorrow or Sunday, but he's calling him first thing Monday morning. It should take about a week.

> (ELGIN *stops pecking at the piano*)

What's the matter, Richie?

ELGIN

Nothing.

> (*Pause. Closes keyboard*)

The Captain had me in again this afternoon.

> (*Pause. Sarcastically*)

I'm a traitor. I'm deforming myself.

FATHER

He spoke that way?

ELGIN

About you too. You're a bad influence.

FATHER

I . . .

ELGIN

You're ruining my whole two years in the Army.

FATHER

He knows that you . . . weren't anxious to pass?

ELGIN

He knows everything. The all-seeing omnipotent Company
Commander.

FATHER

Can he get you into trouble?

ELGIN

(*Standing*)

He could have. <u>Now</u> he can't. He can't <u>touch</u> me now.

FATHER

Then forget about him.

ELGIN

(*Suddenly inflamed*)

What am I supposed to do? Twist myself into something I'm
not, just because they're cracking the whip? Spend two years
testing tubes in a radar station?

FATHER

No!

>   (*He goes to* ELGIN. ELGIN *sits on bench again, looking up
>   at his* FATHER *standing beside the piano.*)

You must do what's best for yourself, keep as much of your private life as you can!

>   (*Pause*)

Do you think <u>my</u> life wouldn't be different if not for the first World War? The years away from my work . . . <u>I</u> could have had a good position, held on to my music—but no, <u>I</u> had to be the hero. . . . I could have become a concert performer, a virtuoso, and what am I now? Old Elgin at the back of the string section. I could have been . . . <u>great</u>—as <u>you</u> will be—if you do what's best for yourself.

>   (ELGIN *is looking up at his* FATHER *with deep sympathy.*
>   FATHER *turns away, goes to cabinet where two violin cases lay.
>   He takes one, brings it back to piano and puts it down.* ELGIN
>   *rises, opens case.* FATHER *goes to desk, picks up sheets of music.*
>   ELGIN *begins tuning violin.* FATHER, *his back to* ELGIN, *is
>   looking beyond the music in his hand. He speaks into space.*)

Do you think your mother would have left me if I'd become anything but a nonentity at the back of the string section?

>   (ELGIN *stops tuning, looks at him.* FATHER *turns, puts
>   music on rack near piano. No emotion.*)

Look at this. It's very difficult.

>   (ELGIN, *after a moment, lifts the violin and begins to play.
>   After a few bars,* FATHER *speaks.*)

Faster there.

ELGIN

My fingers are stiff.

>   (*He begins the piece again*)

(SOUND: DOOR BUZZER)

FATHER

     (*Annoyed*)

Oh . . .

     (*He crosses impatiently to door. Opening door*)

Yes?

(DUGGAN *stands outside*)

DUGGAN

Mr. Elgin?

FATHER

Yes?

(VIOLIN IS STILL PLAYING IN BACKGROUND)

DUGGAN

I'm Captain Duggan, your son's Commanding Officer. Is he
here now?

FATHER

Yes, he is.

DUGGAN

May I speak to him?

FATHER

     (*Opening door wide*)

Come in.

     (*Closing door, he leads* DUGGAN *wordlessly to living room.*

> *Across the room,* ELGIN *is intent on his playing and unaware of their entrance.*)

Richie.

(ELGIN *stops playing and looks up. There is a moment of silence as* DUGGAN *and* ELGIN *look at each other.* FATHER *looks from one to the other, not understanding their silence.*)

DUGGAN

If you're not back by reveille I'll have to report you.

FATHER

Report . . . ?
> (*He looks uncomprehendingly at* ELGIN *and at* DUGGAN *again*)

DUGGAN
> (*Still looking at* ELGIN)

He's AWOL. He has no pass.

FATHER
> (*Surprised reproach*)

Richie . . .
> (*To* DUGGAN)

He'll be leaving here immed —

ELGIN
> (*Over* FATHER)

Ask him why I'm AWOL!

DUGGAN

Why? Why are you? Because of our . . . argument? I think that's just an excuse, Elgin. Why was it so urgent for you to get here tonight? To get reassurance that you did the right thing in deliberately flunking out of school?

(*Pause — turning to* FATHER)

Did you give him that reassurance?

FATHER

(*Pause — quietly*)

This is my living room, Captain, not your orderly room.

DUGGAN

I'm well aware of the difference; it took me an hour and a half to drive between the two. To prevent your son from getting into serious trouble.

ELGIN

(*Over* DUGGAN, *coldly*)

To prevent me from <u>staying</u> AWOL. So there wouldn't be trouble for <u>you</u>.

DUGGAN

(*Pause. Quiet reproach*)

Is that why you think I'm here?

FATHER

(*To* DUGGAN)

Trouble . . . ?

DUGGAN

(*Still looking at* ELGIN)

I treated your son a bit roughly this afternoon. He was about to take a swing at me. Before a witness. If he had —

ELGIN

(*Interrupting with the start of a question*)

I was—?

DUGGAN

(*Cutting in*)

Your hand was coming up threateningly, Elgin. Very threateningly. Before a witness.

(*Turning to* FATHER)

I would have had no choice but to have him court-martialed.

(*Turning back to* ELGIN)

So I grabbed his arm, and pushed him away.

(*Pause*)

I didn't think he would do anyone any good sitting in the stock-
ade. I thought he might still decide to take another crack at
radar school.

ELGIN

(*Pause — taken aback*)

. . . And if I reported you?

DUGGAN

(*Pause — dryly*)

Live dangerously! Command a student company!

(ELGIN *turns away, puts violin and bow on piano and stands
tensely*)

FATHER

Richie will be on his way back in a few minutes, Captain. If I
had known he was here without permission . . .

DUGGAN

On his way back to what, Mr. Elgin? To dismissal from school?
To reassignment to some lesser job that will be a waste of his
time and abilities?

FATHER

(*Pause*)
In a week or so he's going to be assigned to Special Services.

DUGGAN

(*Pause*)
So <u>that's</u> it!
            (ELGIN *turns to face him.* DUGGAN *takes a step back and
            looks ironically from* ELGIN *to his* FATHER.)
The soft deal, the strings being pulled . . .

FATHER

It is <u>not</u> a soft deal! It's a job that he's suited for, that <u>will</u> use
his abilities!

DUGGAN

(*Turns to* ELGIN, *pause, challengingly*)
One question, Elgin! One question and one honest answer!

FATHER

Captain Duggan —

ELGIN

(*Over* FATHER's *protest*)
Go ahead!

DUGGAN

(*Pause*)

Could you have passed the course if you'd wanted to?

(ELGIN, *under strain, doesn't answer*)

An honest answer, Elgin!

ELGIN

(*Strain greater — finally*)

Yes.

DUGGAN

(*Looks at* ELGIN *for a moment, looks at* FATHER. *Puts on cap.*)

The prosecution rests.

(*He turns to go*)

FATHER

(*Looks anxiously at* ELGIN'S *despairing face. To* DUGGAN, *now near door*)

Wait a minute!

(DUGGAN *stops.* FATHER *gropes for some argument, some answer. To* ELGIN)

Play! Play something!

ELGIN

Dad . . .

FATHER

Play something!

(ELGIN, *helpless before* FATHER'S *insistence, takes up violin and bow*)

Listen, Captain Duggan, listen!

(DUGGAN *comes back into living room, interested in* FA-
THER's *intensity.* ELGIN *begins to play. After a moment*
FATHER *begins to speak. Hushed intensity*)
Listen! Do you know anything about music? Captain, listen to that!
(*Pause*)
That left hand! Fourteen years! Since he was seven years old!
Two hours a day! Then three! Then four!

ELGIN

(*Stops playing. Pleadingly*)
Dad . . .

FATHER

Do you know what two years without practicing will do to
that? Do you?

ELGIN

Dad!

(*Pause.* DUGGAN *is silent.*)

FATHER

I do! Second rate, that's what he'll be—a competent member
of some string section!

DUGGAN

(*Gently*)
I don't think that he has to —

FATHER

(*Interrupting*)
Don't contradict me, Captain! I speak from experience! It was
the first World War that killed my career!

(*Pause*)

No, not the war, but my own foolishness. I could have had the
kind of position that Richie is going to have, one where I could
have kept on with my work. But I chose to be the noble hero.
I've paid for that foolishness many times, Captain. Many times.

(*Pause*)

Richie isn't going to make the same mistake.

DUGGAN

I think you're exaggerating the situation a little, Mr. Elgin.
Richard doesn't have to give up his practicing. He's free every
afternoon at five and there's a music room at the service club,
isn't there, Elgin?

FATHER

(*Quickly*)

This is pointless, all pointless! He's already failed the course.
What's the use of —

DUGGAN

It isn't pointless. He can get another chance if he appeals to the
Faculty Board.

FATHER

Why should he? Why compromise after all the work we've gone
through?

DUGGAN

(*Pause. To* ELGIN)

I asked you a question this afternoon, Elgin. I might have asked
it sarcastically then, but I ask it sincerely now.

(*Pause*)

Was it easy to fail?

ELGIN

(*Pause*)

No.

DUGGAN

Why?

ELGIN

(*Pause. His answer is directed to his* FATHER.)

The others, the other men . . . every one of them has something he doesn't want to give up. And he has to. They all have to.

(*Pause*)

Why should I get off easy?

FATHER

I want you to have the chance I didn't have!

DUGGAN

What about the chance you <u>did</u> have, Mr. Elgin. Can't he have that?

(*Pause.* FATHER *turns questioningly to* DUGGAN.)

The chance to be foolish, to be a noble hero. And to keep his self-respect.

FATHER

(*Pause*)

I didn't keep mine long, Captain, once the war was over.

DUGGAN

(*Pause. Gently*)

Were the years in the Army the <u>cause</u> of that—or the excuse?

(*Pause. To* PRIVATE ELGIN)

Elgin, whatever you decide to do, I expect you to be back in the barracks tonight.

ELGIN

Yes, sir.

DUGGAN

(*Pause*)

Good night.

(*He goes out.* ELGIN *and* FATHER *stand motionless at opposite sides of the room until:*)

(SOUND: FRONT DOOR CLOSING)

FATHER

Richie . . .

ELGIN

(*Pause*)

It was awful, Dad. Sitting there during the test and not even trying . . . while everyone else . . .

FATHER

Richie . . .

ELGIN

I know you meant well, but . . . you'd better call Ozzie.
		(*He turns to piano and begins putting violin in case*)

FATHER

		(*He stands motionless for a moment, looking at his son,*
		then goes toward telephone. Trying to speak lightly)

Very well. If you want . . .

(*With his hand on the receiver he stands facing the wall.
The lightness falls away. With sudden vehemence*)
I don't want you to do this!

ELGIN

(*Across room, he turns, surprised by vehemence. Pause.*)
I'm sorry, Dad.

FATHER

A person can not go through two years like this without weaken-
ing his skill and his talent! It can not be done! I <u>know</u> it can not!

ELGIN

(*Pause. Quietly*)
I'll do it, Dad.

FATHER

(*He winces, and then relaxes. He lifts the receiver and
looks down at phone. A beaten voice*)
I know you will, Richie.

(*He begins to dial as* ELGIN *continues packing violin*)

DISSOLVE TO BARRACKS

(GREENLEAF, DOZING ON HIS BUNK. BEIDERMAN
ENTERS FRAME, SHAKES GREENLEAF EXCITEDLY.)

LASKO

Hey, Elgin is back!
(GREENLEAF *sits up*)

I just saw him coming out of the orderly room. Dane said he was in there with the Captain!

BEIDERMAN

Holy Mac!

CALDER

He's had it.

(SOUND: DOOR OPENING/CLOSING)

At ease. Here he comes.

(ELGIN *approaches them, carrying violin case. He takes a few slow steps and stops. There is absolute silence.*)

ELGIN

The bug-out returns.

NORDINGER

(*Chanting*)
AWOL, AWOL, where you been? In New York, a'drinkin' gin.

(ELGIN *advances to his bunk.* GREENLEAF *rises.*)

GREENLEAF

What happened?

ELGIN

Nothing happened. I went home to get my violin. Big deal.

GREENLEAF

I had to tell him, Rich. He asked me right out. Duggan, I mean.

ELGIN

That's okay.

GREENLEAF

What's he gonna do to you?

ELGIN

Company punishment. I <u>will</u> paint the latrine.
> (*Pause*)

CALDER

Is that the violin?

NORDINGER

No, it's a machine gun.

BEIDERMAN

> (*A disgusted glance at* GREENLEAF. *To* ELGIN)

Let's see it.
> (ELGIN *opens violin case, on footlocker.* BEIDERMAN *looks at it.*)

It's dusty there.

ELGIN

That's rosin.
> (*Blows bridge of instrument*)

NORDLINGER

You <u>will</u> GI your violin, soldier!

GREENLEAF

Play something for us.

ELGIN

(*Pause*)

Okay.

(*Takes violin and bow from case, raises violin to chin and plays a few experimental notes*)

BEIDERMAN

Meanwhile, back at the Metropolitan Opera House . . .

CRESCA

(*On loudspeaker*)

Third Platoon! Let's get those lights out!

(*Everybody groans*)

ELGIN

I can play in the dark.

(THE LIGHTS GO OUT AS ELGIN BEGINS TO
PLAY A SLOW, MELODIC THEME. IN SEMI-
DARKNESS, THE CAMERA BACKS AWAY FOR
THE FINAL FADE OUT.)

THE END